BASIC GRAMMAR
OF THE
SPANISH LANGUAGE

Ramón Sarmiento   Aquilino Sánchez

BASIC GRAMMAR
OF THE
SPANISH LANGUAGE

Traducido por:
TERESA TINSLEY

SGEL

SOCIEDAD GENERAL ESPAÑOLA DE LIBRERIA, S. A.

Primera edición, 1996
Sexta edición, 2007

Produce: SGEL - Educación
          Avda. Valdelaparra, 29 - 28108 Alcobendas (Madrid)

© Ramón Sarmiento y Aquilino Sánchez, 1996
© Sociedad General Española de Librería, S. A., 1996
   Avda. Valdelaparra, 29 - 28108 Alcobendas (Madrid)

ISBN: 987-84-7143-554-5
Depósito Legal: M. 42.269-2007
Impreso en España - Printed in Spain

Compone: MonoComp, S. A.
Imprime: Nueva Imprenta, S. A.

SUMMARY

PROLOGUE

The grammar of any language is complex and might pose serious problems both to native and non-native speakers. The attempt at making Spanish grammar easy, yet keeping it complete, coherent and up to date regarding form and usage, is therefore a real challenge. And this is what the **Basic Grammar of the Spanish Language** attempts: it is entitled «basic» because it describes fundamental linguistic principles that govern the language and this is done, we hope, in a clear and direct style, through description and elicitation of rules whenever necessary and with the help of real examples to illustrate every point. Our grammar focuses on usage and therefore it is based on the use of contemporary Spanish; obsolete and outdated uses of the language find no place in this work.

Although the **Basic Grammar of the Spanish Language** relies on the original Spanish version (*Gramática Básica del Español*), it must be stressed that it is not just a translation of the Spanish edition. Teresa Tinsley, translator and adaptor, has done highly professional and useful work in adapting the Spanish Grammar to the linguistic needs of English speakers, while carefully taking into account the contrastive and relevant features of both languages.

Our method has always been to take sentences as the nucleus and procede with an explanation of their forms and functions. Meaning, the semantic component of language, is never left aside and careful attention has been paid to the specification of the different realizations which words and sentences may have depending on a broader communicative context or situation.

In order to make it more useful to the reader, the **Basic Grammar of the Spanish Language** is preceded by a summary of the most important items we deal with in the main parts of the book: Noun Phrase, Verbal Phrase and Sentence. The Index at the end facilitates quick and direct access to topics of possible interest.

RAMÓN SARMIENTO
AQUILINO SÁNCHEZ

1   THE SPANISH LANGUAGE

1. Origins and evolution

Spanish is the official language of Spain. It is also sometimes known as «Castilian», since it was the language of the kingdom of Castile before Spain came into existence as a nation. It became the most important language of literary expression on the Iberian Peninsula and, after Christopher Columbus's voyages of discovery, took root in the New World. It thus became known as the «Spanish language».

At the time of the Reconquest, Castilian was just one of the various languages spoken in the Christian areas in the North of Spain. It absorbed Leonese and Navarrese/Aragonese and advanced southwards as the Reconquest progressed, leaving Catalan and its dialects to the East, and Galician/Portuguese to the West. It reached Andalusia, in the South, last of all, where it flourished and developed many of its present features. Andalusian is now one of the most important varieties of modern Spanish.

After Spain's conquest of the New World, Spanish began to take hold in America, and the language today reflects the contribution made by Latin Americans as well as Spaniards.

2. Spanish: a world language

Spanish is one of the most important languages in the world today, spoken by more than 300 million people. In terms of number of speakers, it is the most important Romance language, and is third in importance overall, after Chinese and English. It is the official language in more than twenty countries and is increasing its importance as a second language.

Spanish is, of course, an important language in Europe, where it is an official language of the EC, but the vast majority of Spanish speakers live in Latin America, where Spanish is spoken in Argentina, Bolivia, Colombia, Costa Rica, Cuba, Chile, Ecuador, Guatemala, Honduras, Mexico, Nicaragua, Panama, Paraguay, Peru, Puerto Rico, the Dominican Republic, El Salvador, Uruguay and Venezuela. Spanish is also spoken in Equatorial Guinea and for a long time held official status in the Philippines, along with English and Tagalog. It is also spoken as a mother tongue by Sephardic Jews (descendants of Jews from Spain in 1492) scattered in communities throughout the Mediterranean, and is of increasing importance throughout the United States.

3. Spanish in America

Spanish arrived in America with Christopher Columbus in 1492 and took root first in the Antilles and then on the American continent itself. Gradually the non-Spanish groups —both the indigenous population and those of African origin— became hispanicised, and this pro-

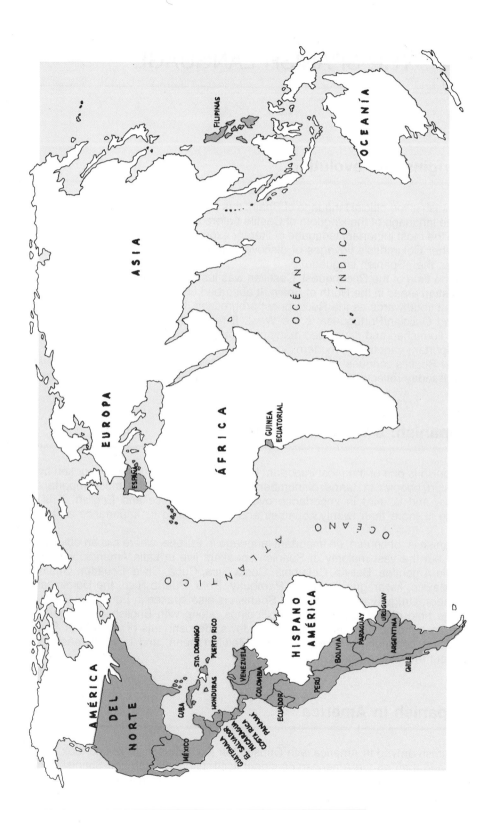

cess had the effect of revitalizing and enriching the language. The process intensified as the Hispanic nations of Latin America achieved independence in the early 19th century. Throughout the 19th and 20th centuries millions of Europeans, including, from Spain, Basques, Galicians and Catalans, have emigrated to Latin America and adopted Spanish as their first language.

4. Varieties of the Spanish language

The Spanish written and spoken by educated Latin Americans is practically the same as that used in Spain. Peculiarities of vocabulary or pronunciation found in certain areas or regions, within Spain as well as within Latin America, do not alter this basic fact. There is a fundamental level of linguistic agreement which guarantees that millions of men and women on both sides of the Atlantic will be able to share a common language for many years to come.

Many features of Latin American pronunciation are also common to the varieties of Spanish spoken in Andalusia and the Canary Islands. These are:

- *Seseo:* the pronunciation of **c** and **z** as **s**.
- *Yeísmo:* the pronunciation of **ll** as **y**.
- *Aspiration or loss* of a final **-s**.
- *Aspiration of* **h** at the beginning of a word.
- *Confusion between* **r** and **l** (*sordado* for *soldado*).

Apart from pronunciation, the most obvious difference between Latin American and Peninsular Spanish is the **voseo**, or the use of the form **vos** instead of **tú** or **ti**.

Differences in vocabulary are minimal. Those that exist are due to the use in Latin America of words derived from indigenous languages, or to the persistence of forms which have become obsolete in Spain.

5. Spelling and pronunciation

5.1. The Spanish alphabet

letter	name	letter	name
a	a	n	ene
b	be	ñ	eñe
c	ce	o	o
ch	che	p	pe
d	de	q	qu
e	e	r	ere
f	efe	rr	erre
g	ge	s	ese
h	hache	t	te
i	i	u	u
j	jota	v	uve
k	ka	w	uve doble
l	ele	x	equis
ll	elle	y	i griega
m	eme	z	zeta

The names of all letters in Spanish are feminine.

There is a high degree of correspondence in Spanish between its spelling and pronunciation systems: most sounds are represented in writing by a single letter and vice versa.

5.2. Vowels and diphthongs

Spanish has a very simple vowel system, consisting of the five vowels, which are pronounced, approximately, as follows:

a	as in English *apple* or *van,*
e	as in English *net,*
i/y	as in the *ea* of *tea* or the *i* of *machine,*
o	as in *orange, not,*
u	as in *cool*, but shorter.

These can be combined to form the following diphthongs:

u+**a**	ag**ua**	pronounced as the *wa* in *wagon,*
u+**e**	c**ue**nca	pronounced as in *wet,*
u+**o**	antig**uo**	pronounced as the *wa* in *watt,*
i+**a**	acac**ia**	pronounced as the *ier* in *barrier* but without any *r* sound,
i+**e**	t**ie**mpo	as in the vowel sound produced by running together the words *extremely embarrassing,*
i+**o**	rad**io**	as in the vowel sound produced by running together the words *extremely honoured,*
i+**u**	c**iu**dad	as in the vowel sound in *few,*
u+**i**	m**uy**	similar to the vowel sound in *chewy,*
a+**u**	c**au**sa	pronounced as in *cow,*
e+**u**	**Eu**ropa	pronounced like the vowel sound in *may you* but with no hint of a *y,*
o+**u**	l**o u**so	found when a word ending in **-o** precedes a word beginning with **u-**: similar to the diphthong in *boat,*
a+**i**	**ai**re	pronounced like the vowel sound in *fight,*
e+**i**	s**ei**s	pronounced like the vowel sound in *pay,*
o+**i**	s**oy**	close to *oy* in *boy.*

5.3. Consonants

The following have a one-to-one correspondence between the way they are written and the way they are pronounced:

d	diente	pronounced further forward than the English *d*, especially when it comes at the end of a word (e.g. *Madrid*), when it may sound more like the *th* in *mouth,*
f	fuente	like the English *f*, but softer,
l	lápiz	like the English *l*,
m	mano	like the English *m*,
n	nadie	like the English *n*, except before **-b**, **-v** and **-p**, when it is pronounced *m*, e.g. *envío,*
ñ	moño	like the *ni* in *onion,*
p	puente	like the English *p*, but softer,
r	arado	like the English *r*, but trilled,
s	soltar	like the *s* in *case,*
t	taza	like the English *t*, but softer,
y	yegua	like the *j* in *jewel*, except when it appears on its own (meaning «and») or at the end of a word, when it is pronounced as a vowel,

| x | exigir | like the *ks* in *socks*. Before a consonant it is pronounced more like a single *s*, e.g. extender, |

The following are written as two letters but pronounced as a single sound:

rr	arrimar	like *r* but doubly trilled,
ll	llano	as in *lli* in *million*,
ch	charco	as in *church*,

The following are different ways of representing the same sound:

b	bellota	}
v	ventana	like the English *b* but not so plosive,
w	wáter	

| c before **-e** or **-i** | } like the *th* in *mouth*, |
| z | zumo |

c before any other letter	}
qu before **-e** or **-i**	like the English *c* in *cat*,
k	kilo	

| j | jota | } a guttural *h* sound, like the Scottish *ch* in *loch*, |
| g before **-e** or **-i** | |

g before any other letter } like the *g* in *goat*,

h and *u* after *g* are not pronounced, e.g.: *harina, guitarra.*
Where *u* needs to be pronounced after *g*, a written accent (*diéresis*) is used: *lingüista, bilingüe.*
The above indications regarding pronunciation are given as a guide only. No Spanish sound is exactly as it is in English, and a clear idea of pronunciation can only be gained by listening to actual examples of spoken Spanish.

5.4. Stress and written accents

Spanish words are normally stressed according to the following rules:

— On the last syllable if the word ends in a consonant which is not -n or -s (which mark the plural in verbs and nouns respectively), e.g.: *reloj, corral.*
— On the penultimate syllable in all other cases, e.g.: *cama, examen.*

If a word is stressed differently from this, it must carry a written accent to mark where the stress falls, e.g.: *lápiz, nación.* This implies that some words require an accent with different inflections (e.g.: *volábamos, ...*), whilst others drop it: *naciones.*
A written accent is also used in the following cases:

— To mark interrogative and exclamatory forms, e.g.: ¿*Cuándo?*, ¡*Qué!*
— To distinguish between words which would otherwise be confused, e.g.:

dé • *give,*	**de** • *of,*
té • *tea,*	**te** • *you,*
sólo • *only,*	**solo** • *alone,*
más • *more,*	**mas** • *but.*

13

1   General description

A noun phrase (NP) is a construction of one or more words which acts as a subject, a direct object, an indirect object, or as a complement. In the example below, the NP is acting as the subject:

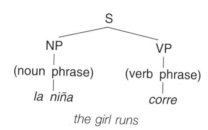

the girl runs

A peculiarity of Spanish is that when the NP is a pronoun functioning as a subject it may be left out, e.g.:

Ellos nos vieron llegar
Nos vieron llegar
     • *They saw us arrive.*

The NP always includes a *head* —an essential noun on which the rest of the phrase turns and which may not be omitted:

Las grandes llanuras se extienden hasta el mar.
• *The great plains stretch down to the sea,*
but not
* *Las grandes .... se extienden hasta el mar.*

Other elements such as determiners and adjectives must agree with the noun in *gender* and *number,* e.g.:

*Tod**os** aquell**os** árbol**es** están amarillent**os.***

2.   Components of the Noun Phrase

The NP is composed of 2 different categories of words:

— *Determiners:* these are described in detail in ch. 4.
— Optional *expansions* of the NP, such as relative clauses, qualifying adjectives, or complements.

COMPONENTS OF THE NP				
GRAMMATICAL WORDS		LEXICAL WORDS		
Determiners		Complements		
	NOUN			
Articles	Determining adjectives	Qualifying adjectives	Complements of the noun	Relative clauses

e.g.: *El otro* día.
Los demás *mozos* **del pueblo.**
Los nuevos *libros* **que habían salido de la imprenta.**

2.1. Essential components

The grammatical words are known as the *essential components* since the presence of at least one of them is always required. Their function is to delimit the meaning of the noun —to distinguish, for example, *las plumas* (the pens) or **unas plumas** (some pens) from the non-specific concept of **plumas** (pens). Below are more examples of grammatical *essential* components of the NP:

Un hombre • A man, **Los** hombres • The men, **El** hombre • The man, **Ningún** hombre • No man, **Aquella** cuestión • That question, **Toda** cuestión • Every question, Plumas **mías** • Pens of mine, **Mis** plumas • My pens, **Cien** plumas • 100 pens, **Sus** promesas • His/Her promises, **¿Qué** problema? • What problem?, Unas **cuantas** palabras • A few words, No tiene problema **alguno** • He doesn't have any problem at all.

These are dealt with in more detail in ch. 4.
The essential components of the NP have the following characteristics:

— Their presence is obligatory:

Le presté **un lápiz** • I lent her a pencil, but not.
* Le presté ..... **lápiz.**

— They always agree with the head noun.
— They belong to a *closed class* of grammatical words (i.e. there is a limited number of them and it would not be possible to add new ones to the language, as in the case of *lexical* words).
— Generally speaking, they precede the noun, *except* for: **aquel, aquella, algún(o)** and **alguna,** which may also follow it, and **mío, mía, míos, mías,** etc., which *must* follow it.

2.2. Optional components

The other components of the NP are optional (lexical) words, that is they can be omitted without the sentence becoming ungrammatical. Their function is to provide more information about the noun:

Casa **barata** • Cheap house.
Pájaro **vistoso** • Brightly coloured bird.

*Hombre **débil*** • *Weak man.*
*Casa **ajena*** • *Somebody else's house.*
*Pájaro **volador*** • *Flying bird.*
*Hombre **instruido*** • *Trained man.*
*Un hombre **débil y confuso*** • *A weak and confused man.*
*El traje **para el baile*** • *The dress for the ball.*
*Un niño **que tiene hambre*** • *A child who is hungry.*

The optional components of the NP can be:

— Qualifying adjectives:

*Un hombre **débil**, Un pájaro **vistoso**.*

— Complements of the noun (prepositional phrases):

*El traje **para el baile**.*
*El libro **de la lengua española*** • *The Spanish language book.*

— Relative clauses:

*Las niñas **que cantan en el coro** sólo tienen seis años.*
• *The girls who sing in the choir are only six.*

— Other nouns used *in apposition:*

*Su amigo, **el médico**, es muy amable.*
• *His friend, the doctor, is very nice.*
Mi otro hermano, Paco, se fue a la mili.
• *My other brother, Paco, went to do his military service.*

The optional components of the NP have the following characteristics:

— They may be omitted without the sentence becoming ungrammatical:

*Me ha llegado una carta **de felicitación**.*
• *I have received a letter of congratulation.*
Me ha llegado una carta • *I have received a letter.*

— The position of the adjective may vary; it may either precede or follow the noun depending on the meaning the speaker wishes to express (see p. 61) (this is in contrast with determiners, whose positioning is restricted):

*La **dulce** miel* • *Sweet honey.*
*El cielo **azul*** • *The blue sky.*

— Noun complements, nouns in apposition and relative clauses always follow the noun:

*El peso **de los años*** • *The weight of years.*
*El rey del corral, **el gallo*** • *The king of the farmyard, the cockerel.*
*El astro **que nos envía luz*** • *The star which gives us light.*

3 | NOUNS

1. General description

In Spanish, as in English, the noun is the essential component of the noun phrase, and is usually preceded by a determiner:

NP = Det + N.
El niño • *The boy.*
Mi mesa • *My table.*
Este perro • *This dog.*

In some circumstances, it may stand alone:

NP = ϕ + N.
Luis trabaja mucho • *Luis works hard.*
Madrid es una ciudad europea • *Madrid is an European city.*

In the absence of a noun as such, some other element —a phrase or other word acting as a noun— must take its place within the sentence:

*El **blanco** es muy bonito* • *White is very pretty.*

(Here «blanco» is being used as an abbreviation for «el color blanco»)

Que tú seas rico no me importa.
• *The fact that you are rich does not matter to me.*
El buen hacer de la gente siempre es apreciado.
• *People acting well is always appreciated.*

Note here that the infinitive of the verb is used in place of the noun —quite a common device in Spanish.

Nouns can perform different syntactic functions without changing their form (as opposed to pronouns, for example, which change their form according to whether they are subjects, objects or indirect objects):

*El **perro** ladra* • *The dog is barking.*
*El niño vio el **perro*** • *The boy saw the dog.*
*Hizo una caricia al **perro*** • *He gave the dog a stroke.*

Él ladra • *It is barking.*
El niño lo vio • *The boy saw it.*
Le hizo una caricia • *He gave it a stroke.*

In the first set of examples, the noun *perro* remains unchanged; however, when pronouns are used instead of nouns, their form depends on their function within the sentence (pronouns are dealt with in detail in ch. 6).

Nouns may appear in different positions within the sentence:

Pedro *llegó a las diez*
A las diez llegó **Pedro** } • *Pedro arrived at 10 o'clock.*
Llegó **Pedro** *a las diez*

When the noun acts as a subject the verb always agrees with it in terms of *number:*

El niño juega • *The boy is playing.*
Los niños juegan • *The boys are playing.*

Spanish nouns may have different forms, or *inflections,* according to whether they are masculine or feminine, singular or plural:

	Masculine	Feminine
Singular Plural	*El niño* • *The boy* *Los niños* • *The boys*	*La niña* • *The girl* *Las niñas* • *The girls*

Nouns are carriers of *lexical* rather than grammatical meaning.
They may denote material objects *(libro* • *book, mesa* • *table)*, animate beings *(hombre* • *man, perro* • *dog)*, qualities *(belleza* • *beauty, bondad* • *goodness)* or actions *(llegada* • *arrival, manifestación* • *demonstration).*

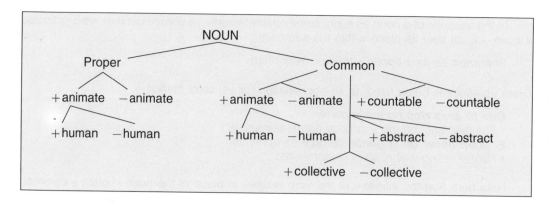

2. Types of nouns

2.1. Common and proper nouns

Common nouns classify reality in that they mark out a group of objects with similar characteristics *(libro* • *book, gato* • *cat, mesa* • *table)*. Proper nouns, in contrast, *particularise* an object or person *(Luis, María,* etc.). Two features distinguish common nouns from proper nouns:

— Common nouns are usually accompanied by a determiner:

La *niña nada muy bien* • *The girl swims very well.*
Pasa **un** *tren* • *A train is passing.*

whilst proper nouns usually stand alone:

> **Antonio** es ingeniero • *Antonio is an engineer.*
> Me gusta **Sevilla** • *I like Sevilla.*

However, some proper nouns always appear with a determiner. These include some cities: *Los Ángeles, Las Palmas, La Coruña,* etc., countries: *el Japón, el Canadá, el Perú...,* and all rivers, mountains and seas: *el Ebro, los Pirineos, el Atlántico,* etc.

— Proper nouns are always written with an initial capital: *María, Carlos, Valencia...*

2.2. Abstract and concrete nouns (+/−abstract)

Abstract nouns express intangible actions or qualities which only exist in the sense that they are produced or possessed by something, or someone:

> La **limpieza** de esta casa es óptima • *The cleanliness of this house is ideal.*

Concrete nouns refer to things which actually exist (or have existed, or will exist) in the material sense:

> Mi **hermano** • *My brother.*
> Este **libro** • *This book.*
> **América** • *America.*

NB: Some nouns may be used either in a concrete or in an abstract sense, or may change from abstract to concrete when used in the plural, for example:

> La construcción de esta casa duró seis meses (+abstract).
> • *The building of this house took 6 months.*
> Las construcciones antiguas abundan en la ciudad (−abstract).
> • *Old buildings are very common in the town.*

2.3. Countable and mass nouns (+/−countable)

If a noun refers to something which can be counted it is known as a *countable* noun (e.g.: *libro*). If it refers to something which is *indivisible,* it is known as a *mass* noun. Logically, this implies that uncountable nouns have no plural:

> El hombre respira **aire** • *Human beings breathe air.*

However, sometimes mass nouns can be used in a countable sense, when their meaning is different:

> Se da **aires** de intelectual • *He likes to think of himself as an intellectual.*

Similarly, countable nouns change their meaning when used as mass nouns:

> Veo una **vaca** en el prado • *I see a cow in the field.*
> Como **vaca** una vez a la semana • *I eat beef once a week.*

2.4. Collective and individual nouns (+/−collective)

Normally nouns only refer to one entity or thing. However, sometimes they may refer to a group of persons or things which is regarded as a single entity and is therefore grammatically singular:

El **ejército** *imperial* **fue** *derrotado* • *The imperial army was defeated.*
El **rebaño** *pacía en los campos* • *The flock was grazing in the fields.*

All grammatical agreements are therefore in the singular. Note also: *el gobierno* • *the government, la gente* • *the people, la junta* • *the board,* etc.

3. Gender

As the essential component or «nucleus» of the noun phrase, the noun requires the other elements to agree with it in *gender* and *number:*

— Determiners:

La *niña* • *The girl.*
Esta *vez* • *This time.*

— Adjectives:

*Batas blanc***as** • *White dressing gowns.*
*El gato es negr***o** • *The cat is black.*
A María la encontré llorosa • *I found Maria tearful.*

— Participles:

*Las órdenes que tengo dad***as** *siguen vigentes*
• *The orders I have given you are still in force.*

— Other nouns used as complements:

A Felipe lo eligieron presidente • *They elected Felipe [as] President.*

All nouns in Spanish have markers which indicate their gender, that is, whether they are masculine or feminine. It is important to distinguish between *grammatical* and *natural* gender. Grammatical gender is imposed by the language with no possibility of choice or variation. Thus nouns such as *libro* and *banco* are masculine, and *mesa* and *manzana* are feminine. All inanimate nouns have a grammatically given gender.

Natural gender is related to the actual sex of living beings. In these cases, the language normally offers both masculine (for males) and feminine (for females):

Juan/Juana,
Antonio/Antonia,
buey/vaca • *bull/cow,*
gallo/gallina • *cock/hen,*
madre/padre • *mother/father,*
ternero/ternera • *bull calf/heifer.*

3.1. Gender markers

In Spanish, gender is commonly marked by the ending of the word. Thus words ending in **-a** are normally feminine, while those ending in **-o**, **-e** or **-ϕ** tend to be masculine:

Masculine endings	Feminine endings
-o **-e** **-ϕ** *hermano* • brother *tío* • uncle *rector* • Vice Chancellor *español* • Spanish man	**-a** *hermana* • sister *tía* • aunt *rectora* • Vice Chancellor *española* • Spanish woman

As in English, gender may also be expressed by the use of different words for masculine and feminine forms of the noun:

Masculine	Feminine
hombre • man *padre* • father *yerno* • son-in-law *marido* • husband *toro* • bull *carnero* • ram *caballo* • horse/stallion	*mujer* • woman *madre* • mother *nuera* • daughter-in-law *mujer* • wife *vaca* • cow *oveja* • sheep *yegua* • mare

In some cases, the noun is invariable in masculine and feminine forms and gender is only marked by the article or other determiner:

Masculine	Feminine
el oculista *el dentista* *el pacifista*	*la oculista* • the oculist *la dentista* • the dentist *la pacifista* • the pacifist

Some nouns have only one grammatical gender, and a descriptive adjective must be used in order to specify a particular natural gender:

*El pez **macho*** • The male fish.
*El pez **hembra*** • The female fish.
*La perdiz **macho*** • The male partridge.
*La perdiz **hembra*** • The female partridge.

A noun's gender may also be identified from the gender of other elements which agree with it:

el caos • *chaos,*
la crisis • *crisis.*

Sometimes it is only in the plural form, or when used with an adjective, that its gender is disambiguated:

*El águila veloz/**Las** águilas veloces* • *The swift eagle/s.*
El águila blanca • *The white eagle.*

3.1.1.   *Gender markers in proper nouns*

— Nouns ending in **-o** (masculine) change into **-a** for feminine:

Alfonso/Alfonsa,　　　　*Antonio/Antonia,*
Francisco/Francisca,　　　*Benito/Benita.*

— Nouns ending in a consonant in the masculine take an **-a** in the feminine:

Agustín/Agustina,　　　　*Ángel/Ángela.*

— Surnames are invariable and take their gender from the sex of the person to whom they refer:

Sr. Roca • *Mr Roca.*
Sra. Roca • *Mrs Roca.*

— Proper names of inanimate objects:

Geographical features tend to be masculine:

— **Seas:** *el Cantábrico* • *the Cantabrian, el Atlántico* • *the Atlantic.*
— **Lakes:** *el Victoria* • *Lake Victoria, el Salado* • *Salt Lake.*
— **Rivers:** *el Rin* • *the Rhine, el Ebro* • *the Ebro.*
— **Capes:** *el Buena Esperanza* • *the Cape of Good Hope,*
　　　　el Cañaveral • *Cape Canaveral.*
— **Mountains:** *los Alpes* • *the Alps, los Urales* • *the Urals.*

Cities, provinces and countries tend to vary in gender according to their endings:

Sevilla bonita • *beautiful Sevilla.*
Bilbao caluroso • *hot Bilbao.*

If the ending does not mark gender, they tend to be masculine:

Madrid festivo • *festive Madrid.*

If a noun of this kind is used with a different gender from that indicated by its ending, this is because there is an agreement with another noun that is «understood», e.g.:

La gran (ciudad de) Toledo • *Great Toledo.*
Todo (el pueblo de) Málaga • *All Malaga.*

3.1.2. *Gender markers in common nouns*

— Animate common nouns:

-o or **-e** become **-a** in the feminine:

sastre/sastra • *tailor,*
presidente/presidenta • *president,*
médico/médica • *doctor,*

primo/prima • *cousin,*
novio/novia • *groom/bride,*
vecino/vecina • *neighbour.*

-d, -l, -n, -r, -s, -z add an **-a** in the feminine:

colegial/colegiala • *school boy/girl,*
león/leona • *lion/lioness,*
profesor/profesora • *teacher,*
marqués/marquesa • *marquis/marchioness,*
rapaz/rapaza • *lad/lass.*

NB. There are also certain «irregular» feminine endings:

-esa: *abad/abadesa* • *abbot/abbess, alcalde/alcaldesa* • *mayor/mayoress,*
príncipe/princesa • *prince/princess.*
-isa: *profeta/profetisa* • *prophet, sacerdote/sacerdotisa* • *priest.*
-ina: *héroe/heroína* • *hero/heroine, rey/reina* • *king/queen.*
-triz: *actor/actriz* • *actor/actress, emperador/emperatriz* • *emperor/empress.*

Some words which refer to persons do not change their form but are nevertheless masculine when referring to men and feminine when referring to women. Gender is marked by the article:

el testigo/la testigo • *the witness,*
el mártir/la mártir • *the martyr,*
el joven/la joven • *the young man/woman,*
el periodista/la periodista • *the journalist,*
el cantante/la cantante • *the singer,*
el idiota/la idiota • *the idiot.*

— Inanimate common nouns:

There is no general rule for inanimate common nouns. The ending of a word is not always a reliable guide to its gender:

el patio • *patio, yard,*
el color • *colour,*
el pan • *bread,*

la radio • *radio,*
el tema • *theme, topic,*
la calle • *street.*

However, nouns ending in **-o, -aje, -an, -ambre, -ete, -il, -ón,** and **-or** are generally masculine, whilst those ending in **-a, -cia, -ción, -dad, -ez, -eza, -idad, -ie, -ncia, -nza, -sión, -tud, -umbre** tend to be feminine.
In some cases, the meaning of a word may give a clue as to its gender, for instance, trees are generally masculine and their fruits feminine (e.g.: *manzano/manzana* • *apple tree/apple.*
Some masculine nouns have feminine forms which express a related but different meaning:

bolso • *handbag,*
manto • *cloak,*
ramo • *bunch* [*of flowers*],
ruedo • *turn, ring,*

bolsa • *bag,*
manta • *blanket,*
rama • *branch,*
rueda • *wheel.*

Sometimes the masculine indicates a person, and the feminine either a person or a machine, place or related object:

cosechador • harvester,	*cosechadora* • harvester,
tejedor • weaver,	*tejedora* • weaver, loom,
cochero • coachman,	*cochera* • coach house,
lechero • milkman,	*lechera* • churn.

With professions, the masculine indicates a person and the feminine the discipline (or person):

físico • physicist,	*física* • physics, female physicist,
músico • musician,	*música* • music, female musician,
astrofísico • astrophysicist,	*astrofísica* • astrophysics, female astrophysicist,
gramático • grammarian,	*gramática* • grammar, female grammarian.

With nouns that are invariable in masculine and feminine, the meaning may change according to whether they are used with the masculine or feminine article:

el capital • economic capital,	*la capital* • capital city,
el cometa • comet,	*la cometa* • kite,
el guardia • policeman,	*la guardia* • guard, watch,
el pendiente • earring,	*la pendiente* • slope.

Days of the week and months of the year are masculine:

el miércoles • Wednesday,
el jueves • Thursday,
un diciembre frío • a cold December.

Some nouns can take either masculine or feminine gender, although in practice one or other usually predominates:

el/la azúcar • sugar,	*el/la mar* • sea,
el/la arte • art,	*el/la esperma* • sperm.

3.2. The gender of compound nouns

The tendency is for these to be masculine, e.g.:

el altavoz • loudspeaker, *el cumpleaños* • birthday, *el puntapié* • kick, *el menosprecio* • contempt, but
la vanagloria • boasting, *la bocacalle* • turning street.

4. Number

In addition to gender markers, Spanish nouns also have markers to indicate whether they are singular or plural.

Plurals are formed in different ways according to the ending of the singular form, as summarized in table below:

Nouns ending in:	To form plural add:	Examples
unstressed vowel stressed -é	-s	el parque/los parques el canto/los cantos la tribu/las tribus el café/los cafés el pie/los pies el canapé/los canapés
all consonants (except -s) stressed vowels (except -é)	-es	el abad/los abades la cruz/las cruces el pan/los panes el rey/los reyes la cárcel/las cárceles esquí/esquíes maniquí/maniquíes tisú/tisúes
(But note papá/papás, mamá/mamás, sofá/sofás, dominó/dominós)		
-s (except words of only one syllable and those with the stress on the last syllable)	invariable	el lunes/los lunes la crisis/las crisis el análisis/los análisis
words ending in -s with one syllable or with the final syllable stressed.	-es	el país/los países el mes/los meses la res/las reses

4.1. Number in different types of nouns

In Spanish, number is based on the opposition between «one» and «many», that is, use of the singular denotes one thing, use of the plural, more than one.

With certain nouns, use of the plural changes the sense of the words, for example, the abstract noun *trabajo* (work) becomes concrete when pluralized: *mis trabajos* (i.e. pieces of work I have done).

The class a noun belongs to is important in order to understand its behaviour as regards pluralization:

		Plural	Indefinite quantifier	Numeral	Article
Common nouns	Countable	+ mesas	− pocos caballos	+ dos mesas	+ la mesa
	Mass	− carne	+ mucho frío	− * dos carnes	+ la carne
Proper nouns		− * Luises	−	−	−

When a noun becomes plural, it is *quantified* in some way. With countable nouns, this is quite clear: *libro-libros, mesa-mesas.* But when we pluralize a mass noun, what we are doing at the same time is subdividing a continuum of meaning (e.g.: *vino* • *wine*) into different semantic categories (*los vinos dulces* • *sweet wines*). If the noun cannot be subdivided into different semantic categories in this way, it cannot be pluralized. For instance, we cannot say:

* Hace muchos fríos • *It is very colds.*

But we can say:

Los fríos del Norte son gélidos • *The colds of the North are freezing.*

In the first instance *frío* is indivisible and in the second we are talking about a number of distinct units of «cold».

When countable nouns are used in the singular without a determiner, they do not denote either singular or plural. For example, in the phrase:

Se busca secretaria • *Secretary wanted,*

the noun «secretaria» remains unquantified.

No countable noun may be used as a subject without quantification:

* pasa vaca • ** cow passes,*
* viene coche • ** car comes,*

pasa una vaca • *a cow is passing,*
viene un coche • *a car is coming.*

Proper nouns referring to people are normally used only in the singular but can be used in the plural in certain circumstances, for instance:

dos Murillos • *two Murillos.*

4.1.1. *Cardinal numbers*

Cardinal numbers may be pluralized when used as nouns:

*Ganó con cinco **treces**, dos **doces** y seis **treinta y cincos***
• *He won with five thirteens, two twelves and six thirty-fives.*
*Tiene **cientos** e incluso **miles** de **millones***
• *He has hundreds, even thousands of millions.*

Mil only takes the plural when used in this way, with other cardinal numbers it is invariable:

dos mil • *two thousand,*
tres mil • *three thousand...*

However, *ciento, millón, billón,* and *trillón* are pluralized in conjunction with other cardinal numbers:

doscientos mil • *two hundred thousand,*
cuatro millones • *four million.*

4.1.2. Nouns borrowed from other languages

In general, foreign words that have become absorbed into the language follow the rules of Spanish. However, there are exceptions and variations where words have unusual endings —for instance, the Real Academia admits both «álbumes» and «álbums». In practice many nouns which retain a Latin structure either remain unchanged in the plural or simply add a final **-s**:

los memorándum/memorándums • *los déficit/déficits.*

4.1.3. Nouns only used in the plural

Some nouns appear almost exclusively in the plural:

alicates • *pliers,*
anales • *annals,*
bártulos • *belongings,*
bragas • *knickers,*
comicios • *elections,*
cosquillas • *as in tener cosquillas —to be ticklish,*
enaguas • *petticoats,*
enseres • *belongings,*
esposas • *handcuffs,*
funerales • *funeral,*
gafas • *glasses,*
termas • *hot springs,*
tinieblas • *shadows.*

Some of these may also, less commonly, be used in the singular, e.g.: *funeral* • *funeral, enagua* • *petticoat.*

With some words, the plural form may be a noun derived from an adjective or adverb, or a noun only used in the plural as part of an idiomatic expression:

adentros • *as in «para sus adentros» —to oneself,*
afueras • *outskirts,*
alrededores • *surrounding area,*
algodones • *as in «tener entre algodones» (pieces of cotton, to pamper),*
credenciales • *credentials,*
mayores • *elders,*
expectativas • *expectations,*
medios • *means,*

4.1.4. *Nouns signifying duality*

These are commonly used in the plural, although some may also appear in the singular:

bigotes • *moustache,*
narices • *nostrils,*
pantalones • *trousers,*
esposas • *handcuffs,*
nalgas • *buttocks,*

calcetines • *socks,*
pulmones • *lungs,*
tenazas • *tongs,*
tijeras • *scissors,*
alforjas • *saddlebags.*

4.1.5. *The plural of compound nouns*

Generally speaking, only the second element in the word is pluralized:

camposantos • *cemeteries,*   *sordomudos* • *deaf and dumb people.*

However, some compound nouns —including those which probably have not become consolidated as such yet— pluralize the first element, whether or not the two parts are written separately:

cualesquier/cualesquiera • *whichever,*   *quienesquier/a* • *whoever,*
hombres-clave • *key men,*   *sofás-cama* • *sofa-beds.*

Some compound nouns have an invariable plural form even though they may be used in the singular:

el/los *cumpleaños* • *birthday-s,*
el/los *espantapájaros* • *scarecrow-s,*
el/los *paracaídas* • *parachute-s,*
el/los *rompecorazones* • *heartbreaker-s.*

4.1.6. *Nouns without a plural*

These include ***el*** *caos* • *chaos* and ***la*** *nada* • *nothingness,* ***nadie*** • *nobody,* ***alguien*** • *somebody,* ***cada*** • *each.*

4 | DETERMINERS

1. General features

Determiners are grammatical words belonging to a closed set—that is, there is only a limited number of them, described below in this chapter. Their function is to identify or particularize the noun, e.g.:

este *libro* • *This book*
el *libro* • *The book*
mi *libro* • *My book*
un *libro* • *A book*

1.1. Use and omission of the determiner

The determiner is in most cases an essential element in the Noun Phrase, especially when the noun acts as a subject, for instance:

El *libro está sobre la mesa*
• *The book is on the table*
Nuestros *amigos regresaron de vacaciones*
• *Our friends came back from holiday*

but not:

Libro está sobre la mesa.
Amigos regresaron de vacaciones.

However, the determiner may be omitted in the following cases:

— With proper nouns:

Julia viste de negro • *Julia dresses/is dressed in black.*
Madrid es la capital de España • *Madrid is the capital of Spain.*

— With common nouns, when they appear:

on labels, notices, etc.: *Azúcar* • *Sugar,* *Huelga* • *Strike.*
as newspaper headlines: *Guerra en Centroamérica* • *War in Central America.*
as titles of books, pieces of music, etc.: *Crimen y castigo* • *Crime and Punishment,*
Sonata de otoño • *Autumn Sonata.*
in the vocative, that is, when they are being used to address someone: *Escucha amigo*
• *Listen, friend,* *Oiga, señor* • *Listen, Sir.*

— In certain prepositional phrases, for example:

Viajar **en tren** • *To travel by train*

*Encontrar algo **por casualidad*** • *To come across something by chance.*
*Comer **con placer*** • *To eat with pleasure.*

— Where two or more nouns appear together as components of a group:

Mujeres y niños *se salvaron del incendio* • *Women and children were saved from the fire.*
Padres y profesores *estuvieron presentes* • *Parents and teachers were present.*

— Where the noun is used as a complement to the subject, especially when describing someone's profession, or role (note the disparity with English here):

*Pepe es **médico** del hospital* • *Pepe is a hospital doctor.*
*Pilar es **profesora de idiomas*** • *Pilar is a language teacher.*
*Pepe es **amigo** de Pilar* • *Pepe is Pilar's friend.*

— With nouns in apposition:

*Valencia, **capital** de la huerta, tiene un clima envidiable* • *Valencia, capital of the fruit and vegetable growing area, has an enviable climate.*

— Where nouns are used in a figurative sense, for example in proverbs:

Obras son amores y no buenas razones • *Actions speak louder than words.*

1.2. Positions

The Determiner (Det) is generally positioned before the noun:

un/el *hombre joven* • *a/the young man*
cierto *día* • *a certain day*
¡qué *promesa!* • *what a promise!*
tal *promesa* • *such a promise*
cien *cuadernos* • *one hundred notebooks*
aquella *señora* • *that lady*

The exceptions to this are *aquel, aquella, algún(o)* and *alguna*, which may follow the noun, and *mío, mía,* etc., which must always follow it.

1.3. Agreement

The determiner agrees with its noun in number and gender:

la cárcel • *the prison*   *las cárceles* • *the prisons*
esta mesa • *this table*   *estas mesas* • *these tables*
poco público • *small attendance*   *pocas personas* • *few people*

Because of this, the determiner serves to mark gender and number in cases where the noun is invariable:

La crisis • *The crisis*   *Las crisis* • *The crises*
Un lunes • *A Monday*   *Los lunes* • *Mondays*

1.4. Types of determiners

Grammarians distinguish the following types of determiners in Spanish (approximate translations are given as a guide only):

Indefinite adjectives: un/a • *a, algún/a* • *some, cierto/a* • *a certain, cualquier/a* • *any, otro/a* • *another, mucho/a* • *a lot of, demasiado/a* • *too much, bastante* • *enough, poco/a* • *little, más* • *more, menos* • *less, tanto/a* • *so much, unos/as* • *some, varios/as* • *several, todo/a, todos/as* • *all, no... alguno/a* • *none, ninguno/a* • *none, cualquiera* • *any, cualesquiera* • *whatever.*

Distributive adjectives: cada, sendos, tal • *each, both, such,* etc.

Numerals: un/a • *one, medio/a* • *half, doble* • *double, triple* • *triple, dos* • *two, tres* • *three, cero* • *none, zero, ambos/as* • *both.*

Articles: el/la/lo, los/las • *the.*

Demonstrative adjectives: este/a • *this, estos/as* • *these, ese/a* • *that, esos/as* • *those, aquel/la* • *that, aquellos/as* • *those.*

Possessive adjectives: mi/mis • *my, tu/tus* • *your, su/sus* • *your/his/her/their, mío/a* • *mine, míos/as* • *of mine, tuyo/a* • *of yours, tuyos/as* • *of yours, suyo/a, suyos/as* • *of his/her/theirs/yours,* etc., *nuestro/a, nuestros/as* • *of ours, vuestro/a, vuestros/as* • *of yours.*

Interrogative and exclamatory adjectives: cuánto/a • *how much, cuántos/as* • *how many, qué* • *what, cuál/es* • *which.*

Relatives: cuyo/a, cuyos/as • *whose.*

2. Indefinite adjectives

As their name suggests, these are used to quantify the noun in a vague or imprecise way.

2.1. *Algún, alguna, algunos, algunas* • *some*

*En **algún** libro tiene que estar lo que buscas.*
• *What you are looking for should be in **some** book (or other).*
*Dirígete a **algún** centro de información.*
• *Ask at an information centre.*

Algún and *alguna* are always used before the noun. They should not be confused with the form *alguno*, which is described below.
The may also be used in the plural:

***Algunos** periódicos y **algunas** revistas publican artículos de interés.*
• *Some (i.e. a few) newspapers and a few magazines publish interesting articles.*

2.2. Cierto/a/os/as • certain

*No deben consultarse **ciertas** obras por inútiles.*
* Certain works are useless and should not be used as reference.
***Cierto** escritor me remitió esta obrita.*
* A certain author sent me this little book.

Note that when used *after* the noun —as a qualifying adjective—, **cierto/a** means certain in the sense of «true»:

*Es una noticia **cierta*** • It is true.

2.3. Otro/a/os/as • another/some other

*Le acompañaba **otra persona que yo no conocía.***
* He was with another person whom I did not know.
*Se había puesto **otros** zapatos.*
* He had put on some other shoes.

Otro/a/os/as are *never* used with the indefinite article (*un/a/os/as*) («an other» in English). However they may be used in combination with the following:

With numerals: *Ponnos **otras dos** copas* • Give us two more glasses.
With demonstratives: *No, te compraré **este otro** coche* • No, I shall buy you this other car.
With quantitatives: *Tiene **otros muchos** libros para ti* • He has many other books for you.

When used as an adjective, *otro* takes on the sense of «different»:

*Ven **otro** día* • Come another day.

Note also the following very common uses of *otro*:

***Otra** vez* • again.
*El **otro** día* • the other day.

2.4. Cualquier • any

***Cualquier** libro es mejor que el que compraste.*
* Any book is better than the one you bought.
*Tomaremos **cualquier** resolución.*
* We will pass any resolution (whatsoever).

There is also a form *cualquiera*, which is used after the noun, and means insignificance or unimportance:

*No se trata de un libro **cualquiera.***
* It's not just any book.

Compare this with:

*No se trata de que me compres **cualquier** libro, sino un libro bueno.*
* I don't want you to buy me any book, just a good book.
Cualquier in this latter example simply means that the noun is unidentified.

2.5. Un/una • one

Un buen día lo encontraron durmiendo en plena calle.
• One fine day they found him asleep in the middle of the street.
No sé, pero vi que paseaba con una alumna por el parque.
• I don't know, but I saw him walking in the park with one of his pupils.

For further explanation of *un/una,* see under Numerals below. Its sense is very close to that of the indefinite article in English (a, an).

2.6. Unos/unas • some

LLegaron unos libros, pero no los miré.
• Some books arrived, but I didn't look at them.
Vinieron a verme unas personas un poco raras.
• Some rather strange people came to see me.

In the above examples, the meaning is of an indefinite quantity. However, it may also mean an indefinite *small* quantity, i.e., a few:

Pasaremos unos días en la playa.
• We will spend a few days at the beach.

It may also have a *partitive* sense, meaning «some» or «a few» of a group:

Surcaban el cielo unos aviones.
• Some (of the) planes were circling overhead.

Or it may be used for emphasis:

Te lo he dicho muchas veces: son unos vagos.
• I've told you time and again, they're a load of good-for-nothings.

Or in an adverbial sense, taking the place of «aproximadamente»:

Sólo he gastado unas dos mil pesetas.
• I've only spent about two thousand pesetas.

2.7. Varios/varias • several

He recibido ya varias postales tuyas.
• I've already received several postcards from you.
Saludé a varios amigos.
• I said hello to several friends.

It is only when used *after* the noun, as an adjective, that *varios* means «various»:

He recibido postales varias.
• I have received a variety of/various postcards.

2.8. Partitives

The words belonging to this group all denote an imprecise quantity or part of something and, in the singular, tend to be used with mass nouns. All have forms for masculine, feminine, singular and plural:

mucho/a = much	poco/a = little	tanto/a = so much	demasiado/a = too much
muchos/as = many	pocos/as = few	tantos/as = so many	demasiados/as = too many

*Este problema presenta **mucha** dificultad.*
* This problem is giving much/a lot of trouble.
*Dispongo de **poco** tiempo.*
* I have little time (to spare).
*Este ejercicio requiere **demasiada** paciencia.*
* This exercise requires too much patience.
***Tanto** sol no es bueno.*
* So much sun is not a good thing.

They may be combined as follows:

— *mucho/a* can be used with the article or possessive in front, or with *otro/a* after it:

*Los **muchos** amigos que tiene le han abandonado.*
* His many friends have abandoned him.
*Sus **muchas** riquezas resultaron inexistentes.*
* His great riches turned out to be non-existent.
*Tiene otras **muchas** cualidades.*
* He has many other qualities.

— *demasiado/a* can only be combined with *poco/a*, which must always follow it:

*Toma **demasiada** poca leche.*
* He/she drinks too little milk.

— *poco/a* may be preceded by an article if there is a complement following on:

*Ya ha perdido las **pocas** fincas que le quedaban.*
* He has already lost the few farms he had left.

but not: *Tiene las **pocas** fincas.

— *poco/a* may also be combined with *muy*:

*Ya le queda muy **poco** dinero.*
* He has very little money left.

— *tanto/a* may be used with a second element in a comparative sense:

*Tiene **tanto** dinero **que** ni él mismo sabe lo que tiene.*
* He has so much money that not even he knows what he's got.
*Tiene **tanta** inteligencia **como** su padre.*
* She/he has as much intelligence as her/his father.

When used without the second element it merely emphasizes amount:

*No se puede ni andar con **tanto** turista.*
* *There are so many tourists you can't even walk.*

Note also the following diminutive and superlative forms which are a feature of Spanish:

poquito/a, poquísimo/a = very little
poquitos/as, poquísimos/as = very few

Ponme poquita leche • *Give me very little milk*
¡Qué poquísima leche me has puesto!
* *What a tiny drop of milk you've given me!*

muchísimo/a = very much
muchísimos/as = very many

tantísimo/a = so very much, such an extraordinary amount, etc.
tantísimos/as = so very many.

Poco and **mucho** combine with the noun «vez» to act as adverbs of time:

pocas veces = rarely
muchas veces = frequently

2.9. *Bastante/bastantes* • quite a lot, a fair amount...

*Perdimos **bastante** tiempo.*
* *We lost a fair amount of time.*
*He estado en Francia **bastantes** veces.*
* *I've been to France on quite a few occasions.*

Note that masculine and feminine have the same form.
When **bastante** is used *after* the noun, as an adjective, it means «enough».

*No disponemos de tiempo **bastante**.*
* *We do not have enough time.*

2.10. Más • *more,* menos • *less*

Both these forms are invariable.

*Volvieron con **más** hombres* • *They came back with more men*
*Tienen **menos** hombres y **menos** fuerza* • *They have less men and less strength.*

Más and *menos* can also function as adverbs:

*Comimos **más**, pero bebimos **menos*** • *We ate more but drank less*
*El león **más** feroz...* • *The fiercest lion...*

2.11. The «zero determiner» (Ø)

What is known as the «zero determiner» (i.e. omitting it altogether) can be used in Spanish as a means of expressing an indefinite quantity of something:

Comen pan • *They eat bread.*
Tomaron vinos en la taberna • *They drank wine in the tavern.*

2.12. Todo • *all,* ningún • *none*

These make reference to the totality of something, or to all items in a set, either positively (todo = all) or negatively (ningún = none). They have both masculine and feminine forms, which agree with the noun to which they are referring:

*No he visto a **ningún** hombre/**ninguna** mujer.*
• *I have not seen any man/woman.*
***Todos** los vecinos deben respetar las normas.*
• *All the occupants (of block of flats, etc.) should respect the rules.*

Although both have singular and plural forms, *todo/a* appears more often in the plural and *ningún/a* in the singular.
Todo in the singular takes on the sense of «every»:

***Todo** vecino debe respetar las normas* • *Every occupant...*

When *ningún/a* is used in the plural the preference is for it to appear after the noun:

*No hay aquí comodidades **ningunas.***
• *There are no comforts here at all.*

Todo/a is often used in the singular with an article.

*Trabajó **todo** el día* • *He worked all day.*
*Se comió **todo** el pan* • *All the bread got eaten/He ate up all the bread.*

Todo/a can be combined with:

— Possessives and demonstratives:

*Me trajeron **todos sus** regalos.*
• *They brought me all their presents.*
*No me digas **todas esas** barbaridades.*
• *Don't tell me all that nonsense.*

— The definite article, plus *que* or *de*:

***Todo el que** estudia, aprueba* • *All those who study, pass the exam.*
***Todos los de** ayer estaban rotos* • *All yesterday's were broken.*

— Personal pronouns:

***Todas vosotras** iréis de excursión* • *You will all go on a trip.*
***Todos ellos** nos miran* • *They are all looking at us.*

There are a number of set phrases and expressions using «todo»:

*de **todo*** = *everything,* as in *Tiene de todo.*

del **todo** = completely, as in *No estaba del todo convencido.*
ante **todo** = first of all,
a **todo** esto = meanwhile,
con **todo** = despite,
así y **todo** = despite.

3. Distributive adjectives

Cada • *each, every* - **Sendos/as** • *each, both* - **tal/tales** • *such.*

As their name suggests, these indicate the distribution of the different elements of something.

3.1. Cada • *each, every* is invariable in gender and is only used with singular nouns:

Cada *día que pasa, su español mejora.*
• *Every day that goes by, their (his, her, your) Spanish improves.*
*A **cada** día le corresponde su preocupación.*
• *Each day brings its own worries.*

Cada may also be used with nouns which are ostensibly plural, but treated as one unit:

Cada *mil soldados tenía(n) un jefe.*
• *Each thousand soldiers had its commander.*

In cases such as this, the verb may be either in singular or plural.

3.2. Sendos/as • *each of two, both;* is always used in the plural and agrees in gender with the noun:

*Sus dos amigos me escribieron **sendas** postales.*
• *His two friends each/both sent me a postcard.*

Sendos/as indicates distribution, as opposed to *ambos/as,* which identifies one element with another.

3.3. Tal/tales • *such, this;* has a vaguer distributive sense than *cada* or *sendos/as,* and can often be translated simply by «*this*» or «*that*»

Tal *conducta no me agrada* = **Esa** *conducta no me agrada.*
• *I don't like that/such behaviour.*
*No me convences con **tal** argumento* = ... *con **ese** argumento.*
• *You don't convince me with such an argument* = *with that argument.*

Although there are both singular and plural forms *tal/tales,* these are invariable in gender:

*No me cuentes **tales** cosas.*
* Don't tell me thing like that.

Tal/tales may also be used adjectivally after the noun:

*No me vengas ahora con cosas **tales.***
* Don't come to me with that sort of thing now.

Or on its own as a pronoun:

*El director no dijo **tal.***
* The head didn't say that/such a thing.

It also appears in set phrases such as:

***tal** vez =perhaps*
*con **tal** que = if*
*¿Qué **tal**? = How're things going?*

4. Numerals

4.1. General features

Numbers in Spanish are as follow:

0 *cero*	10 *diez*	20 *veinte*	30 *treinta*
1 *uno*	11 *once*	21 *veintiuno*	31 *treinta y uno*
2 *dos*	12 *doce*	22 *veintidós*	32 *treinta y dos*
3 *tres*	13 *trece*	23 *veintitrés*	40 *cuarenta*
4 *cuatro*	14 *catorce*	24 *veinticuatro*	50 *cincuenta*
5 *cinco*	15 *quince*	25 *veinticinco*	60 *sesenta*
6 *seis*	16 *dieciséis*	26 *veintiséis*	70 *setenta*
7 *siete*	17 *diecisiete*	27 *veintisiete*	80 *ochenta*
8 *ocho*	18 *dieciocho*	28 *veintiocho*	90 *noventa*
9 *nueve*	19 *diecinueve*	29 *veintinueve*	100 *cien*

101 *ciento uno/a*	102 *ciento dos, etc.*
200 *doscientos/as*	300 *trescientos/as*
400 *cuatrocientos/as*	500 *quinientos/as*
600 *seiscientos/as*	700 *setecientos/as*
800 *ochocientos/as*	900 *novecientos/as*
1.000 *mil*	1.001 *mil uno/a, etc.*
1.100 *mil cien*	1.200 *mil doscientos/as, etc.*
1.234 *mil doscientos treinta y cuatro*	
1.000.000 *un millón*	2.000.000 *dos millones*
1.000.000.000 *mil millones*	1.000.000.000.000 *un billón*

Spanish numerals may be used with or without the article:

*Los **trescientos sesenta y cinco** días del año.*
* The 365 days of the year.

Numbers from 16 to 19 and from 21 to 29 are written as one word:

Dieciséis niños y **veintidós** niñas • *16 boys and 22 girls.*

Uno and *veintiuno* drop their final —**o** before a masculine noun:

Un hombre • *one/a man.*
Veintiún alumnos • *21 pupils.*

Ciento drops its final syllable when it comes before masculine or feminine nouns, and before another number which multiplies it:

Cien coches • *100 cars.*　　**Cien** casas • *100 houses.*
Cien mil pesetas • *A hundred thousand pesetas,* but:
Ciento cincuenta años • *150 years.*

y is used to link tens and units:

Cuarenta **y** *seis* • *46.*

but not when there are no tens:

Ciento ocho • *108.*

(The one exception to this is the phrase *Las mil* **y** *una noches* = *The thousand and one nights.*)

All hundreds between 200 and 900 agree with the noun in terms of gender:

*Doscien**tos** coch**es*** • *200 cars.*
*Ochocien**tas** pesetas* • *800 pesetas.*

Mil is invariable:
Mil *páginas* (1000 pages), **mil** *árboles* (1000 trees), except when it is used substantively, when it may take a plural form:

Miles de visitantes • *Thousands of visitors.*

Note that **un billón** is a million million, not a US billion.
The cardinal number —rather than the ordinal, as in English— is used for centuries:

El siglo XX (veinte) • *the 20th century.*
El siglo XVI (dieciséis) • *the 16th century.*

Cero (zero) can be used as a determiner:

Ganó cero puntos • *He got nought/no points.*

Ambos or **los dos** (both), indicates that two persons or things are being referred to:

*Ganó **ambos** premios en la lotería/Ganó **los dos** premios...*
• *He won both prizes in the lottery.*

4.2. Positioning of numerals

The normal position is in front of the noun:

*Entraron en el puerto **cinco** barcos.*
* *Five boats came into the harbour.*

Sometimes however, the numeral may be separated from the noun:

*Alumnos en el centro sólo hay **venticinco.***
* *There are only 25 pupils in the school.*

Numerals always come after personal pronouns:

*Sentaos conmigo **vosotros dos.***
* *You two sit with me.*

4.3. Fractions and multiples

Fractions are expressed using the following formula:

Una... (ordinal number)... parte de

e.g.: *una cuarta parte* • *a fourth;* *una sexta parte* • *a sixth.*

With lower numbers, the following are used:

1/2   *un medio, la mitad de* • *a/one half.*
1/3   *un tercio, una tercera parte* • *a/one third.*
1/4   *un cuarto, una cuarta parte* • *a/one fourth.*
1/5   *un quinto, una quinta parte* • *a/one fifth.*

To indicate multiple quantities of something, the following are used, preceding the noun:

doble *ración* • *double measure.*
triple *asesinato* • *triple murder.*
cuádruple *alumbramiento* • *quadruple birth.*
quíntuple *posibilidad* • *five times the possibility.*

The following formula may also be used:

numeral + veces $\begin{cases} \text{mayor} \\ \text{más que} \end{cases}$

e.g.:

Cinco veces mayor *que el otro del mismo color.*
* *Five times as big as the other one of the same colour.*

4.4. Un/una • *one, a*

As a numeral, *un/una* has masculine and feminine forms, but no plural inflections (the plural being *dos, tres,* etc.).

Doscientos un pájaros • *201 birds.*
Doscientas una hojas • *201 leaves.* (Note here *doscientos/as*, which take the plural inflection).

40

Before feminine nouns which begin with «ha-» or a stressed «á», the feminine form drops its final -a:

Un hacha • *One/an axe.*
Un águila • *One/an eagle.*

As well as being used in a strictly numeric sense (one), it is also the indefinite article (a):

*Ha llamado **un** señor* • *A gentleman has called.*
*Es **una** cabra montesa* • *It is a mountain goat.*
*He comprado **un** jersey para combinar con **una** falda.*
• *I have bought a jumper to go with a skirt.*

Other uses of **un/a**:

— Emphasizing a negative quality, as in:

*Eres **un** cobarde/**un** infeliz* • *You are a coward/a poor wretch.*

— When used with *todo/a* they perform the function of reinforcing the statement being made:

*Es ya **todo un** hombre/**toda una** mujer.*
• *He-She is already quite a man/woman.*

— In structures expressing a superlative sense after the verb «hace», for example:

*Hace **un** frío que pela* • *It's bitterly cold.*

5. The article

The term «article» is used here to refer to what is traditionally known as the «definite article» (the). This is because the so-called «indefinite article» (a, an) does not exist as such in Spanish and is more appropriately dealt with under indefinite adjectives and numerals.

5.1. General features

The article has different forms for masculine, feminine, singular and plural:

	Masculine	Feminine
Singular Plural	**el** **los**	**la** **las**

When the masculine singular article is combined with «de» or «a», it becomes contracted, as follows:

*de + el = **del***
*a + el = **al***

*Viene **del** mercado* • *He's coming from the market.*

*El libro **del** alumno* • *The pupil's book.*
*Se va **al** monte cada día* • *He goes off to the hills every day.*

(Note that this contraction does not occur with proper nouns which begin with **El**: *Va a El Escorial, Vengo de El Salvador*).

When a feminine noun begins with a stressed *á- or ha-*, **el** is used instead of **la** in the singular:

el *agua/**las** aguas* • *the water, waters.*
el *hacha/**las** hachas* • *the axe, axes,*
but
la *abeja,* **la** *hazaña,* etc., where the stress does not fall on the initial syllable.

Where there is an adjective between article and noun, the article reverts to *la*:

La *terrible hacha de los vikingos.*
• *The terrible axe of the Vikings.*
La *única arma que tenía era la inteligencia.*
• *The only weapon he had was his intelligence.*

Adjectives do not follow this rule:

La *alta sociedad* • *high society.*

The article often carries information about the gender of the noun which is not evident from the form of the noun itself, i.e. when it ends in:

— *e* *la llave* • *the key, la fuente* • *the fountain, el fuerte* • *the fort, el cisne* • *the swan.*
— *í* *el rubí* • *the ruby, el alhelí* • *wallflower, el bisturí* • *the scalpel.*
— *u* *la tribu* • *the tribe, el espíritu* • *the spirit.*
— *d* *el césped* • *the lawn, la salud* • *the health.*
— *l* *la cárcel* • *the prison, la miel* • *the honey, el cincel* • *the chisel.*
— *n* *el pan* • *the bread, la razón* • *the reason.*
— *r* *la flor* • *the flower, el dolor* • *the pain.*
— *s* *el lunes* • *on Monday, la crisis* • *the crisis.*
— *z* *la cruz* • *the cross, el lápiz* • *the pencil.*

The function of the article is to identify the noun, which it precedes:

el *hombre* • *the man.*
la *puerta* • *the door.*

It cannot be combined with indefinite determiners such as *algún, ningún* or *cualquier,* and can only be combined with demonstratives or possessives when these come after the noun:

El *libro **éste*** • *This* (emphatic) *book, but not El este libro.*
El *libro **mío*** • *My* (emphatic) *book, but not El mi libro.*

5.2. Use of the article

It is always used with a singular noun which functions as a subject:

La clase está en la tercera planta
• *The classroom is on the third floor.*

42

La niña sobresalía en la lectura
- *The girl was outstanding in reading.*
El dulce dormir de los bebés
- *The sweet sleep of babies.*

However, it may be omitted in the plural:

Las vacas pasan por la calle
- *The cows are going down the street.*
Pasan vacas por la calle
- *There are cows going down the street.*

The article is omitted in proverbs and sayings which have become part of the language:

Ojos que no ven, corazón que no siente.
- *What the eye doesn't see the heart doesn't grieve over.*
Casa con dos puertas, mala es de guardar.
- *A house with two doors is difficult to protect.*

In certain contexts the use of the article is optional:

Madre e hija caminaban juntas por la acera.
- *Mother and daughter walked down the pavement together.*
La madre y la hija caminaban juntas por la acera.
- *The mother and daughter walked down the pavement together.*

When the noun is a direct object, the use of the article is optional (although the meaning is affected):

— with mass and countable nouns in the singular:

Busco al criado • *I am looking for the servant.*
Busco criado • *I am looking for a servant.*
¿Tienen el asiento? • *Have you got the seat?*
¿Tienen asiento? • *Have you got a seat?*

— with plural nouns:

Perdí las plumas • *I lost the pens.*
Perdí plumas • *I lost some pens.*
Compré las cintas de vídeo • *I bought the video tapes.*
Compré cintas de vídeo • *I bought some video tapes.*

When the noun is an indirect object, it always requires the article:

Dio limosna al pobre • *He gave alms to the poor man.*
Entregó el bolígrafo nuevo al amigo. • *She gave the new pen to her friend.*

However, in the plural, an indirect object may or may not take the article:

Dio limosna a *los hombres* • *He gave alms to the men.*
Dio limosna a pobres • *He gave alms to the poor.*

With nouns in apposition, the presence or absence of the article also changes the meaning:

*Vosotros, **los** españoles, sois alegres y ruidosos.*
• *You, the Spanish, are happy and noisy.*
Vosotros, españoles, sois alegres y ruidosos.
• *You Spanish are happy and noisy.*

The presence of the article serves to identify as opposed to classify:

*Su padre era **el** profesor de inglés.*
• *His father was the English teacher.*
Su padre era profesor de inglés.
• *His father was an English teacher.*

Nouns in the vocative never take an article:

*¡Oye, **papá**!* • *Hey, dad!*
*¡Mira, **mujer**!* • *Look, dear!*

Complements expressing cause or manner do not generally require the article:

*Lo hizo **por compasión*** • *He did it out of compassion.*
*Nos quedamos **sin entradas** para el cine* • *We have been left without tickets for the cinema.*

However, complements indicating place always require an article:

*Se cayó por **las** escaleras* • *He fell on the stairs.*
*Dio un paseo por **el** campo* • *She went for a walk in the country.*

But it may be omitted when two elements appear together:

Caminó por caminos y barrancos. • *She passed over roads and gorges.*

The prepositions *bajo, desde, ante, sobre, tras,* and the phrases *detrás de, frente a, encima de* and *debajo de* all are required to be followed by the article.

Nouns in instrumental prepositional phrases such as the following also require an article:

*El niño juega con **la** pelota* • *The boy is playing with the ball.*
*Juegan **al** tenis* • *They are playing tennis.*

In phrases referring to time, the article must be used as follows:

— with the days of the week:

el *lunes,* **el** *martes...* • *on Monday, on Tuesday, etc.*

but:

hoy es lunes • *today is Monday.*
Se casó en sábado • *He got married on a Saturday.*
*Se casó **el sábado*** • *He got married on Saturday.*

— when referring to the time of day:

*Llegó a **las** seis de **la** mañana* • *She arrived at 6 in the morning.*

but it may be omitted in signs and notices such as:

Abierto de cinco a siete • *Open from five to seven.*

Use of the article with prepositions:

a generally requires it:

*A **los** diez años* • *at age 10.*

but it is not required with:

A mediados de enero • *in mid January.*
*A finales de **los** noventa* • *in the late nineties.*

en does not require an article with:

En 1936 • *in 1936.*
En martes • *on a Tuesday.*
En diciembre • *in December.*

but it does before tens and hundreds:

*En **el** nueve de esta calle* • *At number 9 of this street.*

With seasons, the meaning changes according to whether the article is used or not:

*En **el** otoño* • *in the autumn.*
En otoño • *in autumn.*

Similarly:

*En Navidades/En **las** Navidades* • *At Christmas.*
*En Semana Santa/En **la** Semana Santa* • *At Easter.*

With expressions of movement, the article is not normally used, although it can be, depending on the meaning:

Vamos a casa • *Let's go home.*
*Vamos a **la** casa* • *Let's go to the house.*
Fuimos a misa • *We went to church.*
*Fuimos a **la** misa* • *We went to the mass.*

Similarly:

Dar permiso • *to give permission.*
Dar el permiso necesario • *to give the necessary permission.*
Tener tiempo • *to have time.*
Tener el tiempo necesario • *to have the time necessary.*

Abstract nouns always require an article:

*Detesta **la** pobreza* • *She detests poverty.*
*Admira **la** sencillez de esta persona* • *She admires this person's simplicity.*

5.3. Use of the article with proper noun:

The article is not normally used with the names of countries:

Alemania • *Germany*   *Francia* • *France*
Inglaterra • *England*   *Colombia* • *Colombia*

However, the following countries may sometimes be preceded by an article:

(el) Afganistán	(la) Argentina
(el) Brasil	(el) Camerún
(el) Canadá	(la) China
(el) Ecuador	(los) Estados Unidos (USA)
(el) Indostán	(el) Japón
(el) Paquistán	(el) Paraguay
(el) Perú	(el) Senegal
(el) Uruguay	(el) Yemen

The following proper nouns are always written with an article:

— Cities:
  Los Ángeles, El Escorial, El Ferrol, La Habana, La Haya, Las Palmas.
— Football clubs, etc.:
  el Barcelona, el Real Madrid, el Valencia...
— Some regions:
  la Alcarria, la Mancha, Castilla la Nueva...
— Seas:
— *el Mediterráneo, el Atlántico, el Pacífico...*
— Mountains:
  los Alpes, los Urales, el Cáucaso, el Himalaya, los Andes...
— the names of some streets:
  la Castellana, las Ramblas, los Campos Elíseos...

Proper nouns may also be written with an article when they are being individualized in phrases such as:

La España de los años 90 • *The Spain of the 90s.*
La Alemania de Hitler • *Hitler's Germany.*

The article is always used before personal titles such as: *señora, señorita, señor, capitán, general, rey, papa, presidente, infanta*:

el señor Sánchez • *Mr Sánchez*
la Señorita Julia • *Miss Julia*
el rey Juan Carlos • *King Juan Carlos*
el presidente González • *President González*

However not with the courtesy title *don/doña* or with the religious titles *fray* brother or *sor* sister.
When using surnames in the plural, the article is always used:

los Sánchez • *The Sánchez's*
los Alonso • *the Alonso's*

and when a proper noun is qualified by an adjective:

el famoso Napoleón • *the famous Napoleon*
el gran sultán Almanzor • *the great sultan Almanzor.*

The names of unique objects or beings always take the article:

el Mesías • *the Messiah*
el Sol • *the sun*
el Papa • *the Pope*

With parts of the body and personal objects the article is always used instead of the possessive adjective:

*Ha perdido **el** bolso* • *She has lost **her** handbag.*
*Le han golpeado en **la** cara* • *They hit him in **his** face.*
*Se ha roto **el** pie* • *She's broken **her** foot.*

5.4. *Lo*, the «neuter article»

The «neuter article», *lo*, has no direct translation in English, but its use is widespread and a characteristic of the Spanish language. It has only the one form, which is used as follows:

— With adjectives (**lo** + adj. + *que*):

Lo *guapa **que** eres* • *How beautiful you are.*
Lo *contento **que** está* • *How happy he is.*

Lo serves to emphasize the *quality* the adjective describes. In some cases it may be substituted by an abstract noun (for instance, in the examples above, *tu guapura, su felicidad*) but the meaning is not always exactly the same:

Lo *alto de la torre* • *The highest part of the tower.*
La *altura de la torre* • *The height of the tower.*

— With adverbs (**lo** + adv. + *que*):

Lo *bien **que** escribe* • *How well he writes.*

— *With participles:*

Lo *prohibido gusta más* • *What is forbidden is most pleasurable.*

— With possessive adjectives:

Lo *mío* • *What is mine.*

— With other elements which function as adjectives:

Lo *de Juan* • *what is Juan's, the thing about Juan.*
Lo *del otro día* • *what happened the other day.*

— **Lo** may sometimes be used in an exclamatory sense:

Lo *bien que vive* = *¡Qué bien vive!* • *How well he lives!*

— **Lo** also appears in the following idiomatic expressions:

*A **lo** grande* • *On a grand scale.*
*A **lo** bestia* • *In a monstruous fashion, to extremes.*
*Me da **lo** mismo* • *It's all the same to me.*
*Es **lo** de siempre* • *It's always the same thing.*
*Es **lo** de menos* • *That's the least of (my) worries, what matters least.*

6. Possessive adjectives

The possessive is used to establish a relationship between the noun and a person:

Tu tren • *Your train.*
Mi tren • *My train.*

It also carries information as regards number (*tu* ami*go*, *tus* ami*gos* • *your friend, your friends*) and, in some of its forms, gender (*nuestra casa, nuestro coche* • *our house, our car*).

6.1. Forms of the possessive

A. Expressing relationship with a single person:

		1st person		2nd person		3rd person	
		before noun	after noun	before noun	after noun	before noun	after noun
singular	masc.	*mi*	*mío*	*tu*	*tuyo*	*su*	*suyo*
	fem.		*mía*		*tuya*		*suya*
plural	masc.	*mis*	*míos*	*tus*	*tuyos*	*sus*	*suyos*
	fem.		*mías*		*tuyas*		*suyas*

B. Expressing relationship with more than one person:

		1st person	2nd person	3rd person	
		before & after noun		before noun	after noun
singular	masc.	*nuestro*	*vuestro*	*su*	*suyo*
	fem.	*nuestra*	*vuestra*		*suya*
plural	masc.	*nuestros*	*vuestros*	*su*	*suyos*
	fem.	*nuestras*	*vuestras*		*suyas*

6.2. Positioning

As with other determiners, the possessive generally precedes nouns and adjectives:

Mi libro nuevo • *My new book.*

Tu joven amiga • *Your young friend.*
Su gran ocasión • *Their great occasion.*

The forms *mi, tu, su* and their plurals can only be used in front of the noun.
The forms *nuestro/a, vuestro/a* and their plurals can be used before or after the noun:

Nuestros amigos llegaron tarde
*Los amigos **nuestros** llegaron tarde* } • *Our friends arrived late.*

If the possessive comes after the noun, the use of the article is optional, depending on the shade of meaning being conveyed:

*Hemos recibido **los** saludos **vuestros.***
• *We have received the greetings you sent.*
*Hemos recibido saludos **vuestros.***
• *We have received greetings from you.*

The forms *mío/mía, tuyo/tuya, suyo/suya* and their plurals must always follow the noun:

*Llegó el turno **mío*** • *My turn came.*
*He recibido libros **tuyos*** • *I have received some books of yours.*

6.3. In combination with other elements

Mi, tu, su and their plural forms can be combined as follows:

— with **todo/toda/todos/todas:**

Todas mis cuentas están al día • *All my accounts are up to date.*
Todo mi trabajo resultó inútil • *All my work was in vain.*

— with cardinal and ordinal numbers:

Mis dos libros ya están leídos • *I have read both my books.*
Tu tercera posibilidad aún no ha llegado • *Your third chance has not yet arrived.*

— with demonstratives:

Esta mi primera vez ha sido sólo un intento • *This, my first time, was only a trial run.*

Mío/mía, tuyo/tuya, suyo/suya and their respective plurals can be preceded by:

— the definite article:

*¿Recibiste **la** carta **mía**?* • *Did you get the letter of mine?*

— **un** or **una**:

*Ha llegado **un** paquete **nuestro*** • *A parcel of ours has arrived.*

— numerals or indefinite adjectives:

*No he recibido **ninguna** carta **suya*** • *I have not received any letter of his.*
*Me han llamado **dos** amigos **tuyos*** • *Two friends of yours have phoned me.*

— demonstratives:
*No me gustó nada **ese** amigo **vuestro*** • *I didn't like that friend of yours at all.*

6.4. Use of the possessive

In Spanish the possessive is not used as frequently as in English.

When referring to parts of the body or personal effects where the context makes quite clear to whom they belong, the article is used in preference to the possessive.

Nos metimos las manos en los bolsillos • We put our hands in our pockets.
Luis se quitó el sombrero • Luis took off his hat.

In these cases it is the personal pronoun which identifies the noun in relation to the person.

The possessive is only used for clarification or emphasis:

Me robaron el coche • My car was stolen.
Robaron mi coche • My car was stolen.

7. Demonstrative adjectives

7.1. Forms

Spanish demonstrative adjectives identify the time or space relationship between the noun and the speaker or listener in a system which parallels that of the three grammatical persons (I, you, he/she, etc.);

Esta ventana • This window (near me)
Esa ventana • That window (near you)
Aquella ventana • That window (near them, i.e. over there).

It will be noted therefore that, while English only has a dual system of demonstratives (*this or that*), Spanish has three options. Both **ese** and **aquel** translate as **that**, but **aquel** expresses greater remoteness, either referring to the distant past (En **aquel** tiempo... • *at that time...*) or to a distant object (**Aquel** árbol... • *That tree over there, yonder tree*). However, use is largely a matter of subjective judgment, and even **este** may not always overlap with the English use of *this*.

Spanish demonstratives also carry information concerning the number and gender of the noun:

	1st person		2nd person		3rd person	
	this/these		that/those		that/those	
	masc.	fem.	masc.	fem.	masc.	fem.
singular	este	esta	ese	esa	aquel	aquella
plural	estos	estas	esos	esas	aquellos	aquellas

Note that the forms *esto, eso* and *aquello* (roughly speaking *this, that* and *the other*) are not adjectives, but substantive pronouns. However, they form part of a similar system:

Pon esto aquí • Put this here.
Quita eso de ahí • Take that away from there.
No traigas aquello blanco • Don't bring that white one.

7.2. Positioning

When the demonstrative is used to identify the noun, it always precedes it:

***Este** bello edificio* • *This beautiful building.*
***Aquella** bonita casa* • *That pretty house.*

However, it may be placed after the noun when used in combination with the article or the possessive, which performs the function of identifying the noun:

*El libro **este*** • *This book.*
*La verde pradera **aquella*** • *That green meadow.*
*Mi casa **esta*** • *This house of mine.*

7.3. In combination with other elements

Demonstratives are incompatible with the article when used before the noun, but may be combined with «todo»:

Todas esas** cosas son suposiciones **tuyas.
• *All those things are suppositions of yours.*

They may also be combined with numerals and some indefinite adjectives, as follows:

***Esos** tres niños se han perdido.*
• *Those three boys have got lost.*
***Estas** pocas palabras no convencen a nadie.*
• *These few words don't convince anyone.*
***Estas** muchas ilusiones se desvanecerán pronto.*
• *All these dreams will quickly disappear.*

When a number of determiners are used together in the Noun Phrase, they are used in the following order, counting backwards from the noun:

1. Quantifiers.
2. Possessives.
3. Demonstratives.

Estas	mis	pocas	palabras	convencieron al público
3	2	1	noun	

These few words of mine convinced the public/audience.

7.4. Use of the demonstrative

The most obvious use of the demonstrative is to indicate the situation of something in time or space. Speakers can make reference to:

— something which is near them (first person).
— something which is near the listener (second person).
— something which is near neither the speaker nor the listener (third person).

This is demonstrated in the following exchange:

Me parece que es **esta** *bujía la que falla.*
• *I think it is the spark plug that's not working.*
Sí, **esa** *bujía está muy engrasada.*
• *Yes, that one's very oily.*
Pongamos **aquella** *bujía.*
• *Let's put that other one in.*

Choice of the demonstrative can be a subjective process, as in the above example, dependent on whether speakers view an object as belonging to their personal space or to somebody else's. However, the demonstrative can also be used more objectively to locate an object:

Mira **aquel** *coche rojo* • *Look at that red car over there.*
Quiero **este** *traje* • *I want this suit.*

The demonstrative is also used to indicate location in time. *Este* is used to indicate present time, while *ese* and *aquel* refer to the past:

Sale en **este** *momento* • *He's coming out now.*
Aquel *invierno fue terrible* • *That winter was terrible.*
En **ese** *preciso momento no había nadie en casa.*
• *At that precise moment there was nobody at home.*

In the same way, the demonstrative can be used to indicate *psychological distance* from something. In this case it usually appears after the noun, and takes on a pejorative sense:

No me vengas con la frasecita **esa** *de la jornada legal de 8 horas.*
• *Don't come to me with that little phrase of yours about the 8 hour legal working day.*
Ahí vienen las brujas **esas** • *There they come, those witches.*

8. Interrogative and exclamatory determiners

These are words used to form questions or exclamations. They differ from the relative pronouns *que* and *cuanto*, only in that they carry an accent.

8.1. Interrogatives

¿Qué? • What?, Which?

Qué is invariable in number and gender:

*¿***Qué** *hora es?* • *What time is it?*
*¿***Qué** *días voy?* • *What days shall I go?*
*¿***Qué** *casa es la tuya?* • *Which house is yours?*

¿Cuánto/a/os/as? • How much?, How many?

It agrees with the noun in number and gender:

*¿***Cuántos** *días tiene el año?* • *How many days does a year have?*
*¿***Cuánta** *agua queda?* • *How much water is left?*

8.2. Exclamatory determiners

They have the same forms as the interrogatives:

¡Qué día más hermoso hace hoy!
• *What a (most) beautiful day it is today!*
¡Mira qué ojos tan azules tiene!
• *Look how blue his eyes are!*
¡Cuánta alegría siento! • *How happy I feel!*
¡Cuántos días pasaron sin saber de ti!
• *How many days were gone without a word from you!*
¡Cuánta pobreza hay en el mundo!
• *How much poverty there is in the world!*

9. Relatives: *Cuyo/a/os/as* • whose

Cuyo/a an its plural forms, is an adjective, and always agrees with the noun following it:

Aquellos papeles cuyas fotocopias conservo, no sirven.
• *Those papers which I have photocopies of are no use.*
El libro, cuyo autor no es conocido... • *The book, whose author isn't known...*
Hay negocios cuyas salidas son inciertas.
• *There are pieces of business whose outcome is uncertain.*

5 | ADJECTIVES

1. Qualifying adjectives

1.1. General features

Qualifying adjectives, as opposed to determining adjectives, which have been dealt with in the previous chapter, are *lexical* rather than *grammatical* words. They express the qualities or characteristics of the noun they describe:

*Nos mira una niña **delgada, triste** y **pensativa.***
* *A slim, sad, pensive girl is looking at us.*

They occur either as an optional element in the NP:

Det + N + Adj = *El gato **blanco*** • *The white cat.*
Det + Adj + N = *La **blanca** nieve* • *The white snow.*

or as an *essential* element in a Verb Phrase in structures such as:

Ser + Adj = *(El gato) es **blanco*** • *The cat is white.*
Parecer + Adj = *(El gato) parece **blanco*** • *The cat seems white.*
Estar + Adj = *(El gato) está **enfermo*** • *The cat is ill.*
Llegar + Adj = *(Los corredores) llegaron **cansados*** • *The runners arrived tired.*

Qualifying adjectives have certain features in common with nouns, that is, they take gender and number inflections in order to agree with the noun they are intended to qualify:

Gender: **La** cas**a** blanc**a**/**El** gat**o** blanc**o**.
Number: **Las** cas**as** blanc**as**/**Los** gat**os** blanc**os**.

But unlike nouns, many adjectives have «intensive» forms, derived by adding the suffix **-ísimo**:

Una montaña alta • *A high mountain.*
*Una montaña alt**ísima*** • *A very high mountain.*
Un libro interesante • *An interesting book.*
*Un libro interesant**ísimo*** • *An extremely interesting book.*

They may be combined with **lo**:

***Lo** alto de la sierra* • *The high part of the mountains.*
***Lo** hermosa que parece la noche* • *How beautiful the night seems.*

1.2. Gender

Adjectives take on the gender of the noun they describe. Their endings change as follows:

masculine form	feminine form	example
-o	-a	*pequeño, pequeña* • small
-ete	-eta	*regordete, regordeta* • plump
-ote	-ota	*grandote, grandota* • big, strapping
-án	-ana	*holgazán, holgazana* • lazy
-ín	-ína	*parlanchín, parlanchina* • talkative
-ol	-ola	*español, española* • Spanish
-ón	-ona	*burlón, burlona* • joking
-or	-ora	*trabajador, trabajadora* • hard-working
-és	-esa	*inglés, inglesa* • English
uz-	-uza	*andaluz, andaluza* • Andalusian

Some adjectives are invariable in both the masculine and feminine gender:

Ending in		
	-a	*indígena* • indigenous, native *pueblo indígena, población indígena*
	-e	*célebre* • celebrated *hombre célebre, mujer célebre*
	-ente	*insolente* • insolent *niño insolente, niña insolente*
	-iente	*sonriente* • smiling *niño sonriente, niña sonriente*
	-ense	*oscense* • from Huesca *hombre oscense, mujer oscense*
	-ble	*amable* • friendly *vecino amable, vecina amable*
	-í	*israelí* • Israeli *producto israelí, naranja israelí*
	-ú	*hindú* • Hindu *pueblo hindú, lengua hindú*
	-al	*ideal* • ideal *hecho ideal, hazaña ideal*
	-ar	*lunar* • lunar *frío lunar, luz lunar*
	-az	*feraz* • fertile *campo feraz, tierra feraz*
	-el	*fiel* • faithful *hombre fiel, mujer fiel*
	-il	*pueril* • childish *gesto pueril, acción pueril*
	-iz	*feliz* • happy *hombre feliz, mujer feliz*
	-or	*mejor* • better *huerto mejor, huerta mejor*
	-oz	*veloz* • swift *viento veloz, ave veloz*

1.3. Plural forms

The plural of adjectives is formed in the same way as the plural of nouns:

Adjectives ending in:	Form the plural by adding:
an unstressed vowel	**-s** (*indígena/indígenas, rubio/rubios*)
a stressed vowel or consonant	**-es** (*hindú/hindúes, veloz/veloces*)

1.4. Agreement

The adjective always agrees with the noun in gender and number, whether it appears as part of the Noun Phrase or as part of the Verb Phrase:

*Los días de invierno son **cortos*** • *Winter days are short.*
*Rompió un **hermoso** vaso* • *He broke a beautiful glass.*

When nouns of different genders appear in a group together, the adjective always takes the masculine plural form:

*Recibí una carta y un paquete **curiosísimos.***
• *I received a very strange letter and parcel.*

However, in practice the proximity of and adjective to a particular noun may sometimes override this rule:

*Lo llevó a cabo con una **exquisita** delicadeza y tiento.*
• *He accomplished it with exquisite delicateness and feeling.*

1.5. Shortened forms

Some adjectives drop their final **-o** or have shortened forms in front of a masculine noun:

Bueno • *good*: **buen** hombre, **buena** mujer, hombre **bueno.**
Malo • *bad*: **mal** día, **mala** tarde, día **malo.**
Santo • *Saint*: **San** Antonio, **Santa** Teresa.
Primero • *first*: **primer** paso, **primera** mañana.
Tercero • *third*: **tercer** piso, **tercera** puerta a la derecha.

But note that **Santo** Tomás, **Santo** Domingo and **Santo** Toribio all keep their full forms.

The shortened form of *grande* is used when it appears in front of any singular noun, masculine or feminine, but note the difference in meaning:

grande • *big*   *un coche **grande*** • *a big car.*
gran • *great*   *un **gran** coche* • *a great car.*

1.6. Adjectives derived from other words

A great many adjectives are derived from other words, as follows:

— From nouns:

Semana/semanal • *Week/weekly.*
Trigo/trigueño • *Wheat/olive-skinned.*
Selva/selvático • *Jungle/woodland.*
Sombra/sombrío • *Shade/shady, gloomy.*

— From other adjectives:

Amarillo/amarillento • *Yellow/yellowish.*
Verde/verdoso • *Green/greenish.*
Rojo/rojizo • *Red/reddish*
Alto/altivo • *High/haughty*

— From verbs:

Agradar/agradable • *To please/pleasant.*
Vengar/vengativo • *To avenge/vengeful.*
Decidir/decisorio • *To decide/decisive.*
Sonreír/sonriente • *To smile/smiling.*

— By making a compound word, mostly of two other adjectives:

Agridulce • *Sweet and sour.*
Verdinegro • *Greenish black, dark green.*

1.7. Comparison of adjectives

Qualifying adjectives can express different degrees of meaning, as follows:

The **positive**: indicates the quality being described without making comparisons, e.g.: *valiente* • *brave.*

The **comparative**: indicates the quality being described in relation to others, e.g., *más valiente* • *braver,* ***tan** valiente* • *as brave,* ***menos** valiente* • *less brave.*

The **superlative**: describes the quality in absolute or relative terms in relation to others: ***el más** valiente* • *the bravest,* ***valentísimo/muy** valiente* • *most brave/very brave,* ***el menos** valiente* • *the least brave,* ***muy poco** valiente* • *not at all brave.*

Positive	Comparative	Superlative
valiente	***expressing superiority:*** *más valiente*	***expressing superiority:*** relative: *el más valiente* absolute: *muy valiente* *valentísimo*
	expressing equality: *tan valiente*	
	expressing inferiority: *menos valiente*	***expressing inferiority:*** relative: *el menos valiente* absolute: *muy poco valiente*

The comparative appears in constructions with **más** or **menos** to express superiority or inferiority. A construction with *que* is used when comparing different elements, and with *de* when comparing amounts, e.g.:

Tengo **más** dinero **que** Luis • *I have more money than Luis.*
Tengo **más de** mil pesetas • *I have more than 1000 pesetas.*

Expressing superiority:

más ... que	Soy **más** valiente **que** tú. • *I am braver than you.*
más ... de (+ phrase)	Soy **más** valiente **de** lo que tú crees. • *I am braver than you think.*

Expressing inferiority:

menos ... que	Es **menos** listo **que** tú. • *He is less clever than you.*
menos ... de (+ phrase)	Es **menos** listo **de** lo que tú piensas. • *He is less clever than you think.*

In the examples above + phrase, the phrase is equivalent to an amount and therefore requires the construction with *de.*
In the sentences expressing equality, *tan* is used with *como* or *que*, as follows:

tan ... como	Es **tan** alta **como** tú. • *She is as tall as you.*
tan ... que (+ phrase)	Es **tan** alta **que** parece modelo. • *She is so tall that she looks like a model*

Spanish has a number of irregular comparative forms, derived from Latin, as follows:

bueno/mejor = *good, better*
grande/mayor = *big, bigger*
malo/peor = *bad, worse*
pequeño/menor = *small, smaller*

Comparatives ending in **-or** do not change to form the feminine:

Mi herman**o** may**or** • My elder brother
Mi herman**a** men**or** • My younger sister

In certain expressions, *mayor* and *menor* are used idiomatically, losing much of their comparative sense:

La *calle* **mayor** • *the high street.*
Mi *hermano* **menor** • *my little brother.*

1.8. The Superlative

Superlatives may be **relative**, expressing either superiority or inferiority:

el/la ... **más** *... que*	*El día* **más** *triste* **de** *su vida.* • *The saddest day of his life.*
el/la ... **menos** *... de*	*El viaje* **menos** *largo* **de** *todos.* • *The shortest journey of all.*

or **absolute**, expressing the highest possible degree, but without expressing relation to any other element:

muy + *Adj.*	*Un día* **muy** *triste* • *a very sad day.*
Adj. + **-ísimo/a**	*Un tema interesantísimo* • *A very interesting topic.*

Adjectives with the stress on the antepenultimate syllable (*esdrújulos*) cannot take the suffix **-ísimo**: *férreo* • *iron*, *sanguíneo* • *blood*, *legítimo* • *legitimate*, *lógico* • *logical*, *fructífero* • *productive.*

A superlative sense may also be expressed in other ways in Spanish:

— By use of other adverbs in the place of **muy**:

sumamente • *greatly.*
extremadamente • *extremely.*
altamente • *highly.*
extraordinariamente • *extraordinarily.*

— By use of prefixes:

super- (*superguapo* • *really good looking*).
archi- (*archimillonario* • *multimillionaire*).
requete- (*requetebién* • *«fine and dandy»*).
extra- (*extralargo* • *extra long*).

— By using the suffix **-ito**:

Estás delgadito • *you're very slim.*
Un café calentito • *a nice hot cup of coffee.*

— By using other adverbial constructions:

Estás **la mar de** *guapa* • *You're looking really pretty.*
Está **pero que** *furioso* • *He is absolutely furious.*

Some superlatives have irregular forms which have been handed down from Latin:

máximo/a • *maximum*
mínimo/a • *minimum*
óptimo/a • *optimum, the best*
pésimo/a • *the worst*
(and their plurals).

Some adjectives do not take a superlative form because their meaning cannot be expressed in terms of degrees: for instance, numerals, and words which already contain a sense of the absolute:

inmenso • *immense,* **inmóvil** • *immobile,* **inmutable** • *unchangeable.*
pío > *piísimo* • *very pious.*
vacío > *vaciísimo* • *very empty.*

Spanish also has some irregular superlatives, as follows:

amigo > *amicísimo/amiguísimo* • *very friendly.*
áspero > *aspérrimo/asperísimo* • *very rough.*
cruel > *cruelísimo/crudelísimo* • *very cruel.*
difícil > *dificilísimo/dificílimo** • *very difficult.*
íntegro > *integrísimo/integérrimo* • *very honest.*
simple > *simplicísimo/simplícimo** • *very simple.*
pobre > *paupérrimo/pobrísimo* • *very poor.*
mísero > *misérrimo/miserísimo** • *very wretched.*

* (These forms are obsolete or very rarely used.)

1.9. Use of qualifying adjectives

In Verb Phrases adjectives can be used as follows:

— As an attribute:

*Esta casa es antiqu**ísima*** • *This house is very old.*

— As a predicate:

*El agua viene **turbia*** • *The water is coming (out) cloudy.*

— As an attribute of the complement:

*Tomaron a Juan por **tonto*** • *They took Juan for a fool.*

In Noun Phrases, adjectives may appear:

— Before the noun:

*Las **altas** cumbres están nevadas.* • *The high peaks are snow-covered.*

— After the noun:

*El árbol **seco** ya no retoñará* • *The withered tree will not sprout again.*

— In *apposition* to the noun:

***Indignado** por lo ocurrido, el juez levantó la sesión.*
• *Indignant at what had happened, the judge closed the session.*

1.10. Position of adjectives

Adjectives expressing colour, shape, nationality or religion tend to be placed after the noun:

Llevaba un sombrero **amarillo** • *He wore a yellow hat.*
Era un patio **rectangular** • *It was a rectangular yard.*

Some adjectives change their meaning according to whether they are placed before or after the noun:

Una cierta cosa/una cosa cierta.
• *A certain (some) thing/a certain (beyond doubt) thing.*
Un pobre hombre/un hombre pobre.
• *A poor (wretched) man/a poor (penniless) man.*
Un gran hombre/un hombre grande.
• *A great man/a big man.*
Un buen hombre/un hombre bueno.
• *A good-hearted man/a good man.*
Un raro genio/un genio raro.
• *An unusual genius/a strange genius.*
Una sola mujer/una mujer sola.
• *A single woman (just one)/a single woman (on her own).*
Una bonita escena/una escena bonita.
• *A fine scene/a pretty scene.*
Una extraña persona/una persona extraña.
• *A strange person/an unknown person.*
Una pura ilusión/una ilusión pura.
• *A complete illusion/a pure ideal.*
Una triste figura/una figura triste.
• *A poor figure/a sad figure.*
Un simple colega/un colega simple.
• *A simple colleague (only a colleague)/a simple (-minded) colleague.*
Alta cuna/cuna alta.
• *High birth/a high cot.*
Viejos amigos/amigos viejos.
• *Old (long-standing) friends/old (aged) friends.*
Nueva casa/casa nueva.
• *A new (different) house/a new (brand new) house.*

An adjective before the noun is used as an epithet, whereas and adjective after the noun always has an emphatic sense:

Las **largas** *noches de invierno* • *the long winter nights.*
Los calcetines **largos** *abrigan más* • *long socks are warmer.*

However, the adjective is used after the noun in some set phrases without having this emphatic sense:

El Espíritu **Santo** • *the Holy Spirit.*
El Código **Civil** • *the Civil Code.*

The concept of *restrictive* or *non-restrictive meaning* can be useful for the foreign learner where there is doubt concerning the right position of the adjective. Adjectives placed *after* the noun have a restricted meaning because they mark out a subset of objects having the characteristic they describe (*calcetines **largos,** un sombrero **amarillo***), whereas adjectives placed *before* the noun tend to be non-restrictive since they describe a characteristic common to all objects referred to by the noun (***largas** noches de invierno, **blanca** nieve*) without adding any new information.

Adjectives followed by a preposition must of necessity come after the noun:

*Una regla **fácil de** memorizar* • *An easy rule to remember.*
*Una persona **hábil para** los negocios* • *A skillful person in business.*

1.11. Other factors affecting the meaning of adjectives

Some adjectives can only be applied in a literal sense to certain classes of nouns, e.g.: animate, non-animate. Their meaning may shift when they are used in a figurative sense:

*El campo está **verde*** • *The countryside is green.*
*El niño está aún **verde*** • *The child is still green (immature).*
*La leche está **tibia*** • *The milk is warm.*
*El muchacho está **tibio*** • *The boy is undecided (lukewarm).*

Adjectives which indicate a permanent state or a passing quality may require the use of either *ser* or *estar*.

*La torre es **alta*** • *The tower is high.*
*La mesa es **pequeña*** • *The table is small.*
*María está **guapa*** • *María is looking pretty.*
*El día está **lluvioso*** • *The day is rainy.*

Some may change their sense according to whether they are used with the verb *ser* or *estar*.

2. Ordinal numbers

These are as follows:

Primero • *first*	*segundo* • *second*	*tercero* • *third*	*cuarto* • *fourth*
quinto • *fifth*	*sexto* • *sixth*	*séptimo* • *seventh*	*octavo* • *eighth*
noveno • *ninth*	*décimo* • *tenth*	*undécimo* • *eleventh*	*duodécimo* • *twelfth*

decimotercero • *13th*	*decimocuarto* • *14th*
vigésimo • *20th*	*trigésimo* • *30th*
cuadragésimo • *40th*	*quincuagésimo* • *50th*
sexagésimo • *60th*	*septuagésimo* • *70th*
octagésimo • *80th*	*nonagésimo* • *90th*
centésimo • *100th*	*milésimo* • *1000th*

They agree with the noun in number and gender:

*Un **tercer** alumno* • *a third pupil.*
*La **cuarta** planta* • *the fourth floor.*
*Los **primeros** visitantes* • *the first visitors.*

Primero and *tercero* lose their final vowel if they precede the noun:

*El **primer** día de clase* • *The first day of school.*

Ordinal numbers may come before or after the noun:

El **tercer** día/el día **tercero**
El **cuarto** piso/el piso **cuarto**

Ordinal numbers up to *décimo* • *10 th*, are in common use. From *undécimo* onwards they tend to be substituted by cardinal numbers:

Alfonso Quinto • *Alfonso V.*
Isabel Segunda • *Isabel II.*
Alfonso Trece • *Alfonso XIII.*
Piso catorce • *Fourteenth floor.*

6 | PRONOUNS

1. General features

Pronouns are traditionally regarded as elements which take the place of, or stand in for, nouns or noun phrases, thus avoiding unnecessary repetition, e.g.:

Han llegado mi tío y su novia. Su novia está descansando.
* *My uncle and his fiancée have arrived. His fiancée is resting.*

To avoid repeating *su novia* we can substitute the pronoun **ella** (she):

Han llegado mi tío y su novia. ***Ella*** *está descansando.*
* *My uncle and his fiancée have arrived. She is resting.*

Similarly:

Tengo varios lápices, pero sólo uso **uno**.
* *I have several pencils, but I only use one.*

In these examples, the pronoun refers back to an element which has already been mentioned.

Other pronouns announce an element which is to follow:

*¿**Quién** ha llamado? El cartero.*
* *Who called? The postman.*

Here the pronoun **quién** stands in for the noun phrase following.

Pronouns may also refer to people taking part in the discourse as speakers or listeners. In this case they do not necessarily refer either back or forward, since it is obvious from the context whom they refer to:

***Yo** leo y **tú** escribes* • *I read and you write.*

Here **yo** (I) and **tú** (you) act as subjects in the same way as nouns.

Sometimes pronouns do not just substitute a noun, but another element, such as an adjective, or a whole phrase:

Hace frío. **Lo** *sé* •*It's cold. I know that.*
El vino de Rioja es bueno, pero el de Málaga también **lo** *es.*
* *Rioja wine is good, but so is Málaga's.*

These are known as «neuter forms», since they are neither masculine nor feminine.

Pronouns do not carry any lexical meaning. They are grammatical words whose meaning depends on what they are referring to in a particular context. (The meaning of **yo** (I), for example, cannot be described in a dictionary in the same way as a noun, because it refers simply to «the person speaking»).

Pronouns must always precede the verb, unlike noun phrases:

*Leo un libro. **Lo** leo.*
* *I read a book. I read it.*
*Hace la comida. **La** hace.*
* *He's making the dinner. He's making it.*

Pronouns have different forms according to their function within the sentence, whereas nouns are invariable. In the following examples, the noun, *Luis,* does not change whatever function it is performing in the sentence:

Luis no quiere venir • *Luis does not want to come.*
Lo hice por Luis • *I did it for Luis.*
Vio a Luis en el bar • *He saw Luis in the bar.*

However, if instead of *Luis* we use a pronoun, this has different forms:

*(**Él**) no quiere venir* • *He does not want to come.*
*Lo hice por **él*** • *I did it for him.*
***Lo** (or **le**) vio en el bar* • *He saw him in the bar.*

Pronouns can express number and gender:

Yo	*I (m/f)*	
Tú	*You (m/f)*	Singular
Él/ella	*He/she*	
Nosotros/as	*We (m/f)*	
Vosotros/as	*You (m/f)*	Plural
Ellos/as	*They (m/f)*	

Yo and **tú** have the same form in masculine and feminine. Gender is only expressed through agreements:

***Yo** siempre estoy atenta en clase* • *I (f) always pay attention in class.*
***Tú** no eres serio* • *You (m) are not serious.*

Pronouns can differentiate between + human and − human:

quién/qué • *who* **qué** • *what*	**nadie** • *nobody* **nada** • *nothing*	**alguien** • *somebody* **lo/ello** • *that, it*
e.g.: *¿**Quién** canta?* *Who is singing?* ***Nadie** se mueve.* *Nobody is moving.* ***Alguien** viene.* *Someone is coming.*	*¿**Qué** canta el niño?* *What is the boy singing?* *No se mueve **nada**.* *Nothing is moving.* *Piensa **algo**.* *Think of something.*	*No creo en **ello**.* *I don't believe that.* ***Lo** bello agrada.* *Beautiful things are nice.*

(See below p. 71 for further discussion of **lo**).

Grammarians distinguish the following kinds of pronouns, which are all described in this chapter:

Personal pronouns: *Yo, tú, él, ella...* • *I, you, he, she...*
Demonstrative pronouns: *Éste, ése, aquél...* • *This, that...*
Possessive pronouns: *Mío, tuyo, suyo...* • *Mine, yours, his...*
Indefinite pronouns: *Alguno, ninguno, cualquiera...* • *Someone, no-one, anyone...*
Relative pronouns: *Quien, que, cual...* • *Who, what, which...*
Interrogative pronouns: *¿Quién?, ¿qué?, ¿cuál?...* • *Who?, what?, which?...*
Exclamatory pronouns: *Qué, cuánto, quién...* • *What! how much! who!...*

2. Personal pronouns

Personal pronouns can mark number, gender and case. As we have seen, **yo** and **tú** are invariable as regards gender, and the sex of the person to whom they refer becomes evident only from other agreements.

The first and second persons plural have both masculine and feminine forms:

Nosotros • *We, masculine*   **Nosotras** • *We, feminine*
Vosotros • *You, masculine*   **Vosotras** • *Your, feminine*

Third person differentiate gender in both singular and plural:

Él • *He*   **Ella** • *She*
Ellos • *They, masculine*   **Ellas** • *They, feminine*

Yo and **tú** change form completely in the plural:

Yo • *I*   **Nosotros/as** • *we*
Tú • *you*   **Vosotros/as** • *you*

However the plural forms of **él** and **ella** are regular:

Él   **Ellos**
Ella   **Ellas.**

The meaning of the plural is more complex with pronouns than with nouns. For instance, **nosotros** (we) may mean **I** + **you**, **I** + **he/she**, or **I** + **you** + **he/she**. Similarly, **vosotros** may refer to Name + **you**; **you** + **you** + **he/she** or **you** + **he/she**. **Ellos/as** may represent a plural noun phrase (*los chicos*) or several conjoined noun phrases (**él** + **ella** + NP).

Pronouns are the only grammatical category in Spanish which requires the use of different forms according to the function performed within the sentence: subject, direct object, indirect object, or following a preposition. Consider, for instance, the following sentence:

Llegó el Príncipe Felipe, aunque no vi al Príncipe Felipe; manifestaron al Príncipe Felipe gran afecto.
• *Prince Felipe arrived, although I didn't see Prince Felipe; they showed Prince Felipe great affection.*

The NP *el Príncipe Felipe* performs three different functions, that of subject, direct object and indirect object. However, its form remains the same. But if we use pronouns instead, we must use three different forms to substitute the three uses or *cases* of *el Príncipe Felipe*:

*Él llegó, aunque no **lo** vi; **le** manifestaron gran afecto.*
• *He arrived, although I didn't see him; they showed him...*

The forms of the different pronouns for the different cases are as follows:

	Subject	With preposition	Direct Object	Indirect Object
1.s.m/f	yo	mi, conmigo	me	me
1.pl.m	nosotros	nosotros	nos	nos
1.pl.f	nosotras	nosotras	nos	nos
2.s.m/f	tú	ti, contigo	te	te
	usted	sí, consigo	lo/se	le/se
2.pl.m	vosotros	vosotros	os	os
2.pl.f	vosotras	vosotras	os	os
3.s.m.	él	él/sí/consigo	lo/se	le/se
3.s.f.	ella	ella/sí/consigo	la/se	le/se
3.s.n.	ello	ello	lo/se	le/se
3.pl.m	ellos	ellos/sí/consigo	los/se	les/se
3.pl.f	ellas	ellas/sí/consigo	las/se	les/se

2.1. Subject pronouns

2.1.1. *Omission*

In Spanish the personal pronoun is often omitted when it acts as a subject. This is so because the verb endings themselves provide sufficient information for the meaning to be clear:

(Yo) Temo por su vida • *I fear for his life.*
(Tú) Sabes que es verdad • *You know it is true.*
(Él/Ella) Dice la verdad • *He/she is telling the truth.*

In certain cases, however, it is necessary to retain the pronoun in order to avoid ambiguity or to emphasize the roles of the people to whom they refer:

*No sabía **yo** que **él** vendría tan pronto.*
• *I didn't know he would come so soon.*
*Siempre decía **él** que **yo** no lo podía hacer.*
• *He always said I couldn't do it.*
*Aunque **tú** no me esperes, **yo** estaré allí a las doce.*
• *Even if you don't wait for me, I shall be there at 12.*
*Si **tú** lo dices, **yo** te creo.*
• *If you say so I believe you.*
*Te lo digo **yo**.*
• *I'm telling you.*
*A Marta, no la has visto **tú**.*
• *You haven't seen Marta.*

2.1.2. *Position*

Although in general subject pronouns can be positioned fairly flexibly, there are cases in which they must take fixed positions in the sentence:

— In questions, they come after the verb:

*¿Por qué lo haces **tú**?* • *Why are you doing it?*
*¿Vienes **tú** o no vienes?* • *Are you coming or not?*

— After certain adverbs (*apenas* [hardly], *quizás* [perhaps]...), they come after the verb:

*Apenas había salido **él**, llegué yo.*
• *He had only just left when I arrived.*
*Quizás lo sepas **tú*** • *Perhaps you know.*

— They come after the verb when reporting speech:

*No irá —contestó **ella*** • *«He will not go», she replied.*
*Es Pedro —dije **yo*** • *«It's Pedro», I said.*

— They also come after the verb with orders or commands:

*Vete, **tú*** • *Go away, you.*

2.1.3. *Combined with other elements*

Personal pronouns can be combined with *mismo/a, propio/a,* and *solo/a* for emphasis, as follows:

*Lo hice **yo misma*** • *I (f) did it myself.*
*Vine **yo solo*** • *I (m) came on my own.*
*Lo dijo **él mismo*** • *He said it himself.*

This also has the effect of disambiguating gender in the first and second persons. They can also be combined with numerals, or with indefinites such as *todo*:

***Vosotros dos** vendréis conmigo* • *You two will come with me.*
***Todos nosotros** aplaudiremos* • *We will all applaud.*

Neither ***yo*** nor ***tú*** can be used with prepositions.

2.1.4. *Other features*

Él, ella, ellos and **ellas** as subjects only refer to human beings. When referring to inanimate objects, either the pronoun is omitted altogether, or the demonstrative (see below) is used:

Ésta es mi casa. Es antigua.
• *It (This) is my house. It is old.*

2.1.5. *«Ello»*

Ello is the neuter form of the third person pronoun. It belongs to a rather literary style and is not generally used orally:

*No tienen dinero, pero **ello** no quita que sean generosos.*
• *They have no money, but this doesn't mean they are not generous.*
*Le dolía la cabeza, pero **ello** no le impidió trabajar.*
• *She had a headache, but this did not stop her working.*

2.1.6. *Forms of address*

The forms **tú** and **vosotros/as** are the so-called familiar forms, used to indicate a close or relaxed relationship between speakers:

***Tú** me quieres mucho* • *You are very fond of me.*
***Vosotras** exigís demasiado* • *You are asking too much.*

The polite forms *usted* and *ustedes* (often written as *Vd./Vds.* or *Ud./Uds.*) are Uds. to express courtesy or respect to strangers or persons in authority:

Ustedes *no tenían por qué haberse levantado.*
- *There was no need for you to stand up.*
Usted *se lo merece todo* • *You deserve it all.*

They always take the third person of the verb, and other third person pronouns:

Su *coche (de usted) está preparado* • *Your car is ready.*
A ustedes, **les** *cuidan muy bien.*
- *They are looking after you very well.*
Usted *se lo guarda todo para sí.*
- *You are keeping everything for yourself.*
Este libro es **suyo** *(de ustedes)* • *This book is yours.*

Voseo. In Latin America there also exists the form **vos** which replaces, or in some cases is used along with, **tú.**

* The choice of a familiar or polite form is a difficult one for speakers of English. As a general rule, **tú** can be used in any context in which one might expect to address someone by their Christian name, whereas **usted** occurs in more formal situations.

Other pecularities in forms of personal address:

— As in English, Spanish allows speakers to make general remarks in a depersonalized way by using the third person:

Se *hace lo que* **se** *puede* • *One does what one can.*
Uno *dice lo que sabe* • *One says what one knows.*

— Again, as in English, in colloquial speech the second person may be used when making a general remark as an appeal, perhaps, for comprehension by the listener:

Lo haces con buena intención y ni te lo agradecen.
- *You do it with the best of intentions and they don't even thank you for it.*

— Monarchs, Popes, or persons representing a higher authority may use the first person plural:

Nos *os bendecimos* • *We bless you.*

2.2. Object pronouns

2.2.1. *Direct and Indirect Object Pronouns*

The forms **me, te, nos** and **os** can act as either direct or indirect objects; they do not change their form:

Me/Te *llamaron por teléfono* • *They telephoned me/you:* direct object.
Me/Te *contaron una mentira* • *They told me/you a lie:* indirect object.
Nos/Os *vimos en la fiesta* • *We saw you at the party:* direct object.
Nos/Os *comunicaron que no fuerais* • *They told you not to go:* indirect object.

These forms are not marked for gender either.

However, third person forms vary for gender and number only when they function as direct objects: **lo, la, los, las.**

Lo vi ayer • *I saw him yesterday.*
La vi ayer • *I saw her yesterday.*
Los vi ayer • *I saw them (m) yesterday.*
Las vi ayer • *I saw them (f) yesterday.*

Whereas they only vary in number when they function as indirect objects: **le, les.**

Le haré un regalo • *I will give him/her a present.*
Les compraré unos caramelos • *I will buy them (m/f) some sweets.*

2.2.2. Position

Object pronouns always precede the verb unless used in combination with an infinitive, a gerund, or an imperative (command) to which they may be attached:

Me saludó con efusión • *He greeted me effusively.*
Tienes que avisarme cuanto antes
• *You must let me know as soon as possible.*
Lo resolverás fácilmente informándoles con antelación.
• *You will sort things out easily by letting them know in advance.*
Decídete y vente con nosotros • *Make up your mind and come with us.*

2.2.3. Order

Me always follows **te** or **se**:

No te me escondas • *Don't hide from me.*
Se me paró el coche • *My car stopped on me/The car stopped for me.*

First and second person pronouns always come before third person pronouns:

Me lo contó • *He/she told me about it.*
Nos la dio • *He/she gave it to us.*
Se las entregué en mano • *I gave them to him/her/them personally.*
Os lo remití por correo • *I sent it to you by post.*
Se los devolví • *I gave them back to him/her/them.*

2.2.4. Third person pronouns

The Real Academia recommends the following usage:

	Masculine	Feminine
Direct	*lo/los*	*la/las*
Indirect	*le/les*	

When used in this way, the direct object pronoun carries information concerning gender and number but not the indirect object pronoun, which is only able to distinguish between singular and plural.

*Encontró a dos niñas/os llorando y **las/los** llevó a casa.*
* He found two girls/boys crying and took them (f/m) home.
*Llamó al niño/niña y **le** dio la noticia personalmente.*
* He called the boy/girl and gave him/her the news personally.

2.2.5. *Laísmo/Loísmo/Leísmo*

In practice, the use of **la/lo/le** and their plural forms, in some parts of Spain at least, is often at variance with the Real Academia's recommendations. Whether the noun is animate or inanimate is often a deciding factor in the choice of a particular pronoun, and gender seems to take precedence over case (that is, whether it is a direct or indirect object).

— **Laísmo** is the use of **la** for **le** when the indirect object refers to an animate feminine noun:

> *Miró a la joven y **la** dirigió la palabra.*
> for: *Miró a la joven y **le** dirigió la palabra.*
> > * He looked at the girl and spoke to her.

— **Loísmo,** similarly, is the use of **lo** for **le** when the indirect object refers to an animate masculine noun:

> *Vio a su amigo en la calle, pero no **lo** habló.*
> for: *Vio a su amigo en la calle, pero no **le** habló.*
> > * He saw his friend in the street, but he didn't speak to him.

— **Leísmo** is the use of **le** as a direct object pronoun when refering to an animate masculine noun:

> *Vieron al ladrón y **le** prendieron.*
> for: *Vieron al ladrón y **lo** prendieron.*
> > * They saw the thief and arrested him.

This phenomenom also occurs in the plural, although less frequently:

> *Vieron a los ladrones y **les** prendieron.*
> for: *Vieron a los ladrones y **los** prendieron.*
> > * They saw the thieves and arrested them.

Much argument exists over the correctness of these usages. In educated speech (in Spain), *leísmo* is relatively well tolerated, but not *loísmo* or *laísmo*. With **usted, le** is the preferred form:

Quería conocerle a usted personalmente.
* I wanted to meet you personally.

2.2.6. *The neuter pronoun «lo»*

Lo can be used as follows:

— When it refers back to a preceding phrase:

*Ayer se inauguró la fiesta y yo **lo** ignoraba.*
* The fiesta started yesterday and I didn't know it.

— When it refers back to a preceding adjective:

*Es una señora muy rica, aunque no **lo** aparenta.*
* She is a very rich lady, although she doesn't look it.

2.2.7. *Use of «se»*

The pronoun **se** can present problems for foreign learners because it can stand for different things in different contexts. These are as follows:

— As a substitute for **le/les** when two third person pronouns occur together:

Envió un libro a José • *He sent to José a book.*
***Se** lo envió* • *He sent it to him/her/them.*
***Se** lo entregó* • *He gave it to him/her/them.*

To distinguish number and gender, we must use a further pronoun after the verb:

Se** lo entregó **a ellos • *He gave it to them.*
Se** lo entregó **a ella • *He gave it to her.*

Used in this way, ***se*** is always the indirect object.

— As a reflexive pronoun, when the direct or indirect object refers back to the subject:

*Juan **se** mira en el espejo* (direct).
• *Juan looks at himself in the mirror.*
*La niña **se** compró un helado* (indirect).
• *The girl bought herself an icecream.*

For further clarity or emphasis, the expression **sí mismo/a/os/as** can be used:

*Juan se lava a **sí mismo*** • *Juan washes himself.*

— As a «reciprocal» pronoun, that is, meaning *each other:*

*Juan y Ana **se** odian* • *Juan and Ana hate each other.*

For further clarity, the expression **el uno al otro** can be used:

*Los novios se escribían cartas **el uno al otro**.*
• *The couple wrote letters to each other.*

— As a «grammaticalized» form, that is, when the verb used requires it:

*Los usuarios **se** quejan del servicio de trenes.*
• *Passengers complain about the train service.*
*El asesino **se** arrepintió de su acción.*
• *The murderer was sorry for what he had done.*

Here the relevant verbs are *quejarse* and *arrepentirse.*

— As an intensifier, which modifies the meaning of the verb:

*Ramón **se** fue a Sevilla* • *Ramón went off to Seville.*
Ramón fue a Sevilla • *Ramón went to Seville.*
***Se** comió la paella* • *He ate up the paella.*
Comió la paella • *He ate the paella.*

— As a passive, in the third person, singular and plural:

***Se** rompió el cristal* • *The window pane broke.*
***Se** rompieron los cristales* • *The window panes broke.*

The subject tends to be a thing, rather than a person, and there is no agent, as there is with passive constructions with **ser.**

— In an impersonal sense. This is only possible with the third person singular:

> **Se** vende piso • *Flat for sale.*
> **Se** busca secretaria • *Secretary required.*
> **¿Se** puede aparcar aquí? • *Is it allowed to park here?*

2.2.8. *Enclitic pronouns*

Personal pronouns can be attached to certain forms of the verb and thus make a single word. This is possible with infinitives, gerunds, and imperatives. They are attached in the same order as they would appear separately in front of the verb. The verb is always stressed on the same syllable as it would have been without the pronoun attachment and in writing an accent is sometimes necessary to indicate this.

Infinitives:

> Los dos equipos no **se** pudieron enfrentar.
> Los dos equipos no pudieron enfrentar**se**.
> • *The two teams were not able to play against each other.*

> **Se** lo puedo enviar mañana.
> Puedo enviár**selo mañana.**
> • *I can send it to him/her/them/you tomorrow.*

With verbs indicating a command, a change of order can alter the meaning:

> **Le** mandé construir una casa.
> • *I ordered him/her to build a house.*
> Mandé construir**le** una casa.
> • *I ordered a house to be built for him/her.*

When the infinitive is used with prepositions, the pronoun *must* be attached:

> Al comunicar**le** la sentencia, se derrumbó.
> • *When he was told the sentence, he collapsed.*
> Trabajaba para ayudar**les** en sus estudios.
> • *I/he/she worked to help them study.*
> Demostró gran habilidad en hacer**lo**.
> • *He showed great skill in doing it.*

Similarly, when the infinitive acts as a noun phrase, the pronoun must always be attached:

> Poder ir**se** de vacaciones es lo que le gustaría.
> • *Being able to go on holiday is what he would like most.*

Gerunds:

When the pronoun is a direct object, it may either precede the verb or be attached to the gerund:

> **Los** andaban buscando/Andaban buscándo**los**.
> • *They were looking for them.*

But note that the pronoun must always refer to the verb being used in the gerund, not to a previous one:

> **Lo** vi paseando con su mujer.
> • *I saw him out walking with his wife.*

no

Vi paseándolo con su mujer.

The pronoun must always be attached:

— When the gerund starts the sentence:

Haciéndolo así, gustará a todos.
- *Doing it like that will please everybody.*

— With reflexive verbs followed by the gerund:

El público se aburre escuchándola.
- *The public gets bored listening to her.*

Imperatives:

With imperatives (commands), the pronoun must always be attached:

Cuéntanoslo • *Tell us about it.*
Dímelo • *Tell me.*
Dásela • *Give it to him/her/them.*
Comprádselo • *Buy it for him/her/them.*

Note that in the plural, the final -**d** is sometimes lost:

sentad: *sentaos* • *sit down.*
unid: *uníos* • *unite.*

In colloquial speech, the plural -**d** ending becomes -**r**:

Idos > Iros • *go.*

2.3. Prepositional forms

The forms **mí, ti, usted, ustedes** do not vary according to gender:

Es para mí un honor invitarte a casa.
- *It is an honour for me to invite you to my home.*

However, **nosotros/as, vosotros/as, ellos/ellas**, differentiate gender:

Para nosotras, todo esto es mejor.
- *All this is better for us (f).*

Sí is *only* used in combination with preposition:

Sólo piensa en sí.
- *He only thinks of himself.*

Según cannot be used with **mí, ti,** or **sí**, but with **tú**. Here it acts as an adverb, in the same way as **hasta** and **entre** with **tú** or **yo**.
When **mí, ti** or **sí** are combined with **con**, they produce **conmigo, contigo** and **consigo.**

2.4. Redundant pronouns

In Spanish a second, or «co-referential», pronoun is often used for emphasis or stylistic reasons:

*A **ellas** no **las** he vuelto a ver* • *I haven't seen them (f) again.*
*A **ella** **le** compré un vestido* • *I bought her a dress.*
***Me** temo **yo** que no vengan* • *I'm afraid they won't come.*
Me** lo dieron **a mí • *They gave it to me.*

Note that these pronouns are not redundant in the sense that they are used to no purpose, they always fulfil a communicative function.

3. Demonstrative pronouns

Demonstrative pronouns always agree in number and gender with the noun they are associated with:

***Ésta** es mi casa* • *This is my house.*

The demonstrative pronoun (here **ésta**) is used to indicate which house, in space or time, is being referred to in relation to the speaker and the listener. It performs the function of *indicating* rather than *naming*.

Demonstrative pronouns can be used to refer back to a preceding noun phrase:

Aquélla** fue mucho mejor que **ésta • *That one was much better than this one.*

Or forwards to something about to be mentioned:

***Éste** es el tema: el cese de la violencia.*
• *This is the issue: the end of violence.*

The neuter forms (see below) can refer (again, either backwards or forwards) to a whole sentence:

*Viajar a México es una aventura: **eso** me gusta.*
• *Going to Mexico is an adventure: I like that.*

Demonstrative pronouns appear in the same three variations as demonstrative adjectives and, in their masculine and feminine forms, are usually differentiated from these by a written accent:

	masc.	fem		
singular plural	**éste** **éstos**	**ésta** **éstas**	this (one) these (ones)	near the speaker = 1st person
singular plural	**ése** **ésos**	**ésa** **ésas**	that (one) those (ones)	near the listener = 2nd person
singular plural	**aquél** **aquéllos**	**aquélla** **aquéllas**	that (one) those (ones)	outside the range of both speaker & listener = 3rd person

The neuter forms *esto, eso* and *aquello* are used when there is no association with any particular noun:

Esto *es un desastre* • *This is a disaster.*

The masculine and feminine forms can refer to either animate or inanimate things, but the neuter forms can only refer to inanimate objects or concepts, without distinguishing gender:

Ésta *es la Señora de Roca* • *This is Mrs Roca.*
Ésta *es la piedra que vi antes* • *This is the stone I saw earlier.*
Esto *no me gusta* • *I don't like this.*

The different forms of the demonstrative are used is Spanish to express the idea of *the former* and *the latter.*

Tiene un Rolls y un utilitario; **aquél** *lo usa en los actos oficiales y* **éste** *para desplazarse por la ciudad.*
   • *He has a Rolls and an ordinary car; he uses the former on official occasions and the latter to get around town.*
Has escrito una novela y un libro de poemas. **Aquélla** *fue un éxito y* **éste** *fue un fracaso.*
   • *She has written a novel and a book of poetry. The former was a success and the latter was a failure.*

The demonstrative pronoun is often used in Spanish for emphasis where in English a simple personal pronoun would suffice:

Éste *es un chico simpático* • *He is a nice boy.*
Ésta *sí que es lista* • *She is certainly clever.*

Demonstrative pronouns, like demonstrative adjectives, can have a pejorative sense:

Ése *es un perdido* • *He's a hopeless case.*
¡Qué se habrá creído **éste**! • *Who does he think he is!*

Spanish has a number of set phrases which incorporate the demonstrative pronoun:

Esto es • *That's it. That's what I'm looking for.*
Eso es • *Absolutely. That's right.*
Por eso • *That's why.*
A eso *de las diez* • *At around 10 o'clock.*

4.   Possessive pronouns

These function like adjectives:

El coche es **azul** • *The car is blue.*
El coche es **mío** • *The car is mine.*
El coche **azul** • *The blue car.*
El coche **mío** • *My car.*

Like adjectives, they can also be used substantively:

*El coche no es **el azul**, sino **el rojo**.*
• *The car is not the blue one, but the red one.*
*El coche no es **el mío**, sino **el tuyo**.*
• *The car is not mine, but yours.*

The forms of the possessive pronoun are as follows:

	masc.	fem.	neuter	
singular plural	**el mío** **los míos**	**la mía** **las mías**	**lo mío**	mine
singular plural	**el nuestro** **los nuestros**	**la nuestra** **las nuestras**	**lo nuestro**	ours
singular plural	**el tuyo** **los tuyos**	**la tuya** **las tuyas**	**lo tuyo**	yours* (sing)
singular plural	**el vuestro** **los vuestros**	**la vuestra** **las vuestras**	**lo vuestro**	yours (plur)
singular plural	**el suyo** **los suyos**	**la suya** **las suyas**	**lo suyo**	his/hers/theirs

* Yours as a 2nd person pronoun is used for both sing. and plur.: *El* **suyo** *(de usted* and *de ustedes).*

The masculine and feminine forms always agree with the noun they are replacing:

*Toma tu **libro**, yo me quedo con **el mío**.*
• *Take your book, I'll keep mine.*
*A Pepe le gustan **los coches**, pero sobre todo **el suyo**.*
• *Pepe likes cars, but especially his (own).*
*Aquí están **mis padres**. ¿Dónde están **los tuyos**?*
• *Here are my parents. Where are yours?*

The neuter is used when there is no association with any particular noun:

*Tú te encargas de **lo tuyo**; yo, de **lo mío**.*
• *You get on with your own business and I will with mine.*

5. Indefinite and quantitative pronouns

These have the same form as indefinite adjectives but they stand alone. They are used to indicate —not to identify— persons or things:

***Muchos** participaron en la carrera, pero **pocos** llegaron a la meta.*
• *Many took part in the race, but few reached the finish.*
*Comió **demasiado*** • *He ate too much.*

They can express a scale of quantities:

> *uno* • one, *dos* • two, *tres* • three, *otro* • another, *pocos* • few, *muchos* • many, *todos* • all
> *nadie* • no-one, *alguien* • someone, *dos* • two, *tres* • three, *varios* • several, *muchos* • many
> *nada* • nothing, *algo* • something, *poco* • little, *bastante* • enough, *demasiado* • too much.

In their neuter forms they can function as adverbs of quantity:

Leía **mucho** • *She read a lot.*

If this means *She read constantly,* then *mucho* is being used as an adverb. If the sense is *She read a lot of books,* then *mucho* is a quantitative pronoun. *Mucho, poco, bastante, nada* and *algo* can be either pronouns or adverbs, depending on the sense.

Uno can be used in an impersonal sense:

Persiguen a **uno** *por todas partes.*
• *They pursue one everywhere.*
Uno *se defiende como puede.*
• *One defends oneself as best one can.*

Algo (something) and *nada* (nothing) can be adverbialized:

Está **algo** *cansada* • *She is somewhat tired.*
No es **nada** *tonto* • *He is no fool.*

Todo has masculine and feminine, singular and plural forms (**todo, toda, todos, todas**), and also a neuter form, **todo**, meaning «*everything*»:

Me gusta **todo** • *I like everything.*

Mucho and *poco* tend to keep their agreements when they function as partitives:

Pocas de *nosotras lo sabíamos.*
• *Few of us (fem) knew that.*

Uno and *otro* can be used in correlation:

Uno *llegó, (el)* **otro** *se fue.*
• *One arrived, the other left.*

Cada functions as a pronoun when combined as follows:

Cada uno *se contenta con lo que tiene.*
• *Every one is happy with what they have.*
Cada cual *echa la culpa a su vecino.*
• *Everyone blames the person next to them.*

Cada uno is a less personal usage and so emphasizes the individual less than *cada cual.*

Tal has a plural form: *tales* (such a thing, such things):

No hará **tal** • *He won't do such a thing.*

Tanto has masculine, feminine, singular and plural forms (**tanta, tantos, tantas**) and also a neuter:

*No digo **tanto*** • *I wouldn't go so far as to say that.*

Numbers can be used as pronouns:

*Consulté varios libros, pero sólo me sirvió **uno**.*
• *I looked at several books, but only one was any use.*
*Me visitaron algunos estudiantes, y **dos** me preguntaron por ti.*
• *Some students visited me, and two of them asked after you.*

6. Relative pronouns

Relative pronouns substitute a noun or noun phrase when two sentences are joined together, as follows:

Abre este libro. Este libro está sobre la mesa.
• *Open this book. This book is on the table.*
*Abre este libro **que** está sobre la mesa.*
• *Open this book which is on the table.*

The second phrase thus becomes a *subordinate clause.*

Relative pronouns always refer back to something known as the *antecedent*, which they agree with in number and gender. This antecedent can be:

Explicit:

a) a noun: *Compró el coche **que** le gustaba.*
• *He bought the car he liked.*
b) a pronoun: *No será él **quien** te ayude.*
• *It won't be he/him who will help you.*
c) a phrase: *Estaba cansado*, por *lo que me acosté.*
• *I was tired, so I went to bed.*

Implicit:

***Quien** come mucho, engorda* • *He who eats a lot, gets fat.*
*No me gustó **lo que** dijo* • *I didn't like what he said.*

The different forms of relative pronouns in Spanish are as follows:

	masc.	fem.	neuter
singular	**(el) que** **el cual** **quien**	**(la) que** **la cual** **quien**	**lo que** **lo cual**
plural	**(los) que** **los cuales** **quienes**	**(las) que** **las cuales** **quienes**	
	who/which		what/which

	masc.	fem.	neuter
singular plural	**cuyo** **cuyos**	**cuya** **cuyas**	
	whose		
singular plural	**cuanto** **cuantos**	**cuanta** **cuantas**	cuanto
	what/how much		

Que, el que, el cual, quien and their variants are all to a certain extent interchangeable.

Que is the commonest form. It may follow a noun, pronoun, article or phrase.

*El estudiante **que** no estudia es mal estudiante.*
* *The student who doesn't study is a bad student.*
*Yo, **que** soy responsable, no te lo aconsejo.*
* *As a/the responsible person* (lit. I, who am responsible), *I don't advise it.*
*Feliz el **que** consigue sus objetivos.*
* *Happy is he who attains his objectives.*
*Todo lo dicho, **que** me parece muy bien, no puede cumplirse.*
* *Everything that has been said, which I think is very good, cannot be fulfilled.*

In some cases the article which precedes the relative is equivalent to a demonstrative:

Lo que ⎫
Eso que ⎬ *me dijiste, era verdad.*
* *What you told me was true.*

Only phrases with **el que** and its variants allow combination with *todo*:

Todo lo que *se aprende, es útil.*
* *Everything one learns is useful.*
Todas las que *trabajan, triunfan.*
* *All those (f) who work are successful.*

El que and its variants can be substituted by **que, quien, el cual** and its variants:

*Llegó la señorita **de la que** me hablaste.* ⎫
*Llegó la señorita **de que** me hablaste.* ⎬ *The young lady you told me about arrived.*
*Llegó la señorita **de quien** me hablaste.* ⎬
*Llegó la señorita **de la cual** me hablaste* ⎭

The presence of the article serves to avoid ambiguity as regards the antecedent, since it marks both number and gender:

*Frutas, cebada y trigo, **del que** se hace el pan.*
- *Fruits, barley and wheat, from which bread is made.*

In Spanish, it is clear that the antecedent is *trigo,* not the other elements. However, if we say:

*Frutas, cebada y trigo, **de que** se hace el pan,*

the antecedent remains unclear, as in English.

Prepositions are always placed *in front* of the relative, whichever form is used, as in *correct* English:

*El chico **con quien** salgo.*
- *The boy I am going out with/The boy with whom I am going out.*

Lo que, the neuter form, is used when there is no clear antecedent, or when the antecedent is a whole phrase or concept:

*No recuerdo **lo que** vi.*
- *I don't remember what I saw.*
*Hubo amenaza de bomba, **lo que** me obligó a salir corriendo.*
- *There was a bomb scare, which meant I had to leave in a hurry.*

Lo que, el que, el cual, etc., all function as single units —nothing can be placed between the two words. Prepositions must be placed before both elements:

*Sé **de lo que** eres capaz.*
- *I know what you are capable of.*

Quien is never used in combination with an article, and always refers to a human antecedent. It has a plural form —**quienes**— but does not distinguish between masculine and feminine:

*El joven **de quien** te hablé.*
- *The young chap I told you about.*
*Las jóvenes **con quienes** hablamos eran de Galicia.*
- *The girls we were talking to were from Galicia.*

If **quien** is the subject of the relative clause, this does not serve to restrict the meaning of the noun, only to explain it:

*Los padres, **quienes** tanto habían hablado en su favor, no le apoyaron.*
- *His parents, who had so much spoken for him, did not support him.*

(See p. 182 for further explanation of restrictive and non-restrictive clauses).

Cuyo is the only relative which has an adjectival function. It agrees in gender and number with the noun it accompanies, irrespective of the number and gender of the antecedent:

*Los estudiantes, **cuyas** madres lloraban en el pasillo...*
- *The students, whose mothers were crying in the corridor...*

*La niña, **cuyo** reloj encontré en el patio...*
- *The girl, whose watch I found in the playground...*

It never takes an article and always precedes the noun it accompanies.

El cual, la cual, los cuales, las cuales

No element may be introduced between the two parts. They may be used for people or things. The presence of the article provides information as regards number and gender, thus providing greater clarity. It is a form of the relative which is therefore preferred when it is separated from its antecedent by intervening elements:

*Las causas de la catástrofe fueron el terremoto y la falta de previsión, **las cuales** (causas) constituyeron un ejemplar aviso para el futuro.*
- *The causes of the catastrophe were the earthquake and lack of foresight, which provided an exemplary warning for the future.*

In English the distance between relative and antecedent is so great that the preferred rendering would probably be *and these provided...*

Cuanto implies a vague or unexpressed antecedent, synonymous with **todo, todo lo que**:

***Cuantos** vinieron, recibieron un regalo.*
- *All those who came received a present.*
*Dime **cuanto** sepas = dime **todo lo que** sepas.*
- *Tell me all you know.*

It has masculine, feminine and plural forms:

*Que se levanten **cuantos** sepan la respuesta.* } • *Let those who know the answer*
*Que se levanten **cuantas** sepan la respuesta.* }   *stand up.*

Cuanto appears in the following set phrases and expressions:

***En cuanto** llegó, se puso a comer.*
- *As soon as he arrived he started eating.*
***En cuanto a** nosotros, ya tenemos el problema resuelto.*
- *As far as we are concerned, we have already resolved the problem.*
***Cuanto más** estudia, menos aprende.*
- *The more he studies, the less he learns.*

Cual and **como** can function adverbially. **Cual** has a more intensive meaning:

*Comía **cual si** estuviera muerto de hambre.*
- *He ate just as if he were starving.*
*Comía **como si** estuviera muerto de hambre.*
- *He ate as if he were starving.*

7. Interrogative pronouns

They have the same forms as relative pronouns, but are differentiated in writing with an accent:

masculine		feminine		neuter	
singular	plural	singular	plural		
qué		qué		qué	What?
quién cuál cuánto	quiénes cuáles cuántos	quién cuál cuánta	quiénes cuáles cuántas	cuánto	Who? Whom? Which? How much/many?

*Dime **quién** llama* • *Tell me who is calling.*
*¿**Quién** llama?* • *Who is calling?*
*Dime **cuál** deseas?* • *Tell me which one you want.*
*¿**Cuál** deseas?* • *Which one do you want?*
*¿**Qué** te gusta?* • *What do you like?*
*¿De **qué** se trata?* • *What is it about?*

Quién can only be used when referring to persons.

Cuál is used to ask for individuals of an already known class. It appears in constructions with *ser* where the English translation would be *What*?

*¿**Cuál** es tu nombre?* • *What is your name?*

It is always used when followed by *de*:

*¿**Cuál de** ellos tiene cinco años?* • *Which of them is five?*

However **qué** is always used when a substantive noun follows:

*¿**Qué** mesa tienes en casa?* • *What table do you have at home?*

Cuál is used with *éste, ésta,* etc., but never with *esto*:

*¿**Cuál** es éste?* • *Which one is this?*
*¿**Qué** es esto?* • *What is this?*

8. Exclamatory pronouns

These have the same form as the interrogatives:

— **Qué** is invariable and always neuter:

*¡**Qué** cosas te podría contar!* • *What things I could tell you!*

— **Quién** has the plural form, **quiénes:**

*¡**Quién** estuviera allí!*
lit. • *Who would be there!*
*¡**Quiénes** lo vieran!*
lit. • *Who would see that!*

Note that these are positive exclamations, expressing a wish to take part in the action described.

Cuánto has an adverbial sense, similar to *mucho*:

*¡No sabes **cuánto** me alegro de verte!* • *You don't know how pleased I am to see you!*

<table>
<tr><td>**7**</td><td>## THE VERB PHRASE</td></tr>
</table>

1. General features

1.1. Components of the Verb Phrase

A verb phrase can consist of one or more words but, as its name suggests, it must always include a verb, which supports the other elements:

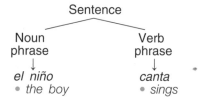

The optional elements may be noun phrases, adjectives, prepositional phrases or adverbial phrases:

VP (verb phrase): **Canta** *canciones* • *She/he sings songs.*
NP (noun phrase): *Escribe* **una carta** • *He/she is writing a letter.*
Adj (adjective): *El niño es* **bueno** • *The boy is good.*
Prep. P. (prepositional phrase): *Ha escrito un poema* **de amor** • *He/she has written a love poem.*
Adv. P. (adverbial phrase): *El perro juega* **continuamente** • *The dog plays continuously.*

The characteristics of the VP, or the verb within it, determine what other elements are necessary.

1.2. The verb

The verb is the key element in the verb phrase. It indicates a process, an action or a state (although it is not the only element capable of doing so: *Un paseo* • *A walk).* If it appears alone, it contains within itself all the information needed in the verb phrase. For example:

Amaré • *I will love.*

contains the following information:

indicative mood
future tense
first person
singular in number.

84

1.3. Auxiliaries

Sometimes the verb is accompanied by elements which produce more complex verbal structures. Some of these elements may have lost some or all their lexical meaning and perform a mainly grammatical function. These grammaticalised elements are known as *auxiliaries*. Auxiliary verbs always precede the main verb and carry information relating to tense, number, person, mood, modality and aspect:

Auxiliary verb	Main verb
Puede haber estado He may have been	leyendo reading

Here *puede* carries the information relating to person and number (3rd person singular), and also the meaning of «possibility». *Haber* carries a perfective meaning, and *estado* a progressive sense, which is completed with the **-ndo** form of the main verb.

The participle **(-do)**, infinitive and gerund **(-ndo)** always come last in any verbal structure and carry the semantic information. The other grammatical information is carried by the auxiliary verbs, which must be used according to a strict sequence:

1. Modal auxiliaries, which consist of a basic verb form.
2. Perfective auxiliaries, which require the form **-do.**
3. Passive auxiliaries, which require the form **-do**.
4. Progressive auxiliaries, which require the form **-ndo.**

This can be schematized as follows:

Modal	Perfective	Passive	Progressive	Basic form
—	—	—	—	ama (he/she loves)
—	—	—	—	amar (to love)
—	—	es (he/she is)	—	amado/a (loved)
—	—	—	está (he/she is)	amando (loving)
—	—	está (he/she is)	siendo (being)	amado/a (loved)
—	ha (he/she has)	—	—	amado (loved)
—	ha (he/she has)	sido (been)	—	amado/a (loved)
—	ha (he/she has)	—	estado (been)	amando (loving)
—	ha (he/she has)	estado (been)	siendo (being)	amado/a (loved)
puede (he/she can)	—	—	—	amar (love)
puede (he/she can)	—	ser (be)	—	amado/a (loved)
puede (he/she can)	—	—	estar (be)	amando (loving)
puede (he/she can)	—	estar (be)	siendo (being)	amado/a (loved)
puede (he/she can)	haber (have)	—	—	amado (loved)
puede (he/she can)	haber (have)	sido (been)	—	amado/a (loved)
puede (he/she can)	haber (have)	—	estado (been)	amando (loving)
puede (he/she can)	haber (have)	estado (been)	siendo (being)	amado/a (loved)

1.4. Other elements in the verb phrase

As we noted above, the other elements which may appear in the verb phrase depend on the characteristics of the verb in question. Some verbs produce what are known as *attributive structures*, others give rise to *predicative structures*.

1.4.1. *Attributive structures*

VP =	Cop + Adj.	(copula, or linking word + adjective)
	Cop + NP	(copula + noun phrase)
	Cop + Adv.	(copula + adverb)
	Cop + Prep. P.	(copula + prepositional phrase)

In these structures the verb, which can be a copula or linking word (**ser, estar**), or a verb such as **parecer** or **resultar**, indicates a quality which is attributed to the subject:

Mis **primos** son **simpáticos** • *My cousins are nice.*
Mis **primos** parecen **simpáticos** • *My cousins seem nice.*
Mis **primos** resultan **simpáticos** • *My cousins turn out to be nice.*

If the word being attributed is an adjective, it must agree with the subject, as in the examples above. However, the attribute may be a noun, in which case it may not agree:

Mis **primos** son la **ruina** de la casa.
• *My cousins are the ruination of this house.*
Las **huelgas** son un **derecho** de los trabajadores.
• *Strikes are a workers' right.*

1.4.2. *Predicative structures*

VP =	V	(verb)
	V + NP	(verb + noun phrase)
	V + NP + Prep. P.	(verb + noun phrase + prepositional phrase)
	V + subordinate clause	

In this type of structure the verb describes an action or a process and is often accompanied by elements which act as complements:

El conductor   ha evitado el obstáculo.
• *The driver*   *has avoided the obstacle.*
NP   VP = V + NP

Some verbs (**considerar, encontrar, dejar, convertir**, etc.) may allow an attribute to the object, which may be an adjective:

Consideró esta solución **difícil**.
• *He considered this solution difficult.*

or a noun:

Eligieron a González **presidente.**
• *They elected González president.*

(Note here that the preposition **a** precedes the noun rather than the attribute.)

2. The verb

All the other elements of the verb phrase fall into place in direct or indirect relation to the verb:

Ayer ganó una bicicleta azul en la tómbola.
* *Yesterday she/he won a blue bicycle in the fair raffle.*

Here all the elements relate to *ganó; ayer* is an adverb of time; *bicicleta azul*, a direct object; and *en la tómbola*, an adverbial phrase relating to place:

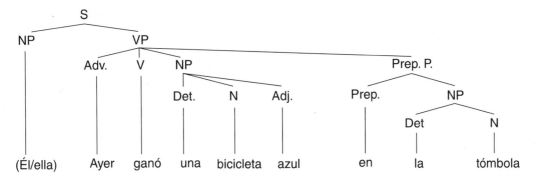

2.1. Characteristics of the verb

The verb can take different forms (inflections) to express:

person
number (singular or plural)
tense (past, present, future)
mood (indicative, subjunctive, conditional)
aspect (perfective, continuous)

Certain other grammatical elements can express person and number (e.g. pronouns), but only the verb can express the other possibilities.

2.2. Morphology of the verb

The verb can be broken up into *morphemes* which perform different functions:

Morphological structure of the verb					
1	2	3	4	5	
prefixes	stem	theme vowel	mood aspect tense	number person	
des-	-arm-	-a-	-ro-	-n	**desarmaron = they disarmed**
re-	-vel-	-	-ó	-	**reveló = he revealed**

2.2.1. Prefixes (morpheme 1)

These are optional components which provide a way of making new words:

hacer (do)	*deshacer* • *undo* *rehacer* • *do again*
poner (put)	*reponer* • *put back* *imponer* • *impose* *suponer* • *suppose* *anteponer* • *to put in front* *trasponer* • *to put behind* *disponer* • *have at one's disposal*
partir (break)	*repartir* • *to share out* *impartir* • *impart* *compartir* • *to share*

2.2.2. The stem (morpheme 2)

The stem is an essential component, since it carries the lexical meaning of the verb. In some verbs, the vowel becomes diphthongized or changes when stressed.

acertar	acierto	(e→ie)
adquirir	adquiero	(i→ie)
mover	muevo	(o→ue)
jugar	juego	(u→ue)
decir	digo	(e→i)
poder	pudo	(o→u)
tener	tuvo	(e→u)

2.2.3. The «theme» vowel (morpheme 3)

This vowel depends on which *conjugation* the verb belongs to:

1st conjugation verbs end in **-ar**
2nd conjugation verbs end in **-er**
3rd conjugation verbs end in **-ir**

2.2.4. Endings (morpheme 5)

It is these which show the greatest variation, since they have the power to express a wide range of meanings (number, person, tense, etc.).

In some cases confusion can arise when the verb ending is the same in the first and third person singular:

— Imperfect:

Amaba • *I/he/she loved.*
Temía • *I/he/she feared.*
Partía • *I/he/she left.*

— Present Subjunctive:

Ame • *that I/he/she should love.*
Tema • *that I/he/she should fear.*
Parta • *that I/he/she should leave.*

— Conditional:

Amaría • *I/he/she would love.*
Temería • *I/he/she would fear.*
Partiría • *I/he/she would leave.*

In these cases a pronoun is generally used to avoid ambiguity:

Yo amaba • *I loved.*   *Él amaba* • *He loved.*
Yo temía • *I feared.*   *Ella temía* • *She feared, etc.*

2.3. Mood (morpheme 4)

Spanish verbs have different forms according to their *mood*:

Amáis • *You love.*   Indicative
Améis • *You should love.*   Subjunctive
 Amad • *love.*   Imperative

All three of the above are second person plural forms and differ only in mood.
The *indicative mood* is used to express something which is either real, or which the speaker is presenting as real:

*En España **luce** un sol espléndido.*
• *In Spain the sun shines beautifully*: lit. *a beautiful sun.*
*Sabía que tu avión **había aterrizado** a las ocho.*
• *I knew that your plane had landed at eight o'clock.*
*Mañana **no iré** a clase.*
• *I shall not go to school tomorrow.*

The *subjunctive mood* is used to express uncertainty or possibility, or something which is presented as uncertain by the speaker:

*Temo que en España **luzca** un sol espléndido.*
• *I am afraid that in Spain a beautiful sun may be shining.*
*No sabía que tu avión **hubiera aterrizado.***
• *I did not know whether your plane had landed.*
*Es posible que mañana **no vaya** a clase.*
• *It is possible that tomorrow I may not go to school.*

The *imperative mood* is used for commands:

***Ven** mañana*   • *Come tomorrow.*
***Sal** de aquí*   • *Get out of here.*
***Invíta**le a comer*   • *Invite him to lunch.*

Mood therefore expresses the attitude of the speaker towards what is being expressed:

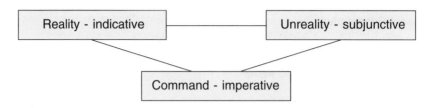

Mood may also be expressed *analytically* through the use of different auxiliary verbs:

— To express obligation, verbs such as **haber de, haber que, deber,** or **tener que,** can be used instead of the imperative:

Has de *pasear después de cenar.*
• *You should go out for a walk after dinner.*
Hay que *escuchar al que habla.*
• *You must listen to the person speaking.*
Debes *acudir a la cita con tu novia.*
• *You should keep your date with your girlfriend.*
Tienes que *acompañarnos.*
• *You must come with us.*

— To indicate possibility or uncertainty, the verbs **deber de, poder,** or **tener que** can express the same sense as the subjunctive:

Debe de *haber llegado ya.*
• *He should have arrived by now.*
Puede *saber ya la noticia.*
• *He may know the news by now.*
Tienen que *ser aproximadamente las seis.*
• *It must be about six o'clock.*

These verbs are known as *modal auxiliaries*:

Haber + de ⎫ Haber + que ⎬ Tener + que ⎭	*To have to, must*
Poder	*To be able to, can*
Deber	*To have to*
Soler ⎫ Acostumbrar ⎬	*To be in the habit of*
Atreverse a	*To dare*

2.4. Aspect (morpheme 4)

Aspect refers to the duration of the action expressed by the verb. Like mood, it may be expressed through the use of different verbal forms, or by using auxiliary verbs.

The *perfective* aspect of the verb expresses a completed action:

Juana **fue** *al colegio* • *Juana went to school.*

Whereas the *imperfective* aspect expresses a continued action:

Juana **iba** *al colegio* • *Juana was going/went/used to go to school.*

The fact that the action has now finished is irrelevant. Aspect expresses completed or incompleted action within the past, present or future time frame being used.

The *perfective* aspect is present in the simple perfect forms of the verb (*estudié* • *I studied*), and in all compound forms using *haber*:

He estudiado • *I have studied.*
Había estudiado • *I had studied.*
Habré estudiado • *I will have studied.*
Haya estudiado • *I may have studied.*
Hubiera estudiado • *I might have studied.*

The *imperfective* aspect is present in all the other verb forms:

Estudio • *I study.*
Estudiaba • *I was studying/studied/used to study.*
Estudiaré • *I will study.*
Estudie • *I may study.*
Estudiara • *I might study.*

These forms allow speakers to express a situation which was in existence for an indefinite period of time, whereas the perfective forms pinpoint the moment at which something occurred.

Íbamos a ir al cine, pero llovió y nos quedamos en casa.
• *We were going to go to the cinema, but it rained and we stayed at home.*

In Spanish, aspect can also be expressed through the use of auxiliary verbs, which offer a subtle range of meanings:

Ir a/estar para + infinitive:

These express a moment before some action which did not in the end take place:

***Iba a** venir, pero finalmente se quedó en casa.*
• *She was going to come, but in the end she stayed at home.*
***Estaba para** llover, pero no llovió.*
• *It looked like it was going to rain, but it didn't.*

Echarse a, ponerse a, romper a, comenzar a, resolverse a + infinitive:

These express the point when the action of the verb begins:

***Comienza a** estudiar idiomas.*
• *She is starting to learn languages.*
***Se echó** a reír* • *She burst out laughing.*
***Se puso** a leer un libro* • *She started reading a book.*

Ir, estar, venir, seguir, andar, llevar + gerund:

These express the progressive development of an action:

***Va** mejorando día a día* • *He is improving steadily all the time.*
***Sigue** trabajando mucho* • *He is still working a lot.*
*No **viene** saliendo como queríamos.*
• *It's not working out as we wanted.*

Ir, seguir, venir, andar + participle:

These substitute **estar** to express a lasting action or state still going on:

*El equipo **anda** cansado* • *The team is tired (now).*
*Mamá **sigue** enfadada conmigo* • *Mum is still mad at me.*
*La modelo **va** peinada a la última moda.*
• *The model has got her hair done in the latest fashion.*
*Este niño **viene** muerto de miedo.*
• *This boy is dead scared.*

Terminar de, dejar de, cesar de, concluir de/por, acabar de/por, llegar a, venir a + infinitive:

These express completion of an action:

***Dejé de** fumar* • *I stopped smoking.*
***Terminó de** leer el cuento* • *He finished reading the story.*

They can express different shades of meaning concerning the state of the subject as a result of a past action:

***Llegó a** gustarme Alemania* • *I ended up liking Germany.*
(Implying a neutral previous attitude towards that nation).
***Acabó por** gustarme Alemania* • *I ended up liking Germany.*
(Implying a negative previous attitude).

Ser, estar + participle (passive auxiliaries):

These make the subject the receptor of the action described by the verb:

*María **es amada*** • *María is loved.*
*El perro **ha sido mordido*** • *The dog has been bitten.*
*La casa **ha sido construida** con piedra* • *The house is built of stone.*

Note that the participle always agrees with the subject.
Only *transitive* verbs, that is, the ones which have a direct object, can take the passive.

Llevar, dejar, tener, traer, quedar + participle:

These express the cumulative result of an action:

***Llevo leídos** dos libros* • *I've read two books.*
***Quedé asustado** por la fiera* • *I got scared by the wild animal.*
***Tengo contados** muchos cuentos* • *I've told a lot of stories.*

2.5. Tense (morpheme 4)

Tense allows speakers to situate the action of the verb in the past, present or future. The past may be expressed in absolute terms (perfect):

*Su llegada me **sorprendió*** • *His arrival surprised me.*

or in a relative relation to another point in time (past perfect):

*No la **había previsto** (la llegada)* • *I had not expected it.*

2.6. Impersonal forms of the verb

These are the infinitive, the gerund and the participle. They express the process described by the verb but cannot in themselves differentiate tense, number or gender.

2.6.1. *The infinitive*

The infinitive may be thought of as the «name of the verb», e.g.:

Hablar • *To talk.*
Comer • *To eat.*
Ir • *To go.*

In Spanish, infinitives have certain features in common with nouns. They can take determiners and complements in the same way as any other noun:

Fumar *es pernicioso para la salud.*
• *Smoking is harmful to one's health.*
Es difícil de **encontrar.**
• *It is difficult to find.*
Espera **hablar** *bien el español.*
• *She hopes to speak Spanish well.*

In some cases they have actually become nouns:

El pesar • *Regret.*
El deber • *Duty.*
Los haberes • *Assets.*

The infinitive can also be used with prepositions:

— To express conditionality:

De haberlo *sabido, no habríamos venido.*
• *If we had known that, we would not have come.*
A no ser *por ti, no hubiéramos comprado este coche.*
• *If it hadn't been for you, we would not have bought this car.*

— Or to express a point in time:

Al salir *de clase, nos fuimos todos al cine.*
• *When we came out of school, we all went to the cinema.*
Al llegar *mi hermano, nos esconderemos.*
• *When my brother comes, we'll hide.*

The infinitive is also used for negative commands (prohibitions), especially where an impersonal sense is required:

No **fumar** • *No smoking.*
No **tirar** *objetos por la ventanilla* • *Do not throw objects out of the window.*

Note also the following uses:

Concessive: **Con tener** *dinero, no es más feliz* • *He's no happier now he's got money.*
Imperfect: *El crimen está* **por investigar** • *The crime has yet to be investigated.*
Final: *Vine* **a veros** • *I came to see you.*

2.6.2. *The gerund*

The gerund cannot be used with determiners, but it takes on verb complements in the normal way:

Estoy **leyendo** una novela de Cela. • *I'm reading a novel by Cela.*
Le vi paseando por el parque • *I saw him walking in the park.*

The gerund is used to express:

— The duration of an action, or an action which takes place at the same time as another:

Caminando, todo parece más fácil.
• *Walking (i.e. as one is walking) everything seems easier.*
Viene **leyendo** el periódico.
• *He is reading the paper on his way here.*
Enseñando se aprende.
• *By teaching, one learns.*

— The way in which an action is carried out (in which case it functions as an adverb):

Contestó **sonriendo** • *He answered smiling (with a smile).*
Pasaron **corriendo** • *They went running past.*

— The state of something (descriptive or adjectival function):

Encontré a su madre **llorando.**
• *I found her mother crying.*
El profesor, **viendo** a los alumnos cansados, concluyó la clase.
• *The teacher, seeing the pupils were tired, ended the lesson.*

— Some gerunds, such as *ardiendo*, and *hirviendo* have themselves become adjectives:

Se quemó con agua **hirviendo.**
• *He scalded himself with boiling water.*
Vio el horno **ardiendo.**
• *He saw the burning oven.*

— The *compound gerund* is used to indicate an action which has been completed before that described by the main verb:

Habiendo acabado su trabajo, se fue a casa.
• *Having completed her work, she went home.*

— Note also the following usages:

conditional: **Estando** tú conmigo, no me pasará nada.
        • *If you are with me, nothing will happen to me.*
concessive: **Estando** reñidos, todavía se hablan.
        • *Even though they've fallen out, they still talk to each other.*
copulative: Es muy inteligente, **sobresaliendo** entre todos sus compañeros.
        • *She is very intelligent and stands out amongst all her friends.*

2.6.3. *The participle*

The participle is a form of the verb which has many features in common with adjectives. It varies in number and gender, except when used with the auxiliary *haber* in compound tenses:

*Visto **el** museo, iremos a descansar al hotel.*
• *Having seen the museum, we will go to the hotel to rest.*
*Vist**as las** aves, el zoo carece de interés.*
• *The zoo is of no interest once you have seen the birds.*

but

*Isabel **ha visto** a su hermana en Sevilla.*
• *Isabel has seen her sister in Seville.*

The participle can be an attribute to verbs such as *ser* and *estar*.

*Juan **está disgustado*** • *Juan is upset.*
*María **viene dormida*** • *María has arrived half asleep.*

It can also act as a complement to transitive or pronominal verbs:

*La dejé **contenta*** • *I left her happy.*
*Me quedé **aturdido*** • *I was stunned.*

Or it can act as a complement to a noun:

*Del **árbol caído**, todos hacen leña.*
• *Everyone makes firewood from a fallen tree = proverb*
*Comieron **patatas asadas*** • *They ate roast potatoes.*

The participle can have an active or a passive meaning, for example:

*Un libro **leído*** • *A book that has been read.*
*Una persona **leída*** • *A well read person.*

The participle of an intransitive or reflexive verb cannot have a passive sense and can only refer back to the subject:

*Es muy **atrevido*** • *He is very daring.*
*Está **acostumbrado*** • *He is used to it.*
*El custard es **parecido** a las natillas.*
• *Custard is similar to «natillas».*

Some verbs have two forms of the participle, one regular and one irregular:

bendecido, bendito • *blessed*
confundido, confuso • *confused*
convencido, convicto • *convinced*
corrompido, corrupto • *corrupted*
difundido, difuso • *spread, disseminated*
elegido, electo • *elected*
eximido, exento • *exempted*
expelido, expulso • *expelled*
expresado, expreso • *expressed*
extinguido, extinto • *extinguished, extinct*
freído, frito • *fried*
hartado, harto • *fed up*
imprimido, impreso • *printed*
insertado, inserto • *inserted*
maldecido, maldito • *cursed*

prendido, preso • caught
presumido, presunto • presumed
proveído, provisto • provided
sepultado, sepulto • buried
suspendido, suspenso • suspended

The participle can be used to form what is known as an *absolute construction* (where the noun agreeing with the participle does not agree with or form part of the rest of the sentence):

Omitidos *los informes del presidente, la reunión careció de sentido.*
• *Since the president's reports had been left out, the meeting was pointless.*
Acabado *el banquete, se retiraron los camareros.*
• *When the meal was over, the waiters withdrew.*

2.7. Personal forms of the verb

The personal forms of the verb can be used in either the *indicative* or the *subjunctive* mood.

2.7.1. *The indicative mood*

The indicative denotes fact, or reality. Within the indicative mood there are five simple tenses and four compound tenses:

2.7.1.1. *The present*

In general terms, the present tense indicates that the action is occurring at the time of speaking:

Ahora **estudio** • *I'm studying now.*
Hablo *por teléfono con mi hija* • *I'm on the phone to my daughter.*

Note that the simple present in Spanish often translates as the present continuous in English.
However, as in English, it can be used to express actions which are not necessarily limited to the immediate present:

— The *habitual present* indicates actions which may have begun in the past and continue into the future:

   Paso *los veranos en la playa* • *I spend my summers at the beach.*
   Aquí **llueve** *poco* • *It does not rain much here.*
   Trabajo *para una empresa* • *I work for a company.*

— The *historic present* is used to describe actions which took place in the past. It is used:

   — when describing historical events:

      Colón **descubre** *América en 1492.*
      • *Columbus discovers America in 1492.*

   — to give immediacy to a story being recounted, either in literary style or colloquial speech:

      Llega *pronto la primavera y María* **se encuentra** *otra vez sola.*
      • *Spring comes early and María finds herself alone once more.*

Voy *a la tienda y* **pido** *que me cambien el traje.*
- *I go to the shop and ask them to exchange the suit.*

— to express actions about to take place in the immediate future: it is usually accompanied by *mañana, después,* etc. (the markers of future time).

Mañana **salgo** *para Moscú* • *I am leaving for Moscow tomorrow.*
Después **regreso** *a Madrid* • *Afterwards I'll come back to Madrid.*

— to express actions which take place or exist outside any limitation of time, especially in the style of proverbs or aphorisms:

La tierra **gira** *en torno al sol.*
- *The earth revolves around the sun.*
El dinero no lo **es** *todo en la vida.*
- *Money is not everything in life.*

— The *mandatory present* is used to express or underline an order. It is more emphatic than the simple imperative:

Tú **obedeces** *cuando yo lo digo.*
- *Do obey when I tell you (to do) something.*
Ahora mismo **te pones** *a estudiar.*
- *Get down to work immediately.*

2.7.1.2. *The imperfect*

The imperfect tense indicates that the action of the verb took place in the past, but it does not give any indication as to whether it has ended or not, either because the action is still going on, or because whether the action has ended or not is irrelevant:

Llovía *mucho aquella noche.*
- *It was raining hard that night.*
Estudiaba *una hora cada día en aquella época.*
- *He used to study an hour a day at that time.*

It always expresses time in relation to either another action, or to the time of speaking. The two actions may be simultaneous:

Ayer **llovía** *torrencialmente mientras* **comíamos.**
- *It was raining hard yesterday whilst we were eating.*

or one may take place at a particular point whilst the other is going on:

Ayer **llovía** *torrencialmente cuando me llamaste.*
- *It was raining hard yesterday when you called me.*

The imperfect can also be used in the following ways:

— To indicate an action which is repeated over time:

Llovía *y* **llovía** *sin cesar.*
- *It rained and rained endlessly.*

— As an alternative to the conditional tense in colloquial speech:

Poco **cambiaba** *el mundo sin tu existencia.*
- *The world wouldn't be much different without you.*

— As a polite form of asking a question:

> *¿**Quería** usted un libro?*
> • *Did you want a book?*
> ***Quería** que me explicara este problema.*
> • *I wanted you to explain the problem to me.*

2.7.1.3. *The pretérito (or simple past)*

The **pretérito** expresses an action which has been completed at the moment of speaking (as opposed to the imperfect, where no completion is implied). The length of time elapsed between completion of the action and the moment of its expression is irrelevant:

> ***Hablé** con tu padre* • *I spoke to your father.*
> *Hace solamente unos minutos que le **vi** pasar por la calle.*
> • *It was only a few minutes ago that I saw him go past in the street.*

The **pretérito** is almost always used with expressions such as *ayer, la semana pasada, anoche, aquel día*, etc., since they show that the action happened and was completed within a time which is separate from the moment of speaking.

2.7.1.4. *The future*

Use of the **futuro** makes reference to a future point in time separate from the time of speaking:

> *El mes que viene **acabaré** mi trabajo.*
> • *I shall finish my work next month.*
> *Mañana **hará** sol* • *It will be sunny tomorrow.*

It may also be used to express the following:

— Obligation:

> ***Amarás** a tus padres* • *You must love your parents.*
> *A las ocho, **irás** a ver al Director.*
> • *You will go and see the Head at eight o'clock.*

— Probability or supposition:

> ***Serán** las diez de la mañana* • *It must be about 10 am.*
> ***Tendrá** doce años* • *He must be 12.*

— Surprise or anger:

> *¡**Serás** tonta!* • *You must be stupid!*
> *¿Te **atreverás** a negarlo?* • *Would you dare to deny it?*

2.7.1.5. *The conditional*

This expresses a hypothetical future:

> *Me dijeron que **llegarías** hoy* • *They told me you would arrive today.*
> *Me **gustaría** salir con María* • *I would like to go out with María.*

However, depending on the context, it can also refer to past time:

> *Me dijiste que **estudiarías*** • *You told me that you would study.*

It can also be used as follows:

— As a polite way of asking questions:

¿Podría decirme qué hora es?
- Could you tell me what time it is?

— When giving advice:

Deberías descansar más.
- You should get more rest.

— To express probability:

Serían las doce cuando sonó la alarma.
- It must have been about 12 when the alarm rang.

2.7.1.6. Compound tenses of the indicative

These are formed with the auxiliary verb **haber.**
When a speaker wishes to express a past action which has been completed, but which is linked in some way with the present, the *present perfect* tense is used:

Este año **he jugado** mucho al tenis.
- I've played a lot of tennis this year.
Lo **hemos aguantado** suficientemente.
- We have put up with it/him for long enough.

The actual time elapsed between the action having been completed and the moment of speaking is irrelevant. What matters is the speaker's intention to draw the action into relation with the present:

En nuestro siglo **ha nevado** mucho.
- It has snowed a lot this century.
En la historia de la humanidad, **ha habido** momentos de especial importancia.
- In the history of mankind, there have been moments which have had special importance.

Unlike English, the present perfect can be used for any event which has taken place in the very recent past:

Esta mañana me **he duchado.**
- I had a shower this morning.
Me **he caído** en la calle.
- I fell over (just now) in the street.

The other compound tenses present few problems to English speakers. They are the *past perfect*, the *future perfect* and the *past conditional*.
The *past perfect* describes events which took place at a time previous to another past event:

Llegué a las ocho, pero ya se **había marchado** Pepe.
- I arrived at 8, but Pepe had already left.

The *future perfect* looks forward to a time when an action will have taken place:

Cuando llegues, ya **habré terminado** todo el trabajo.
- When you arrive, I will have already finished all the work.

The *past conditional* looks back to an event which would have been completed, had the situation been different:

*Si no hubieras llegado tan pronto, ya **habría terminado.***
- *If you hadn't arrived so soon, I would have finished already.*

(Conditional sentences of this type are dealt with in greater detail on p.194-196.)

There is also a further compound tense, the **pretérito anterior**, which expresses the idea of an event having just been completed immediately prior to another past event. It is never used in speech, and rarely in writing:

*Apenas **hube llegado** cuando se puso a llover.*
- *I had only just arrived when it started to rain.*

2.7.2. *The subjunctive*

In contrast to the indicative, it is more difficult to locate the different forms of the subjunctive within an overall time frame, since the point in time they refer to is often determined by the context, e.g.:

*Me dijeron que te **visitara** en casa.*
- *They told me to visit you at home.*

Here the *visit* referred to might take place in past, present or future time, depending on the context.

The subjunctive refers to an action or process which is not real, and is used to express doubt, hope, fear, desire, etc. It can also be used either on its own, or in a subordinate clause.

It often has no straightforward translation in English: its meaning can be expressed in a variety of different ways, depending on context:

Expressing doubt:

Independent clause	Subordinate clause
Quizás lo sepas • *Perhaps you know.* *Tal vez llegue* • *He may arrive.*	*Dudo que lo sepas* • *I doubt you know.* *Temo que llegue* • *I'm afraid he'll arrive.* *Lamento que venga* • *I'm sorry he's coming.*

Expressing a wish:

Independent clause	Subordinate clause
¡Ojalá venga! *Oh, that he would come!* *¡Que venga!* • *Let him come!*	*Quiero que venga* • *I want him to come.* *Conviene que venga* • *It's a good idea for him to come.*

In subordinate clauses, the subjunctive is used with:

— Verbs of language or perception:

*Te aconsejo que lo **hagas*** • *I advise you to do it.*
*Me sorprende que **venga** tan pronto.*
- *I am surprised he's coming so soon.*

When the negative is used with verbs of perception, the subjunctive *must* be used:

*Creo que **viene**.*   *No creo que **venga**.*
- *I think he's coming.*   • *I don't think he will come.*

*Veo que **estudia**.*   *No veo que **estudie**.*
- *I see he's studying.*   • *I can't see he's studying.*

— Verbs expressing orders, wishes, desires or hopes:

*Ordenó que **vinieras*** • *He ordered you to come.*
*Deseo que **llegues**, juegues y ganes.*
- *I want you to come, play and win.*
*Espero que nos **veamos** pronto.*
- *I hope we will see each other soon.*

— Verbs expressing emotion:

*Me molesta que **hables** alto.*
- *I don't like you talking in a loud voice.*
*Temo que no **puedas** hacerlo solo.*
- *I'm afraid you won't be able to do it alone.*
*Siento que lo **tomes** así.*
- *I am sorry you have taken it like that.*

There is a correspondence between the different tenses of the indicative and the subjective, as follows:

Indicative	Subjunctive
Present or Future	Present
*Creo que **viene** Juan.* • *I think Juan is coming.* *Creo que **vendrá** Juan.* *I think Juan will come.*	*No creo que **venga** Juan.* • *I don't think Juan is coming/will come.*
Present perfect or Future perfect	Present perfect
*Creo que **ha venido** Juan.* • *I think Juan has come.* *Creo que **habrá venido** Juan.* *I think Juan will have come.*	*No creo que **haya venido** Juan.* • *I don't think Juan has/will have come.*
Imperfect, Conditional or Simple Past	Imperfect
*Creí que **venía** Juan.* • *I thought Juan was coming.* *Creía que **vendría** Juan.* *I thought Juan would come.* *Creo que **vino** Juan.* *I think Juan came.*	*No creí que **viniera** Juan.* • *I didn't think Juan was coming.* *No creía que **viniera** Juan.* • *I didn't think Juan would come.* *No creo que **viniera** Juan.* • *I don't think Juan came.*

Although the subjunctive has different tenses, its main purpose is to express mood, and the tenses are to a large extent dependent on the requirements of the main verb which sets the time frame for the action being described.

2.7.2.1. *The present subjunctive*

The subjunctive cannot distinguish between present and future time: the present subjunctive indicates both:

*Quiero que **cantes*** • *I want you to sing.*

In this example, the action expressed by the subjunctive can take place either now or later, but never in the past.

The present subjunctive can be used in an independent clause as follows:

— To express negative commands:

*No **vengas** pronto* • *Don't come early.*

— To express doubt:

*Quizás te lo **cuente** todo* • *I/he/she may tell you everything.*

Adverbs expressing doubt or scant probability (*quizá[s], acaso, tal vez*) always require the subjunctive when they come before the verb, except *a lo mejor,* which always takes the indicative. When they come after the verb, the verb may be in the indicative:

***Llegaremos**, quizá, mañana a las diez.*
• *We will arrive, perhaps tomorrow at 10.*

Seguramente and *posiblemente* can take either the indicative or the subjunctive, according to the shade of meaning being expressed:

*Seguramente **vendrá** mañana* • *He will certainly come tomorrow.*
*Seguramente **venga** mañana* • *He will probably come tomorrow.*

— In exclamations:

*¡Ojalá **tenga** suerte en la lotería!*
• *If only I'm lucky in the lottery!*
*¡Que **seas** muy feliz!*
• *May you be very happy!*

— In special constructions where the verb is repeated with a *concessive* meaning:

***Digan lo que digan**, lo haremos.*
• *Whatever they may say, we will do it.*
***Trabajes lo que trabajes,** nunca lo lograrás.*
• *You will never achieve it, however much you work.*

In subordinate clauses, the present subjunctive is required when:

— A verb of perception or communication is used in the negative:

*No ve que **hagas** nada por ella.*
• *She can't see you are doing anything for her.*
*No creen que tú les **aventajes.***
• *They don't think you will get ahead of them.*

— A verb of wishing or demanding is used, which exerts an influence on the subject of the verb in the subordinate clause:

*Te ordeno que **bajes** del coche.*
• *I'm telling you to get out of the car.*
*Me aconsejan que no **oculte** la verdad.*
• *They advise me not to hide the truth.*

— A verb expressing emotion or reaction is used where there is a change of subject in the subordinate clause:

*Le molesta que **hables** tanto.*
* *He doesn't like you talking so much.*
*No le gusta que la **califiques** de «descuidada».*
* *She doesn't like you calling her «unkempt».*

— The structure is of the form *Es + adj + que,* where the adjective is *bueno, importante, indiferente, fácil, lógico, probable, posible, verosímil, necesario, mejor, natural,* etc. and their opposites:

*Es **bueno que adelgace** un poco.*
* *It's good for him to slim down a bit.*
*Es **importante que tome** el sol.*
* *It's important for you/him/her to sunbathe.*

— The subjunctive is also required with the structure *Es mentira que...* (It's not true that...):

*Es **mentira que sea** tu profesora.*
* *It's not true that she's your teacher.*

— The present subjunctive is used too when the subordinate clause is presented as something «unreal» or which hasn't taken place yet:

*Cuando **hable,** verás cuanto sabe.*
* *Whe she speaks, you will see how much she knows.*
*Aunque **trabaje** día y noche, no podrá acabarlo.*
* *Even if she works day and night, she won't be able to finish it.*

2.7.2.2. *The imperfect subjunctive*

There are two forms of the imperfect subjunctive, one ending in **-ra** and one in **-se** (see p. 112 for table). They may be used interchangeably, except in special cases when the **-ra** form takes the place of the conditional.

As stated above, the use of the imperfect subjunctive depends on the time frame given by the main verb: its use in independent clauses is fairly restricted.

In subordinate clauses, it is used as follows:

— When verbs expressing wish, fear, hope, perception and communication, are used in the main clause in the past tense:

*No **creía** que lo **hicieras** tan bien.*
* *I didn't think you would do it so well.*
*Les **aconsejaba** que se **lavaran** los dientes antes de ir a la cama.*
* *He advised them to brush their teeth before they went to bed.*
*Le **gustó** que le **alabaras** en público.*
* *He liked you praising him in public.*
*No **quiso** que le **ayudaras** a pagar la deuda.*
* *He didn't want you to help him pay off the debt.*

— When the subordinate clause is expressed as something unreal not experienced before, in various contexts or environments:

*Aunque me **quisiera**, no me **casaría** con ella.*
* *I wouldn't marry her even if she loved me.*

*Si **fuera** cierto, ya lo **habrían** publicado.*
• *If that were true, they would already have printed it.*

In independent clauses, the imperfect subjunctive is used as follows:

— In exclamations with *quién, ojalá* or *así*:

*¡Quién lo **dijera**!*
• *Who would say that!/Who could expect anything like that (to happen)!*
*¡Ojalá **comprara** la casa!*
• *If only she/he/you would buy the house!*

The use of the imperfect as opposed to the present subjunctive with *ojalá* implies less possibility of the action coming true.

— As a polite way of expressing obligation or desire with *querer, deber,* etc.:

***Quisiera** ir con usted* • *I would like to go with you.*
***Debiera** venir conmigo* • *You ought to come with me.*

— With constructions such as the following, where the verb is repeated:

***Dijeran lo que dijeran**, no es cierto.*
• *Say what they might, it is not true.*
***Escribiera lo que escribiera**, sus argumentos son siempre flojos.*
• *Whatever he might write, his arguments are always weak.*

2.7.2.3. *Compound forms of the subjunctive*

The compound forms of the subjunctive are formed with *haber* and always refer to actions which are being expressed as (hypothetically) having been completed:

*Lo dirá cuando todos **hayan abandonado** la sala.*
• *He will say it when everyone has left the room.*
*Le habría gustado que lo **hubieras dicho** tú.*
• *He would have liked you to have said it.*
*¡Ojalá **hayan encontrado** a la familia reunida!*
• *I hope they've found the family reunited.*
*¡Quién **hubiera creído** que España era así!*
• *Who would have thought Spain was like that!*

2.7.3. The imperative

The imperative is used to express direct orders, requests or wishes. It has the following peculiarities:

— It only exists in the 2nd person singular and plural:

Salta • *Jump,* sing.
Saltad • *Jump,* pl.

— The endings (**-o** in the singular and **-d** in the plural), differ from those corresponding to the second person in other forms of the verb (**-s** and **-is**).

— Pronouns must be postponed to the imperative:

*Cánta**lo*** • *Sing it.*

except in the negative:

No lo cantes • *Don't sing it.*

— When the plural form is used with **-os**, it loses its final **-d**:

Sentaos • *Sit down* (not *sentados*).

The exception to this is **idos**, which keeps the **-d** for phonetic reasons.

— The imperative form cannot be used in the negative. To express this, the present subjunctive is used:

No **vengas** • *Don't come.*
No **cantéis** • *Don't sing.*

In this case, the pronoun precedes the verb, as normal:

No lo **cantes** • *Don't sing it.*

— There is a marked tendency in present day Spanish to substitute the infinitive for the second person plural form of the imperative:

Sentaros por **sentaos** • *Sit down.*
Quedaros por **quedaos** • *Stay.*

2.8. The conjugation of regular verbs

All regular verbs conjugate, that is, form their different inflections for tense, mood, number, person, etc., according to one of the following models. The verbs *amar, temer* and *partir* are used as models of 1st, 2nd and 3rd conjugation verbs respectively.

	1st conjugation **amar**	2nd conjugation **temer**	3rd conjugation **partir**
IMPERSONAL FORMS			
SIMPLE FORMS			
Infinitive • to love, etc.	amar	temer	partir
Gerund • loving, etc.	amando	temiendo	partiendo
Participle • loved, etc.	amado	temido	partido
COMPOUNDS FORMS			
Infinitive • to have loved, etc.	haber amado	haber temido	haber partido
Gerund • having loved etc.	habiendo amado	habiendo temido	habiendo partido

	1st conjugation *amar*	2nd conjugation *temer*	3rd conjugation *partir*
PERSONAL FORMS			
Indicative mood:	**SIMPLE TENSES**		
Present: • *I love, etc.*	*amo* *amas* *ama* *amamos* *amáis* *aman*	*temo* *temes* *teme* *tememos* *teméis* *temen*	*parto* *partes* *parte* *partimos* *partís* *parten*
Imperfect: • *I used to love,* *etc.*	*amaba* *amabas* *amaba* *amábamos* *amabais* *amaban*	*temía* *temías* *temía* *temíamos* *temíais* *temían*	*partía* *partías* *partía* *partíamos* *partíais* *partían*
Simple past: (Pretérito) • *I loved, etc.*	*amé* *amaste* *amó* *amamos* *amasteis* *amaron*	*temí* *temiste* *temió* *temimos* *temisteis* *temieron*	*partí* *partiste* *partió* *partimos* *partisteis* *partieron*
Future: • *I will love, etc.*	*amaré* *amarás* *amará* *amaremos* *amaréis* *amarán*	*temeré* *temerás* *temerá* *temeremos* *temeréis* *temerán*	*partiré* *partirás* *partirá* *partiremos* *partiréis* *partirán*
Conditional: • *I would love,* *etc.*	*amaría* *amarías* *amaría* *amaríamos* *amaríais* *amarían*	*temería* *temerías* *temería* *temeríamos* *temeríais* *temerían*	*partiría* *partirías* *partiría* *partiríamos* *partiríais* *partirían*
	COMPOUND TENSES		
Present perfect: • *I have loved,* *etc.*	*he amado* *has amado* *ha amado* *hemos amado* *habéis amado* *han amado*	*he temido* *has temido* *ha temido* *hemos temido* *habéis temido* *han temido*	*he partido* *has partido* *ha partido* *hemos partido* *habéis partido* *han partido*
Past perfect: (pluscuam- perfecto) • *I had loved,* *etc.*	*había amado* *habías amado* *había amado* *habíamos amado* *habíais amado* *habían amado*	*había temido* *habías temido* *había temido* *habíamos temido* *habíais temido* *habían temido*	*había partido* *habías partido* *había partido* *habíamos partido* *habíais partido* *habían partido*

	1st conjugation **amar**	2nd conjugation **temer**	3rd conjugation **partir**
Anterior Preterite: • I had loved, etc.	hube amado hubiste amado hubo amado hubimos amado hubisteis amado hubieron amado	hube temido hubiste temido hubo temido hubimos temido hubisteis temido hubieron temido	hube partido hubiste partido hubo partido hubimos partido hubisteis partido hubieron partido
Future perfect: • I will have loved, etc.	habré amado habrás amado habrá amado habremos amado habréis amado habrán amado	habré temido habrás temido habrá temido habremos temido habréis temido habrán temido	habré partido habrás partido habrá partido habremos partido habréis partido habrán partido
Perfect conditional: • I would have loved, etc.	habría amado habrías amado habría amado habríamos amado habríais amado habrían amado	habría temido habrías temido habría temido habríamos temido habríais temido habrían temido	habría partido habrías partido habría partido habríamos partido habríais partido habrían partido

Subjunctive mood:

SIMPLE TENSES

	1st conjugation **amar**	2nd conjugation **temer**	3rd conjugation **partir**
Present: • that I love, etc.	ame ames ame amemos améis amen	tema temas tema temamos temáis teman	parta partas parta partamos partáis partan
Imperfect: • that I loved, etc.	amara/amase amaras/amases amara/amase amáramos/-ásemos amarais/-aseis amaran/-asen	temiera/temiese temieras/temieses temiera/temiese temiéramos/-iésemos temierais/-ieseis temieran/-iesen	partiera/partiese partieras/partieses partiera/partiese partiéramos/-iésemos partierais/-ieseis partieran/-iesen
Future: • I will love, etc.	amare amares amare amáremos amareis amaren	temiere temieres temiere temiéremos temiereis temieren	partiere partieres partiere partiéremos partiereis partieren

COMPOUND TENSES

	1st conjugation **amar**	2nd conjugation **temer**	3rd conjugation **partir**
Perfect: • that I have loved, etc.	haya amado hayas amado haya amado hayamos amado hayáis amado hayan amado	haya temido hayas temido haya temido hayamos temido hayáis temido hayan temido	haya partido hayas partido haya partido hayamos partido hayáis partido hayan partido

	1st conjugation *amar*	2nd conjugation *temer*	3rd conjugation *partir*

Past perfect:
• *that I had*
  loved, etc.
	hubiera/hubiese amado
	hubieras/-ieses amado
	hubiera/-iese amado
	hubiéramos/-iésemos
	  amado
	hubierais/-ieseis amado
	hubieran/-iesen amado
		hubiera/hubiese temido
		hubieras/-ieses temido
		hubiera/-iese temido
		hubiéramos/-iésemos
		  temido
		hubierais/-ieseis temido
		hubieran/-iesen temido
			hubiera/hubiese partido
			hubieras/-ieses partido
			hubiera/-iese partido
			hubiéramos/-iésemos
			  partido
			hubierais/-ieseis partido
			hubieran/-iesen partido

Compound future:	*hubiere amado* *hubieres amado* *hubiere amado* *hubiéramos amado* *hubiereis amado* *hubieren amado*	*hubiere temido* *hubieres temido* *hubiere temido* *hubiéramos temido* *hubiereis temido* *hubieren temido*	*hubiere partido* *hubieres partido* *hubiere partido* *hubiéramos partido* *hubiereis partido* *hubieren partido*
Imperative mood:			
Present: *(love, etc.)*	*ama* amad	*teme* temed	*parte* partid

* Note the two forms of the imperfect subjunctive and the past perfect subjunctive (which is formed with the imperfect subjunctive of *haber*), one ending in **-ra**, the other in **-se**.

2.9. Verbs which undergo spelling changes

These are not regarded as irregular since the change in spelling is merely to preserve phonological regularity. The most common spelling changes are:

— Changes in the final consonant of the stem:

c → qu	*expli*c*ar, expli*qu*e*
g → gu	*obli*g*ar, obli*gu*e*
z → c	*alcan*z*ar, alcan*c*e*

— Changes which occur before the vowel **-o**:

c → z	*ven*c*er, ven*z*o*
g → j	*prote*g*er, prote*j*o*
gu → g	*conse*gu*ir, consi*g*o*
qu → c	*delin*qu*ir, delin*c*o*

— Dropping of the theme vowel. This occurs, again for reasons of pronunciation, in verbs which end in **-llir, -ñer**, and **-ñir**, giving, for example, **gruñó** and **gruñera** instead of **gruñió* and **gruñiera*. Similarly:

bullir   *bulló, bullera*
tañer   *tañó, tañera*

— The substitution of **i** for **y** between two vowels:

leer   *leyó, leyera*
roer   *royó, royera*

— Variations in the use of the written accent, especially with verbs ending in **-uar** and **-iar**:

confiar   *confío, confíe, confiaban*
continuar   *continúo, continúe, continuaba*

2.10. The conjugation of irregular verbs

2.10.1. *Irregular verbs*

A large number of verbs conjugate differently from the models given above in that either their stem or their endings do not conform to the regular pattern. These are known as *irregular verbs*. Irregularities in the Spanish verb are the result of phonetic mutations in the language which have affected vowels, consonants, or both.

2.10.2. *Radical changing verbs*

In these verbs, the stem vowel either changes or becomes a diphthong when stressed. Verbs where the vowel changes may be like *pedir*, where **e** becomes **i** (*pido*) or *podrir*, where **o** becomes **u** (*pudrió*):

Pedir:

e becomes **i** in all forms where the stress falls on the stem vowel or where the following syllable is not a syllabic **i** (pedí, pidió; pido, pedimos):

Present indicative: *pido, pides, pide, pedimos, pedís, piden*
Present subjunctive: *pida, pidas, pida, pidamos, pidáis, pidan*
Imperative: *pide, pedid*
Simple past: *pedí, pediste, pidió, pedimos, pedisteis, pidieron*
Imperfect subjunctive: *pidiera/pidiese, pidieras, pidiera, pidiéramos, pidierais, pidieran*
Gerund: *pidiendo*

Verbs which follow this pattern include: *concebir, conseguir, corregir, derretir, despedir, elegir, impedir, medir, perseguir, repetir, seguir, servir, teñir, vestir(se)*.

Podrir:

The **o → u** mutation affects only the simple past, imperfect subjunctive and gerund:

Simple past: *podrí, podriste, pudrió, podrimos, podristeis, pudrieron*
Imperfect subjunctive: *pudriera/-iese, pudrieras, pudriera, pudriéramos, pudrierais, pudrieran*
Gerund: *pudriendo*

When the stem vowel becomes a diphthong, this involves one of the following changes:

e → ie	*querer*	*quiero*
o → ue	*poder*	*puedo*
i → ie	*adquirir*	*adquiero*
u → ue	*jugar*	*juego*

This occurs when the stress falls on the stem vowel, in the present indicative, present subjunctive and the singular form of the imperative.

---

e → ie: *acertar.*

Present indicative: *acierto, aciertas, acierta, acertamos, acertáis, aciertan*
Present subjunctive: *acierte, aciertes, acierte, acertemos, acertéis, acierten*
Imperative: *acierta, acertad*

Verbs conjugated like **acertar:** alentar, apacentar, apretar, atravesar, calentar, cegar, cerrar, cimentar, confesar, despertar, empezar, encomendar, enmendar, fregar, gobernar, helar, manifestar, merendar, negar, pensar, plegar, reventar, sentir, tentar, tropezar.

---

o → ue: *contar.*

Present indicative: *cuento, cuentas, cuenta, contamos, contáis, cuentan*
Present subjunctive: *cuente, cuentes, cuente, contemos, contéis, cuenten*
Imperative: *cuenta, contad*

Verbs conjugated like **contar**: *acostar, almorzar, apostar, avergonzar, colar, consolar, costar, forzar, mostrar, poblar, probar, recordar, renovar, soltar, sonar, soñar, tostar, volar, volver.*

Some verbs combine both diphthongization and alternation of the stem vowel:

mentir, miento, mintió
morir, muero, murió

2.10.3. *Verbs with consonantal irregularities*

The forms most affected by this type of irregularity are the first person singular of the present indicative, and the present subjunctive.

— **c** changes to **g**:

decir	*digo*
hacer	*hago*

Decir:

Present indicative: *digo, dices, dice, decimos, decís, dicen.*
Present subjunctive: *diga, digas, diga, digamos, digáis, digan.*

— **c** becomes **zc**:

nacer	*nazco*	*nazca*
conocer	*conozco*	*conozca*
enardecer	*enardezco*	*enardezca*

Nacer:

Present indicative: *nazco, naces, nace, nacemos, nacéis, nacen*
Present subjunctive: *nazca, nazcas, nazca, nazcamos, nazcáis, nazcan*

Verbs following this pattern include: *renacer, pacer, conocer, reconocer, desconocer, lucir, relucir, traslucir, deslucir, inducir, conducir, deducir, introducir, producir, reducir, seducir, traducir, placer, yacer, complacer.*

— Insertion of an additional consonant, e.g.:

l → lg	*salir, sal**g**o, sal**g**a*
n → ng	*poner, po**ng**o, po**ng**a*
s → sg	*asir, a**sg**o, a**sg**a*
u → uy	*huir, hu**y**o, hu**y**a*

Salir:

Present indicative: *salgo, sales, sale, salimos, salís, salen*
Present subjunctive: *salga, salgas, salga, salgamos, salgáis, salgan*

— Insertion of an additional consonant and vowel:

e → ig	*caer, ca**ig**o, ca**ig**a*

Caer:

Present indicative: *caigo, caes, cae, caemos, caéis, caen*
Present subjunctive: *caiga, caigas, caiga, caigamos, caigáis, caigan*

Verbs following this pattern include *oír (o**ig**o), traer, (tra**ig**o), roer, (ro**ig**o)* and *raer (ra**ig**o).*

— Mutation of both vowel and consonant:

*ca*ber	***que**po, **que**pa*
*sa*ber	***sé**, **sepa***

Caber:

Present indicative: *quepo, cabes, cabe, cabemos, cabéis, caben*
Present subjunctive: *quepa, quepas, quepa, quepamos, quepáis, quepan*

Saber:

Present indicative: *sé, sabes, sabe, sabemos, sabéis, saben*
Present subjunctive: *sepa, sepas, sepa, sepamos, sepáis, sepan*

2.10.4. *Haber, Ser, Ir*

These verbs show such a high degree of irregularity that their forms are presented in full:

	Haber	Ser	Ir
Present indicative:	*he*	*soy*	*voy*
	has	*eres*	*vas*
	ha/hay	*es*	*va*
	hemos	*somos*	*vamos*
	habéis	*sois*	*vais*
	han	*son*	*van*
Imperfect:	*había*	*era*	*iba*
	habías	*eras*	*ibas*
	etc.	etc.	etc.
Future:	*habré*	*seré*	*iré*
	habrás	*serás*	*irás*
	etc.	etc.	etc.
Simple past (Pretérito):	*hube*	*fui*	*fui*
	hubiste	*fuiste*	*fuiste*
	hubo	*fue*	*fue*
	hubimos	*fuimos*	*fuimos*
	hubisteis	*fuisteis*	*fuisteis*
	hubieron	*fueron*	*fueron*
Conditional:	*habría*	*sería*	*iría*
	habrías	*serías*	*irías*
	etc.	etc.	etc.
Imperative:	*he*	*sé*	*ve*
	habed	*sed*	*id*
Present subjunctive:	*haya*	*sea*	*vaya*
	hayas	*seas*	*vayas*
	haya	*sea*	*vaya*
	hayamos	*seamos*	*vayamos*
	hayáis	*seáis*	*vayáis*
	hayan	*sean*	*vayan*
Imperfect subjunctive:	*hubiera/hubiese*	*fuera/fuese*	*fuera/fuese*
	hubieras/hubieses	*fueras/fueses*	*fueras/fueses*
	etc.	etc.	etc.
Gerund:	*habiendo*	*siendo*	*yendo*

2.10.5. *Verbs with irregularities relating to the theme vowel*

These fall into the following categories:

— Verbs which drop the theme vowel in the future and conditional tenses:

caber	*cabré*	*cabría*
haber	*habré*	*habría*
poder	*podré*	*podría*
querer	*querré*	*querría*
saber	*sabré*	*sabría*

— Verbs which drop their theme vowel in the singular form of the imperative:

poner	**pon**
hacer	**haz**

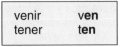

salir	**sal**

All forms derived from these vebs (*anteponer, retener, prevenir,* etc.) follow the same pattern.

— Verbs which drop their theme vowel and add **-d-** in the future and conditional tenses:

poner	*pon**d**ré*	*pon**d**ría*
salir	*sal**d**ré*	*sal**d**ría*
tener	*ten**d**ré*	*ten**d**ría*
valer	*val**d**ré*	*val**d**ría*
venir	*ven**d**ré*	*ven**d**ría*

and their derived forms.

— Verbs which drop a syllable in the future and conditional tenses:

hacer	*haré*	*haría*
decir	*diré*	*diría*

and forms derived from these verbs.

2.10.6. *Verbs with irregular simple past endings*

The following verbs have irregular preterites:

andar	*and**uve***	poder	*p**u**de*
conducir	*cond**uje***	poner	*p**u**se*
caber	*c**u**pe*	querer	*q**u**ise*
decir	*d**ije***	saber	*s**u**pe*
estar	*est**uve***	tener	*t**uv**e*
haber	*h**u**be*	venir	*v**i**ne*
hacer	*h**i**ce*	ver	*v**i***

They are nonetheless regular in the sense that they all follow one of the following patterns:

andar	**hacer**	**decir**	**poner**	**tener**	**querer**
anduve	*hice*	*dije*	*puse*	*tuve*	*quise*
anduviste	*hiciste*	*dijiste*	*pusiste*	*tuviste*	*quisiste*
anduvo	*hizo*	*dijo*	*puso*	*tuvo*	*quiso*
anduvimos	*hicimos*	*dijimos*	*pusimos*	*tuvimos*	*quisimos*
anduvisteis	*hicisteis*	*dijisteis*	*pusisteis*	*tuvisteis*	*quisisteis*
anduvieron	*hicieron*	*dijeron*	*pusieron*	*tuvieron*	*quisieron*

The verbs *ver, dar, ser* and *ir* have contracted forms in the first and third persons singular (*vi/vio, di/dio, fui/fue*).

2.10.7. *Defective verbs*

Defective verbs are only conjugated in certain tenses or persons (they may, of course, show other irregularities as well, such as those described above). They are as follows:

— Verbs which, in general, only appear in the third person (*gustar, doler, placer,* etc.), either singular or plural:

*Me **gusta** el té •* I like tea.
*Me **gustan** los vestidos floreados •* I like flowery dresses.
*Me **duele** la cabeza •* I have a headache.
*Me **duelen** las costillas •* My ribs ache.

— Verbs which have an impersonal sense (generally translated by *It ...* in English) and are therefore only used in the third person (*suceder, acontecer, pasar, ocurrir, convenir,* etc.):

***Sucede** con frecuencia •* It happens frequently.
***Parece** mentira •* It doesn't seem true.
***Conviene** hacerlo inmediatamente •* It's a good idea to do it straightaway.

— Verbs which describe the weather (*nevar, llover, helar,* etc., also *anochecer, amanecer*) are only used in the third person:

***Llueve** •* It's raining.
***Está** diluviando •* It's pouring.

— The modal auxiliary *soler*, which expresses the sense of *usually* and is always followed by an infinitive:

***Suele** llegar pronto •* He/she usually arrives early.
***Suelen** decirlo con claridad •* They usually say it clearly.

— Other verbs which only tend to appear in set phrases, for example:

*En lo que **atañe** a... •* With respect to..., regarding...
*No nos **compete...** •* It is not our responsibility/business to...

3. Types of verbal construction

The characteristic of a particular verb, or the way in which it is used, may give rise to different types of syntactical constructions, as follows:

3.1. Transitive constructions

In these the verb is followed directly by a complement or direct object:

*El abuelo **lee el periódico.***
• The grandfather is reading the newspaper.
*El perro **come un hueso.***
• The dog is eating a bone.
*Juan **vive una vida** feliz.*
• Juan lives a happy life.

3.2. Intransitive constructions

Here, in contrast, the verb does not take any complement or direct object:

El pájaro **vuela** • *The bird is flying.*
El niño **corre** • *The child is running.*
Juan **vive** • *Juan lives/is alive.*

It will be noted from the examples given above that some verbs may be used either transitively or intransitively.

3.3. Pronominal constructions

These occur with verbs which are conjugated with personal pronouns agreeing with the subject, e.g. *arrepentirse:*

Yo **me** *arrepiento* • *I'm sorry.*
Tú **te** *arrepientes* • *You are sorry.*

Some verbs may be used with or without the **-se** form:

Ir • *To go.*   *Irse* • *To go away.*
Marchar • *To go.*   *Marcharse* • *To go away.*
Dormir • *To sleep.*   *Dormirse* • *To go to sleep.*

Pronominal constructions may be either:

Reflexive, e.g.: *Juan* **se** *lava* • *Juan is washing (himsefl).*
Reciprocal, e.g.: *Juan y Marta* **se** *quieren mucho* • *Juan and Marta are very fond of each other.*
Passive, e.g.: *Este coche* **se** *fabrica en Pamplona* • *This car is made in Pamplona.*

An *impersonal construction* with **se** occurs when the subject and the direct object are not the same:

Se *alquila piso* • *Flat for rent.*

3.4. Copulative verbs

The two most frequent copulative or «linking» verbs is Spanish are *ser* and *estar*. However, the following also give rise to similar constructions:

parecer: *Juan parece listo* • *Juan seems intelligent.*
llegar a ser: *Juan llegó a ser famoso* • *Juan became famous.*
quedar: *Isabel quedó entristecida* • *Isabel was left saddened.*
venir: *Pedro vino cansado* • *Pedro arrived tired.*
llegar: *El paquete llegó roto* • *The parcel arrived torn.*

The most significant feature of this type of construction is the agreement required between subject and predicate:

Los *libros* **son** *viejos* • *The books are old.*

However, as noted above, in some cases complete agreement may not be possible:

Lo que tú dices **son** cosas imposib**les.**
• *You talk about impossibilities.*
El problema **son** los viejos • *The problem is the old people.*

4. Peculiarities of auxiliary verbs

The most common auxiliary verbs in Spanish are *ser, estar* and *haber.* Both *ser* and *estar* may also be used as verbs in their own right, but *haber* almost always appears as an auxiliary, forming the perfect tense of another verb (*he comido,* etc.). *Ser* and *haber* are highly irregular, and appear conjugated in full on p. 112.

4.1. Haber

Haber as an auxiliary verb provides the «*perfective aspect*» to the main verb (the sense of having completed the action it describes):

Ha cantado • *She has sung.*
Hemos llegado bien • *We have arrived safely.*
Habían comido a las dos • *They had eaten at 2 o'clock.*

When used in this way it requires agreement in number with the subject. The main verb does not agree in any way with the subject.

Haber is also an impersonal verb in its three forms: *hay, había,* and *hubo,* which are used in the singular only:

Hay muchos problemas • *There are many problems.*
Había muchos problemas • *There were many problems.*
Hubo un gran problema • *There was a great problem.*

It may also be used in relative constructions:

Los **hay que** no me gustan • *There are those I don't like.*
Siempre **hay quienes** llegan tarde • *There are always those who arrive late.*

The construction *hay que* (*había que, hubo que*) expresses obligation:

Hay que volver mañana
• *We'll (You'll) have to come back tomorrow.*
Había que regar las plantas todos los días
• *It was necessary to water the plants every day.*

4.2. Ser

Both *ser* and *estar* are complex verbs which may cause some difficulties to students of Spanish as a foreign language and are therefore dealt with at some length here.

Ser may be used as follows:

— In a predicative sense, meaning *to be*:

Tu cumpleaños **será** *mañana.*
● *It will be your birthday tomorrow.*
La fiesta **fue** *en la discoteca.*
● *The party was in the discotheque.*

— In an attributive or copulative sense, linking one element with another. The second element may be a noun, in which case *ser* performs the function of identifying the subject with it:

Mi hermano **es** *profesor* ● *My brother is a teacher.*
El león **es** *un animal salvaje* ● *Lions are wild animals.*
Juan Carlos **es** *el rey de España* ● *Juan Carlos is the king of Spain.*

The second element may also be a verb. In conjunction with the preposition *para* it signifies purpose:

Eso **es** *para cortar madera* ● *That is for cutting wood.*
Este libro **es** *para estudiar* ● *This book is to study.*

Or the verb may follow on from the following type of construction with *de*:

Es de *desear que tu hija vaya a la universidad.*
● *It is to be hoped that your daughter go to university.*
Es de *temer que no te haga caso.*
● Lit: *It is to be feared that he should take no notice of you.*

If the second element is an adjective, then it serves to describe a quality of the subject:

Esta mesa **es** *muy cara* ● *This table is very expensive.*
Este coche **es** *bonito* ● *This car is nice.*

As an auxiliary verb, forming the passive:

El animal **fue** *atado por sus guardianes.*
● *The animal was tied up by its keepers.*
Los ladrones **fueron** *descubiertos por la policía.*
● *The thieves were found by the police.*

In the structure *Es que* or *Es (+ adj) que*:

Es *mejor* **que** *vengas* ● *It's better for you to come.*
Es *posible* **que** *llueva* ● *It may rain.*
Es *importante* **que** *salga bien.*
● *It's important it should turn out well.*
Es que *no había llegado* ● *The thing is, he hadn't arrived.*

In idioms and set usages, as follows:

— to express the time:

Son *las dos y media* ● *It is half past two.*

— to express someone's origin or nationality:

Es de León • *He's from León.*
Es alemana • *She is German.*

— to describe what something is made out of:

*Este collar **es** de oro* • *This necklace is (made of) gold.*
*El mío **es** de plástico* • *Mine is plastic.*

— to express possession:

*El lápiz **es** mío* • *The pencil is mine.*

— to describe what something costs:

*¿Cuánto **es** esto?* • *How much is this?*
***Son** mil pesetas* • *It's 1000 ptas.*

— to refer to the days of the week:

Es sábado • *It is Saturday.*

In idiomatic expressions such as *esto es (that's it), es a saber (that is to say), es más (not only that), no ser para menos (quite right too),* etc:

*Le dio 100.000; **no era para** menos, después de lo que había hecho por él.*
• *He gave him 100.000. Quite right too, after what he had done for him.*
*Sacó el primer premio; pero **es más,** lo sacó por unanimidad.*
• *He won first prize. Not only that, he won it by unanimous decision.*

To refer to age:

Es un joven de 18 años • *He is a young man of 18.*

To describe colour:

*¿De qué color **es** tu nuevo coche?* • *What colour is your new car?*
Es verde • *It is green.*

To refer to the time or season:

Es verano • *It is summer.*
Es temprano • *It is early.*

In the set phrase ***Érase** una vez...* • *Once upon a time...*

4.3. Estar

Estar is used as follows:

Meaning *to be* in predicative structures when expressing:

— the location of something in space:

*Mis padres **están** en Berlín* • *My parents are in Berlin.*
*La secretaria **está** en la oficina* • *The secretary is in the office.*

— the location of something in time:

Estamos en invierno • *We are in winter.*
Estamos en 1992 • *We are in 1992.*
Estamos a dos horas de Madrid • *We are two hours away from Madrid.*

— a temporary state with a fixed duration:

Estuvo dos horas con ella • *He was with her for two hours.*
Estaba mejor antes • *I/he/she was better off before.*

— readiness:

El traje **estará** para mañana a las dos.
• *The suit will be ready by tomorrow at two.*

As a copula or *linking word,* as follows:

— with adjectives expressing a temporary state, or the result of a process:

Los niños **están** castigados • *The children have been punished.*
El tejado **está** sucio • *The roof is dirty.*
El árbol **está** seco • *The tree is dried up.*

— with the preposition *de*, expressing a function fulfilled temporarily:

Estuve de niñera mientras fueron de compras.
• *I acted as a nanny whilst they went shopping.*
Está de auxiliar de conversación.
• *He is a language assistant.*

— with other prepositions expressing a temporary situation:

Estuvieron un mes **a** régimen.
• *They were on a diet for a month.*
El suelo **está con** manchas • *The floor has dirty marks on it.*

As an auxiliary verb:

— Followed by the gerund it makes the continuous forms of the verb:

Estaba comiendo el pastel • *She was eating the cake.*
Están trabajando mucho últimamente.
• *They are working a lot lately.*

— Followed by the participle it describes a state resulting from a process having been completed:

La casa **está acabada** • *The house has been finished.*
La muchacha **está agotada** • *The girl is exhausted.*

Note that both *ser* and *estar* can be used to form the passive, but *estar* adds a *perfective* sense in that it expresses not only the action, but the result of the action:

Las entradas **fueron** compradas • *The tickets were bought.*
Las entradas **están** compradas • *The tickets have been bought.*

— Followed by the prepositions *sin, para* or *por* plus the infinitive:

Estuvo un mes **sin** comer • *He went for a month without eating.*
No **estoy para** tonterías • *I'm not in the mood for silliness.*

*Su novia **estaba por** darle plantón.*
  • *His girlfriend was tempted to stand him up.*

In the construction *Estar que* + verb:

Está que revienta • *He's fit to bursting.*
La niña está que trina • *The girl's absolutely furious.*

In idiomatic expressions, as follows:

— *Estar de más* = *to be unnecessary:*

*En esta empresa tan pequeña, una secretaria **está** de más.*
  • *In such a small firm, a secretary is surplus to requirements.*

— *Estar de acuerdo* = *to agree.*
— *Estar al caer* = *to be about to happen.*
— *Estar en ello* = *to be working on it.*
— *Estar bien* = *to be OK, to be in good health.* It may also mean «to have done enough»:

*No trabajes más, ya **está bien** por hoy.*
  • *Don't work any more, you've done enough for today.*

— *Estar en todo* = *to keep track of everything.*

4.4. Comparison of *ser* and *estar*

As it will be evident from the above, in general terms *ser* is used to describe a permanent state, whilst *estar* usually refers to a temporary condition. The following examples make this contrast clear:

*Este hombre **está** borracho* • *This man is drunken.*
*Este hombre **es** un borracho* • *This man is a drunkard.*
*El queso **es** bueno para la salud* • *Cheese is good for one's health.*
*Este queso **está** bueno* • *This cheese is (tastes) good.*

Ser followed by an adjective describes a quality which is inherent to the subject, whereas **estar** + adjective describes a transient quality which is the result of a change or process:

*Los libros **son** útiles* • *Books are useful.*
*El agua del mar **es** azul* • *Sea water is blue.*
*El ser humano no **es** perfecto* • *Human beings are not perfect.*

*La fruta **está** madura* • *The fruit is ripe.*
*El queso **está** duro* • *The cheese is hard.*
*El niño **está** despistado* • *The boy is confused.*

4.4.1. *Agreement*

When functioning as predicates or passive auxiliaries, both **ser** and **estar** require agreement between the subject and other elements:

*Mi amiga es director**a** de un colegio.*
  • *My friend is a headteacher.*
*Mis amig**as** son guapas.*
  • *My girlfriends are pretty.*

Luisa fue recibida por el ministro.
• Luisa was received by the minister.
Las entradas están ya compradas.
• The tickets have already been bought.
El pescado está fresco.
• The fish is fresh.

Many adjectives change their meaning according to whether they are used with **ser** or **estar**, e.g.:

Estar atento • to pay attention
Ser atento • to be attentive
Estar blanco • to be white (after washing)
Ser blanco • to be white (naturally)
Estar bueno • to taste good
Ser bueno • to be good for one/to be a good person
Estar ciego • to be temporarily blinded by something
Ser ciego • to be a blind person
Estar limpio • to be clean (after washing)
Ser limpio • to be clean (naturally)
Estar triste • to feel sad
Ser triste • to be a miserable person
Estar malo • to be/feel ill
Ser malo • to be a bad person/thing
Estar nuevo • to be like new
Ser nuevo • to be brand new
Estar negro • to be furious
Ser negro • to be black
Estar vivo • to be alive
Ser vivo • to be a lively person
Estar listo • to be ready
Ser listo • to be a clever person
Estar fresco • to be fresh
Ser (un) fresco • to be cheeky

8 | ADVERBS

1. General features

Adverbs are elements which perform the function of modifying other words: either adjectives, verbs, or other adverbs:

*Ha sido un día **muy** agradable.*
* It has been a very pleasant day.

Here the adverb *muy* modifies the adjective *agradable*. (Adverbs which modify adjectives are always *adverbs of quantity* [*muy, bastante, demasiado,* etc.].)

***Siempre** piensa en todo.*
* She always thinks of everything.

In this example, *siempre* modifies the verb *pensar*.

*En invierno **casi siempre** nieva.*
* In winter it almost always snows.

Here the adverb *casi* modifies another adverb, *siempre*. Adverbs which modify other adverbs also tend to be adverbs of quantity.

— Adverbs often form the nucleus of Adverbial Phrases:

*La casa queda **muy cerca**.*
* The house is very near.
*La excursión no estuvo **nada mal**.*
* The trip was not at all bad.
*Carlos llegó **excesivamente temprano**.*
* Carlos arrived excessively early.
*El director habló **muy seriamente**.*
* The head spoke very seriously.

— Adverbs are invariable, and distinct from adjectives and nouns in that they do not mark either number or gender:

*Llegó **medio** muerta* • She arrived half dead.
*Lo hicieron todos **salvo** ella* • They all did it except her.
***Incluso** nosotros lo afirmamos* • Even we say that.

— Some adverbs, like adjectives, can take comparative or superlative forms:

*El avión llegó **más tarde** de lo previsto.*
* The aeroplane arrived later than expected.
*Vuelve **lo más pronto** que puedas.*
* Come back at the earliest you can.

*Las gestiones van **lentísimamente.***
* Matters are going very slowly.

The following adverbs cannot be used in the comparative or superlative:

hoy • today
ayer • yesterday
siempre • always
aquí • here
apenas • hardly
quizá(s)/acaso • perhaps

ahora • now
entonces • then
ya • already
ahí, allí • there
nada • nothing

Many adverbs can take diminutive forms and their meaning (in Spain mainly) becomes slightly emphatic:

cerca • near
despacio • slowly
junto • close
temprano • early

cerquita • very near
despacito • nice and slowly
juntito • right next to
tempranito • nice and early

This phenomenon is particularly common in Latin American Spanish, though the meaning is not altered in such a way. (In Mexico, for instance, they say *hasta lueguito*, instead of *hasta luego* • So long/I'll see you later).

— Many adjectives, used in the masculine singular, function as adverbs:

*Habla **alto*** • Speak up.
*Canta **bajo*** • Sing quietly.
*Lo dijo **muy claro*** • He said it very clearly.

— The adverbs **tanto** and **cuanto** become shortened when used before an adjective, another adverb or adverbial phrase:

*Lo hace **tan** suavemente* • He/she does it so gently.
*¡**Cuán** aprisa escribe!* • He/she writes so quickly!

However, before **peor**, **mejor** and **mayor** they appear normally:

***Tanto peor** para ti* • So much the worse for you.
***Cuanto mejor** sea, más te beneficiará.*
* The better it is, the more you will benefit from it.

— New adverbs can be formed by adding **-mente** to the feminine singular form of an adjective:

Rápida -mente • Quickly.
Correcta -mente • Rightly.

When a number of adverbs ending in **-mente** appear together, all except the last one drop this ending:

*Obró **sabia, noble** y **discretamente.***
* She acted wisely, nobly and discreetly.

Some words function as other parts of speech as well as adverbs:

	Determiner	Pronoun	Adverb
mucho	*Tardó mucho tiempo.* • *He took a long time.*	*Leyó mucho.* • *He read a lot.*	*Leyó mucho.* • *He read a lot.*
poco	*Tardó poco tiempo.* • *He took a short time.*	*Leyó poco.* • *He read little.*	*Leyó poco.* • *He read little.*
bastante	*Tardó bastante tiempo.* • *He took a fair time.*	*Ya digo bastante.* • *I have already said enough.*	*Está bastante enfermo.* • *He is rather ill.*
nada		*No digo nada.* • *I'm not saying anything.*	*No es nada fácil.* • *It is not at all easy.* *No le interesa nada.* • *He is not at all interested.*
tanto	*Tanto tiempo.* • *So much time.*	*Bebió tanto.* • *He drank so much.*	*Es tanto peor.* • *It is so much worse.*
cuanto	*Cuánto tiempo.* • *How much time/* *Such a long time.*	*Bebió cuanto quiso.* • *He drank as much as he wanted.*	*¡Cuán aprisa escribe!* • *She writes so quickly.*

Adverbs are the only words capable of modifying the lexical meaning of verbs. In this sense, they have a parallel function to adjectives, which modify the lexical meaning of nouns:

Carlos llegó **bien** • *Carlos arrived safely.*
Carlos parece **contento** • *Carlos seems happy.*

In the first example, the adverb **bien** modifies the meaning of the verb *llegar*. In the second, the adjective **contento** modifies the noun (*Carlos*), and therefore must agree with it. Adverbs refer to the action, not to the noun, and therefore do not require agreements.

2. Types of adverbs

2.1. Adverbs of manner

These express the way in which the action of the verb is carried out. They include:

bien • *well*   *como* • *how*   *apenas* • *hardly*
aprisa • *quickly*   *adrede/aposta* • *on purpose*   *despacio* • *slowly*
cómo/cuán • *how*   *hasta* • *until*   *así* • *like that.*

However, most adverbs of manner are derived from adjectives by using the suffix **-mente** (*suavemente, correctamente,* etc.). Sometimes adverbs may also be formed in this way from the superlative form of the adjective:

Facilísimo • *Very easy.*   *Facilísimamente* • *Very easily.*

Only qualifying adjectives can be made into adverbs. The only adverbs derived from determining adjectives are:

Mismamente • *Precisely.*
Primeramente • *Firstly.*
Últimamente • *Lastly.*

124

Adverbs ending in **-mente** cannot be derived from adjectives which describe physical characteristics or qualities (such as *rojo, español,* etc.).

The adverbs *bien (well), mal (badly)* and *recién (newly/recently)* exist in addition to the adjectivally derived forms *buenamente, malamente* and *recientemente.*

The form *inclusive* is preferred to *inclusivamente,* but *exclusivamente* is perfectly acceptable:

*Lo hicieron todos, ellas **inclusive.***
● *They all did it, including the women.*
*La responsabilidad es **exclusivamente** suya.*
● *The responsibility is his alone.*

As stated above, the masculine singular form of the adjective is often used in preference to the adverbial form:

*Pisa **fuerte*** ● *Tread heavily.*
*Habla **claro*** ● *Speak clearly.*

Así can be used in a variety of ways:

*Una cosa **así** no se hace todos los días.*
● *You don't do a thing like that every day.*
*Era **así** de alta la torre.*
● *The tower was as high as this.*
*Las cosas le van **así así.***
● *Things are going fairly middling for her.*

2.1.1. *Adverbial phrases of manner*

Spanish has many ways of forming adverbial phrases which can be used as an alternative to adverbs themselves:

— **A la** + feminine singular adjective:

A la inglesa ● *In the English way.*
A la española ● *Spanish style.*

— **A lo** + masculine singular adjective:

A lo grande ● *In grand style.*
A lo loco ● *In a crazy/haphazard way.*

— **A** + feminine plural adjective:

A escondidas ● *Secretly, behind someone's back.*
A medias ● *By halves.*
A ciegas ● *In the dark.*

— A + noun:

A hurtadillas ● *Stealthily.*
A caballo ● *By horse.*
A pie ● *On foot.*
A mano ● *By hand.*
A cuadros ● *Checkered.*
A rayas ● *Striped.*

— **De** + noun:

De pie • Standing.
De hecho • In fact.
De prisa • In a hurry.
De memoria • By heart.

De paso • By the way.
De rodillas • On one's knees.
De veras • Honestly.
De buena gana • Willingly, gladly.

— **Con** + noun:

Con gusto • With pleasure.
Con razón • Rightly.

— **En** + noun:

En un santiamén • In a trice.
En cuclillas • Squatting.

— The gerund can also function as an adverb of manner:

*Habla **gritando*** • He/she speaks in a loud voice.
*Contestó **sonriendo*** • He/she replied with a smile.
*Pasó **corriendo*** • He/she/it went past at a run.

2.2. Adverbs of place

These express the place where the verb action is carried out.

aquí/acá • here.	*ahí/allí/allá* • there.	*cerca* • near.
lejos • far away.	*enfrente* • opposite.	*junto* • next to.
atrás/detrás • behind.	*dentro/adentro* • inside.	*fuera* • outside.
adelante • forward.	*delante* • in front.	*arriba* • above.
abajo/debajo • below.	*alrededor* • around.	*donde/adonde* • where.

Adverbs of place have, in many cases, the same form as prepositions.

*Él va **delante*** • He's going in front - Adverb.
*Él va **delante de mí*** • He's going in front of me - Prepositional phrase.

The choice between the forms **aquí, ahí** and **allí** depends on the distance being expressed in relation to the speaker; **allí** expresses a greater distance than **ahí**. The system parallels that which exists for demonstratives:

yo • I
mío • mine
éste • this
aquí • here

tú • you
tuyo • yours
ése • that
ahí • there

él/ella • he/she
suyo/a • his/hers
aquél/aquélla • that
allí • there

Acá and **allá** have a less precise meaning than **aquí** and **allí**. They are used particularly with verbs of movement, and can be combined with **más**:

*Vete **más allá*** • Go further over there.
*Ven **más acá*** • Come nearer here.

They are the preferred forms in Latin America.

Allá can be combined with a personal pronoun to express absence of interest:

Allá tú si no trabajas • *So much for you if you don't work.*

Some adverbs of place may also refer to distance in time:

Vivió allá por los años 1200.
• *He lived back in the 1200s.*
De aquí en adelante • *From now on.*
Ya lo trataremos más adelante • *We'll deal with that later on.*
*Te lo dije meses **atrás*** • *I told you months ago.*

Adonde can only be used with verbs of motion:

*Es el cine **adonde** vamos* • *There is the cinema we are going to.*

but

*Lo encontré **donde** nos habíamos citado.*
• *I met him where we had arranged.*

A donde is written separately with a non-specific antecedent:

*Se acercaron **a donde** yo estaba y me escondí.*
• *They drew near to where I was and I hid.*

Adverbial phrases of place:

calle arriba • *up the street.*	*calle abajo* • *down the street.*
río arriba • *upstream.*	*río abajo* • *downstream.*
aquí y allí • *here and there.*	*aquí abajo* • *down here.*
acá y allá • *here and there.*	*allá arriba* • *up there.*
a/de/por todas partes • *everywhere.*	*a/en ninguna parte* • *nowhere.*

2.3. Adverbs of time

These show when the action of the verb takes place, and include:

ahora • *now.*	*antes* • *before.*	*después* • *afterwards.*
hoy • *today.*	*ayer* • *yesterday.*	*anteayer* • *the day before yesterday.*
anoche • *last night.*	*mañana* • *tomorrow.*	*luego/entonces* • *then.*
tarde • *late.*	*temprano* • *early.*	*presto* • *at once.*
pronto • *soon.*	*siempre* • *always.*	*nunca/jamás* • *never.*
mientras • *meanwhile.*	*ya* • *already.*	*todavía/aún* • *still.*
recién/recientemente • *recently.*		*cuándo/cuando* • *when.*

Nunca and **jamás** require a negative construction if they follow the verb. Before the verb they can stand alone:

*No fui **nunca** a esa ciudad.* ⎫
Nunca fui a esa ciudad. ⎭ • *I never went to that city.*
*No descubrí **jamás** el secreto.* ⎫
Jamás descubrí el secreto. ⎭ • *I never discovered the secret.*

For extra emphasis, both words can be used together, in which case **nunca** always precedes **jamás**:

Nunca jamás *lo había visto por esas tierras.*
* *I had never ever seen him in those parts.*

Ya, which generally translates as *already,* implies that the action of the verb is finished and therefore belongs to the past:

El tren **ya** *ha llegado* • *The train has already arrived.*

However, it can also be used to reinforce an action expressed in the present or future tense, in which case its meaning is somewhat different:

Ya *te lo digo ahora* • *I'll tell you right now.*
Ya *te lo diré a su debido tiempo* • *I'll tell you all in good time.*

Aún and **todavía** are interchangeable and may be used before or after the verb. They translate as both *still* and *yet* in English:

Aún/todavía *está trabajando* • *He/she is still working.*
¿Está **todavía/aún** *en casa?* • *Is he/she still at home?*
No he acabado **todavía/aún** • *I haven't finished yet.*
El tren no ha llegado **aún** ⎫
Todavía *no ha llegado el tren* ⎬ • *The train has not arrived yet.*

Aun (without an accent) means *even*:

Aun *si habla en voz alta, no se le oye.*
* *You can't hear him/her even when he/she speaks up.*

Recién, a shortened form of *recientemente*, is used before a participle:

Están **recién** *casados* • *They are newly-married.*
Es un **recién** *nacido* • *He is newly-born.*

In other positions, where its meaning is *recently,* **recientemente** is preferred, especially in Castilian Spanish.

Luego can mean *then, later, afterwards*, but refers to a more immediate future than **después**:

Primero *haremos la maleta,* **luego** *comeremos y* **después** *saldremos.*
* *First we will pack the bag, then we'll eat and afterwards we'll go out.*
Ven **luego** • *Come a bit later on.*

2.3.1. *Adverbial phrases of time*

en breve • *shortly*
en el futuro • *in future*
al principio • *at first*
antiguamente • *formerly*
hoy en día • *nowadays*
entretanto • *meanwhile*
de vez en cuando • *from time to time*
en ningún momento • *at no time*

de ahora en adelante • *from now on*
dentro de poco • *soon*
la semana pasada • *last week*
el año que viene • *next year*
a partir de ahora • *starting from now*
a veces • *sometimes*
a menudo • *often*

2.4. Adverbs of quantity

mucho • a lot	*muy* • very	*poco* • little
algo • somewhat	*nada* • not at all	*demasiado* • too much
medio • half	*bastante* • rather	*más* • more
menos • less	*casi* • almost	*sólo* • only
además • besides, also	*excepto/salvo* • except	*cuán/cuánto* • how
tanto • so much	*tan* • so	
cuan/cuanto • as much	*apenas* • hardly	

These intensify or moderate the meaning of the verb or other element:

*Lo **veo mucho** este año* • I'm seeing a lot of him this year.
*Camina **demasiado lentamente*** • He's walking too slowly.
*Los paquetes son **demasiado pesados*** • The parcels are too heavy.
*Javier es **muy hombre*** • Javier is a real man.

Muy is used with adjectives, **mucho** with verbs:

*Está **muy** contento* • He is very happy.
*Llueve **mucho*** • It's raining a lot.

Tan and **tanto** have a similar relationship: **tan** is used with adjectives, adverbs and participles, and **tanto** is used with verbs:

*¡Es **tan** bueno!* • It's so good!
*Es **tan** temido como amado* • He is feared as much as he is loved.
*¡No empujes **tanto**!* • Don't push so!

Cuan and **cuanto** function in a similar way.

Más and **menos** can come before or after the noun, with or without a preposition:

*No comas **más** pastel* • Don't eat any more cake.
*No come ni un caramelo **más*** • He/she doesn't eat even one sweet more.
*Serían **menos de** las ocho* • It must be before 8 o'clock.
*Tendrá **más de** veinte años* • He must be over twenty.

(For further discussion of *más* and *menos* see Comparison of Adjectives, p. 57-59).

The idea of *approximately* can be expressed in a variety of ways:

*Leí diez páginas, **más o menos.***
• I read 10 pages, more or less.
*Eran **cosa de** cinco o seis* • There were about 5 or 6 of them.
*Asistieron **alrededor de/cerca de/unas** cien personas.*
• About 100 people attended.
*Conté **aproximadamente** cuarenta* • I counted about 40.

Sometimes certain adjectives may function as adverbs of quantity:

*Durmió tres horas **escasas*** • He slept barely 3 hours.
*Habló **largo y tendido*** • She talked long and hard.

al menos • *at least*
poco más o menos • *more or less*
al por menor • *at retail, in detail*
al tanto por ciento • *at so much per cent*
poco a poco • *little by little*
a lo sumo • *at most*
cuanto más • *as much as possible*
no más (de) • *no more (than)*
a lo menos • *at least*
por lo menos • *at least*
nada más • *nothing more/else*
por poco • *almost*
al por mayor • *wholesale*
al ciento por ciento • *one hundred per cent*

2.5. Adverbs of negation

No can be used on its own or in combination with other adverbs to produce a variety of meanings:

No • *no*   *ni* • *neither/nor*
jamás • *never*   *no... ya* • *not... yet*
no... más que • *no... more than*   *no... casi* • *hardly*
no... tampoco • *not... either*
no... nunca • *not... ever*
no... nadie • *not... anybody*
no... nada • *not... anything*
no... ninguno • *not... anybody*

In Spanish, two negatives *do not* make a positive:

No lo han llamado **nunca** • *They have never called him.*
(**Nunca** lo han llamado)
No he visto **nada** • *I haven't seen anything.*
(**Nada** he visto)
No me habrían informado **tampoco** • *They wouldn't have told me either.*
(**Tampoco** me habrían informado)

Ya or **casi** at the beginning of a sentence give emphasis to the negation:

Ya no salgo con él • *I don't go out with him any more.*
Ya no trabaja aquí • *He/she doesn't work here any longer.*
Casi no lo veo • *I hardly see him at all.*

If a sentence has two verbs but a single subject, the negation is reinforced with another negative adverb before the second verb.

No come **ni** deja comer • *He/she neither eats him/herself nor lets other people eat.*

No trabaja y *tampoco* deja trabajar.
* He/she doesn't work and he/she doesn't let others work either.

A restrictive negation (*only*) can be expressed by using:

— **Sólo:**

Sólo ha llamado una vez • He/she has only called once.
Sólo bebe agua • He/she only drinks water.

— **No... más que** (signifying an exact amount):

No me quedan *más que* cien pesetas • I only have 100 ptas. left.
No ha llamado *más que* una vez • He has only called once.

— **No... más de** (signifying an upper limit):

No me has escrito *más de* tres veces.
* He has not written to me more than three times.

— **No... hasta:**

No llamará *hasta* el lunes • He will not call until Monday.

2.5.1. Adverbial phrases of negation

de ninguna manera • in no way	
de ningún modo • in no way	
ni hablar • not in your life	
ni con mucho • no way	
que no • no!	
claro que no • of course not	
nada de eso • none of that	
ni por asomo • by no means	
eso sí que no • not that	
en mi vida • not ever	
¡qué va! • no way!	
en absoluto • absolutely not	
casi nada • almost nothing	

2.6. Affirmative adverbs

These are used to confirm or emphasize a positive statement:

sí • yes	
también • also	
desde luego • indeed	
ciertamente • certainly	
seguramente • surely	
verdaderamente • really	
por cierto • certainly	
sin duda • doubtless	
¡cómo no! • of course!	
a buen seguro • very probably	

Seguramente/ciertamente llegará hoy • *He will certainly come today.*
Claro que llegará • *Of course he will come.*

Sí may be used with or without **que**, for extra emphasis:

Sí, llegará hoy • *He/she will come today.*
Sí que llegará hoy • *He/she will come today.*

También is used in affirmative statements, **tampoco** in negative ones:

María canta bien y Carlos también.
• *María sings well and so does Carlos.*
María no canta bien y Carlos tampoco.
• *María does not sing well and neither does Carlos.*

2.7. Adverbs of doubt

These are:

> *quizá/quizás/tal vez/a lo mejor/acaso* • *perhaps, maybe.*
> *probablemente* • *probably.*   *posiblemente* • *possibly.*
> *sin duda* • *doubtless.*

2.8. Conjunctive adverbs

Some adverbs have meanings implying causality or a sequence of events and can therefore be used to link two sentences together:

> *entonces* • *then*   *así* • *so*   *además* • *moreover*
> *también* • *also*   *tampoco* • *neither*
> *en efecto* • *in fact*   *en conclusión* • *finally*
> *no obstante* • *nevertheless*
> *sin embargo* • *however*

*Había corrido mucho, **así** que estaba cansada.*
• *She had run a long way, so she was tired.*
*El detenido no habló. **Tampoco** comió en todo el día.*
• *The detainee did not speak. Neither did he eat all day.*

2.9. Adverbs expressing modality

These introduce an opinion or judgment on the part of the speaker and are therefore closely associated with the use of mood.

Quiza venga • *He might come.*
Posiblemente no esté enfermo • *He might not be ill.*
Tal vez esté enfermo • *Perhaps he is ill.*

3. Comparison of adverbs

Adverbs can be used comparatively in a similar way to adjectives:

— To express *superiority:*

*Come **más** aprisa* • *Eat more quickly.*
*Vive **más** cerca de aquí* • *He lives nearer here.*

— To express *equality:*

*Avanza **tan** lentamente que no llegará nunca.*
• *He is progressing so slowly that he will never arrive.*

— To express *inferiority:*

*Vive **menos** intensamente su vida.*
• *She lives her life less intensively.*

4. The superlative degree of adverbs

— Absolute superiority:

*Vive **lejísimos*** • *He/she lives very far away.*
*Está **muy lejos** de aquí* • *He/she/it is very far from here.*

— Relative superiority:

*María es la que vive **más lejos** de aquí.*
• *María is the one who lives farther away from here.*

1. General features

Prepositions are grammaticalized words whose function is to express the relation between the other words in a sentence:

*Llegó su novia **a** recogerla **en** moto **delante de** su casa.*
• *Her boyfriend arrived to pick her up by motorbike in front of her house.*

Prepositions are invariable, and can form part of a verb phrase or a noun phrase:

*Vive **en** la ciudad* • *She lives in the city.*
• *No es un buen día **para** negocios* • *It is not a good day for business.*

Prepositional phrases can provide a complement to an adjective or an adverb:

*Un árbol cargado **de** fruta* • *A tree loaded with fruit.*
*Vive **lejos de** la ciudad* • *She lives a long way from the town.*

Some prepositions depend directly on verbs rather than functioning independently:

*Obedecer **a** alguien* • *to obey somebody.*
*Confiar **en** una persona* • *to trust someone.*
*Morirse **de** algo* • *to die of something.*

2. Types of prepositions

It is generally recognized that there are two types of prepositions in Spanish: *simple* prepositions derived from Latin, and *prepositional phrases* that have come into the language more recently:

2.1. Simple prepositions

(Translations are only approximate, since meaning depends on the context in which they occur. A summary of their main uses appears below.)

a • *to*	*ante* • *before*	*bajo* • *beneath*
con • *with*	*contra* • *against*	*de* • *of*
desde • *since*	*en* • *in/on*	*entre* • *between*
hacia • *towards*	*hasta* • *until*	*para* • *for*
por • *for*	*según* • *according to*	*sin* • *without*
sobre • *on*	*tras* • *after, behind*	

There are also, traditionally, two others, now obsolete: *cabe* *near*, and *so, under.*

2.2. Prepositional phrases

mediante • by means of	*durante* • during
excepto/salvo • except	*acerca de* • about
además de • as well as	*alrededor de* • about, around
a pesar de • in spite of	*antes de* • before
cerca de • near	*debajo de* • under
delante de • in front of	*dentro de* • inside, within
después de • after	*detrás de* • behind
encima de • on top of, above	*en cuanto a* • as regards
enfrente de • opposite	*frente a* • opposite, as opposed to
fuera de • outside	*junto a* • near
lejos de • far from	*con respecto a* • as regards

The use of these is fairly straightforward for English speakers.

The choice of preposition is dependent on the semantic possibilities of the other words in the sentence. For instance, we can say:

*El reloj es **de** oro* • *The watch is made of gold.*

or

*El reloj es **para** decir la hora* • *The clock is to tell the time.*

but not

*El reloj es **para** oro.*

2.3. Prepositions indicating movement

— **a, hasta, contra, hacia** and **para** can all express *movement towards* something:

*Iré **a** tu casa* • *I will go to your house.*
*Iré **hasta** tu casa* • *I will go to your house.*
*El enemigo viene **contra** nosotros.*
• *The enemy is coming towards (lit. «against») us.*
*Va **hacia** su casa* • *He's going to his house.*
*Va **para** su casa* • *He's going to his house.*

Used with other verbs they can have different meanings, in particular they can refer to time:

*Estará en casa **a** las diez* • *He/she will be home at 10.*
*Estará **hasta** las diez* • *He/she will be here until 10.*
*Estará **hacia** las diez* • *He/she will be here around 10.*
*Estará en casa **para** las diez* • *He/she will be home by 10.*

— **de** and **desde** both express *movement away* from something. Only de expresses origin:

*No sale **de** casa* • *He does not go out of the house.*
*Es **de** Salamanca* • *He is from Salamanca.*

Whereas **desde** emphasizes distance:

Desde *aquí no veremos nada* • *We won't see anything from here.*
Viene **desde** *París* • *He's coming (all the way) from Paris.*
Viene **de** *París* • *He's coming/he comes from Paris.*

Desde can also be used with expressions of time, when it means *since*:

No lo he visto **desde** *enero* • *I haven't seen him since January.*

— **Por** expresses the idea of movement *within* a certain context:

Vino **por** *París* • *He/she came through/via Paris.*
Viajaron **por** *autopista* • *They travelled on the motorway.*
Estará aquí **por** *la mañana* • *She will be here in the morning.*
Vendrá **por** *la tarde* • *She will come in the afternoon.*

2.4. A

The main uses of **a** are as follows:

— Before an indirect object:

Dio limosna **a** *los pobres.*
• *He/she gave alms to the poor.*
Entregó el premio **a** *los ganadores.*
• *He/she presented the prize to the winners.*

— Before a human direct object (*personal* **a**):

Busco **a** *mi secretaria* • *I'm looking for my secretary.*
Vi **a** *María anoche* • *I saw María last night.*

a is also used to personalize non-human direct objects:

Encontró **a** *su perro* • *She found her dog.*

It may be omitted in cases where two **a**'s in the same sentence might cause confusion:

Prefiero **el** *hermano mayor al menor.*
• *I prefer the older brother to the younger one.*
Recomendó **su** *sobrino al director.*
• *She recommended her nephew to the director.*

— To express a price or rate:

Las manzanas están **a** *doscientas el kilo.*
• *Apples are at 200 a kilo.*
Conducía **a** *cien kilómetros por hora.*
• *She was driving at 100 kilometres per hour.*

— With infinitive, to form commands:

*¡***A** *trabajar!* • *To work!*
*¡***A** *dormir!* • *Off to sleep!*

or where the infinitive stands alone in a phrase:

A decir verdad, me gustó la película. • *To tell the truth, I liked the film.*
A no ser por ti, me engañan. • *If it hadn't been for you, they would have tricked me.*

Words requiring **a**:

*Dedicarse **a*** • *To spend one's time doing something.*
*Tener derecho **a*** • *To be entitled to something.*
*Oler **a*** • *To smell of something.*
*Saber **a*** • *To taste of something.*
*Igual **a*** • *Equal to.*
*Parecido **a*** • *Similar to.*
*Jugar **a*** • *To play (a game).*
*Ayudar **a*** • *To help to.*
*Acostumbrarse **a*** • *To get used to something.*

2.5. Con

Con presents few problems, since it combines with nouns in the same way as *with*:

*Le contestó **con** una sonrisa* • *He/she replied with a smile.*
*Escribe **con** un lápiz negro* • *He/she is writing with a black pencil.*

However, it may also be used with verbs:

***Con** decirle unas palabras dulces, se le pasará el enfado.*
• *If you say a few gentle words to him, he'll stop being angry.*
***Con** que no te molestes, ya me basta.*
• *As long as you're not upset, that's enough for me.*

Words which require **con**:

*Meterse **con*** • *To pick a quarrel with.*
*Soñar **con*** • *To dream of.*
*Relacionarse **con*** • *To have contact with.*
*Competir **con*** • *To compete with.*

2.6. De

As noted above, **de** is used to express origin:

*Viene **de** León* • *He comes from León.*
*Ha ido **de** Tokio a Londres* • *She has gone from Tokyo to London.*
*La tradición arranca **de** la Edad Media.*
• *The tradition originates from the Middle Ages.*

Other uses of **de** are as follows:

— to describe possession, reference or something pertaining to something:

*La cartera **de** Paquita* • *Paquita's briefcase.*
*La cola **del** caballo* • *The horse's tail.*
*Las plantas **del** patio* • *The plants in/on the patio.*

— to demarcate a period of time, in combination with **a**:

*Trabaja **de** nueve **a** cinco* • *He works from 9 to 5.*
*Abierto **de** abril **a** septiembre* • *Open from April to September.*

— to describe what something is made of, or consists of:

*La mesa es **de** madera* • *The table is made of wood.*
*Tortilla **de** patatas* • *Potato omelette.*
*Un libro **de** poesía* • *A poetry book.*
*Clases **de** español* • *Spanish lessons.*

— to form an adverbial phrase of manner:

*Pintó la casa **de blanco*** • *She painted the house white.*
*Se disfrazó **de payaso*** • *He dressed up as a clown.*
*Fue **de embajador** a Tokio* • *He went to Tokyo as ambassador.*

— to express the *cause* of something:

*Esta rojo **de** vergüenza* • *He is red with embarrassment.*
*Se volvió loco **de** tanto leer* • *He went mad with so much reading.*
*Se murió **de** frío* • *He died of cold.*

— to denote *age, colour* or some other quality pertaining to something:

*Una casa **de** color marrón* • *A brown-coloured house.*
*Una niña **de** seis años* • *A girl of six.*
*Un billete **de** mil pesetas* • *A 1000 pesetas note.*
*Una máquina **de** afeitar* • *An electric razor.*

— With the infinitive, to express *condition:*

***De** no ser por ti, no lo habría hecho.*
• *If it hadn't been for you, I would not have done it.*
***De** haberlo sabido antes, estaríamos atentos.*
• *If we had known beforehand, we would have paid attention.*

— Words which require **de** to introduce a complement:

*Entender **de*** • *To understand about something.*
*Alegrarse **de*** • *To be pleased about something.*
*Ser imposible **de*** • *To be impossible to.*
*Tener un deber **de*** • *To have a duty to.*

Note also:

***De** día* • *During the daytime.*
***De** noche* • *At night.*

2.7. En

En often translates as *in* and can express:

— Time:

***En** primavera* • *In the spring.*
***En** 1992* • *In 1992.*
*Lo hizo **en** cinco minutos* • *He did it in five minutes.*

— Manner:

> *En voz baja* • *In a low voice.*
> *En zapatillas* • *In slippers.*
> *En avión* • *By plane.*

— Place:

> *Vive todo el año **en** Murcia.*
> • *He lives in Murcia all year round.*
> *La falda está expuesta **en** el escaparate.*
> • *The skirt is on display in the window.*
> *Entró **en** la habitación* • *She entered the room.*

When referring to place it may also have the sense of *on*:

*El libro está **en** la mesa* • *The book is on the table.*

Or translate as *into* or *onto*, depending on the meaning of the verb accompanying it:

> *Metió el libro **en** la caja* • *She put the book in(to) the box.*
> *Puso el libro **en** la mesa* • *She put the book on(to) the table.*

— Amount, price or a calculation:

> *Vendió la casa **en** veinte millones.*
> • *She sold the house for 20 million.*
> *Las acciones subieron **en** un cinco por ciento.*
> • *The shares went up five per cent.*

— For qualifications:

> *Licenciado **en** Pedagogía* • *A graduate in education.*
> *Perito **en** industrias químicas* • *A technician in industrial chemistry.*

Words which require ***en***:

*Pensar **en*** • *To think of, about.*
*Pobre **en*** • *Poor in.*
*Abundante **en*** • *Rich in.*
*Dudar **en*** • *To hesitate to.*
*Interesarse **en*** • *To be interested in.*
*Quedar **en*** • *To agree to.*
*El primero/último **en*** • *The first/last to.*

2.8. Entre

Entre can mean *between* or *among/st*:

*Está **entre** la multitud* • *He is amongst the crowd.*
*Está **entre** Madrid y Barcelona.* • *She is between Madrid and Barcelona.*

2.9. Para *and* por

These often translate as *for* and their use is often confusing for English speakers.

Para is used as follows:

— to express movement towards:

*Salió **para** la oficina* • *He left for the office.*
*Ven **para** acá* • *Come over here.*

— to express future time:

*Te esperamos **para** Navidad* • *We will expect you at Christmas.*
*Quedamos **para** el miércoles* • *We'll meet on Wednesday.*

— to express a limitation:

*Es muy espabilado **para** su edad* • *He's very lively for his age.*
***Para** sus posibilidades, es más que suficiente.*
• *It's more than enough, for all he can do with it.*
*Dispone de poco tiempo **para** estar contigo dos horas.*
• *He has too little time to spend two hours with you.*

— to express utility or disadvantage:

*Bueno **para** la salud* • *Good for one's health.*
*Es nocivo **para** la vista* • *It's harmful to one's sight.*

— to express purpose:

*Vino **para** arreglar la lavadora.*
• *She came to mend the washing machine.*
*Fue enviado por el Presidente **para** negociar la paz.*
• *He was sent by the President to negotiate a peace settlement.*

— to indicate an action about to begin:

*Está **para** salir* • *She is about to go out.*
*Estaba **para** llover, pero luego salió el sol.*
• *It looked like rain, but then the sun came out.*

— to introduce an indirect object:

*Envió flores **para** María* • *He sent flowers for María.*
*Me dio esto **para** ti* • *She gave me this for you.*

— Words which require *para:*

*Apto **para*** • *Good at/fit for.*
*Embarcarse **para*** • *To embark for.*

Por is used to express:

— Cause (meaning *on account of*):

*Fue criticado **por** su actuación.*
• *He was criticized for his performance.*
*Lo castigaron **por** culpa tuya* • *He was punished on your account.*
*Se echó a llorar **por** encontrarse sola.*
• *She burst out crying on finding she was on her own.*

— Time:

*Nunca salimos **por** la noche* • *We never go out in the evenings.*
*Se ausentó **por** dos días* • *She was away for 2 days.*

— Place (in a fairly imprecise sense):

*Pasea **por** el jardín* • *She is walking in the garden.*
*No lo hemos visto **por** aquí* • *We haven't seen him around here.*

— Price, equivalency, or substitution:

*Vendió el coche **por** dos millones* • *She sold the car for 2 million.*
*Trabaja **por** poco dinero* • *He works for little money.*
*Trabaja **por** dos* • *He does the work of two.*
*Esta empleada vale **por** cinco* • *This employee is worth five.*
*Juan puede firmar **por** su padre.*
• *Juan can sign on behalf of his father.*

— Means:

*Envió su coche a León **por** tren* • *He sent his car to León by train.*
*Ya podemos hacer las compras **por** teléfono.*
• *Now we can do shopping by telephone.*

— Distribution or proportion (*per*):

*Pagaron medio millón de pesetas **por** vecino.*
• *They paid half a million pesetas per occupant.*
*Paga un interés del cinco **por** ciento.*
• *He pays interest at five per cent.*

— In passive constructions (*by*):

*Este puente fue construido **por** nuestra empresa.*
• *This bridge was built by our company.*
*Fue detenido **por** la policía* • *He was arrested by the police.*

— To describe something at the point of happening:

*Estuvo **por** irse* • *He was on the point of leaving.*
*Esto está **por** ver* • *We'll see about that.*

— Words which require **por**:

*Interesarse **por*** • *To take an interest in.*
*Luchar **por*** • *To fight for.*
*Velar **por*** • *To look out for.*

A complete list of verbs and other elements requiring particular prepositions would be too long to reproduce here. Guidance concerning this should be sought in a good dictionary.

10 | CONJUNCTIONS

1. General description

Conjunctions are words which join phrases and other elements together. For instance, the two sentences:

Hizo calor • *It was hot.*
Salimos de paseo • *We went out for a walk.*

can stand independently of each other, or they can be joined together by a conjunction:

*Hizo calor **y** salimos de paseo.*
• *It was hot and we went out for a walk.*
*Hizo calor **pero** salimos de paseo **y** fuimos al parque.*
• *It was hot but we went out for a walk and we went to the park.*

In the first example the ideas contained in the two sentences are simply added together. In the second, two divergent ideas are joined together, and a third added. The choice of conjunction used determines the relationship between the two parts joined; they may be simply linked together, they may be placed in opposition to each other, or they may be presented as alternatives.

The units which are added together must always be syntactically equivalent:

*La clase **grande** y **espaciosa** está vacía.*
• *The big spacious classroom is empty.*
***Este hombre** y **el que vino ayer** son de la misma región.*
• *This man and the one that came yesterday are from the same region.*
*Antonia **canta** y **baila.***
• *Antonia sings and dances.*
*Isabel **lo escucha** pero **no lo ve.***
• *Isabel can hear him but she can't see him.*

2. Simple conjunctions

Simple conjunctions consist of a single word.

— **y** (*and*):

*Va **y** viene* • *He comes and goes.*

— **y** changes to **e** before words which begin with the sound /i/:

*Geografía **e** historia* • *Geography and history.*
*Estado **e** Iglesia* • *State and Church.*

142

— **ni** (*neither/nor*):

Ni hace **ni** deja hacer a nadie.
* He neither does anything nor lets anyone else do anything.

— **que** is sometimes used as a conjunction:

Dale **que** dale.
* Over and over again - no literal translation.

— **o** (*either/or*):

This changes to **u** before words beginning with the sound /o/:

O estudias **o** trabajas.
* Either you study or you work.
O mandas **u** obedeces.
* Either you give orders or you obey (them).

— **pero, sino** (*but*):

Sino is only used when the first element is negative:

No es inteligente, **sino** estudioso.
* He's not intelligent, but studious.
Es inteligente, **pero** estudia poco.
* He is intelligent, but he doesn't study much.

3. Conjunctive adverbs

Conjunctive adverbs may consist of one or more words and link elements in the same ways as simple conjunctions. They are invariable:

igualmente (*in the same way*), **también** (*also, so*), **asimismo** (*likewise*), **luego** (*so*), **en consecuencia/ por (lo) tanto** (*therefore*), etc., all perform the function of linking ideas which are similar.

mas (*but*), **empero** (*however*), **al contrario** (*on the other hand*), **sin embargo** (*however*), **salvo/excepto/menos** (*except*), **no obstante** (*nevertheless*), **aunque** (*although*), etc., act to place the two elements in opposition to each other.

ya, ora, bien, sea, ahora, etc., put two ideas in a position of equivalency or alternation. They are often repeated in front of both halves of the sentence:

Bien puede ser su madre, **bien** puede ser su tía.
* She may be her mother or she may be her aunt.
Ahora dicen esto, **ahora** dicen lo otro.
* Now they say this, now they say that.

WORD FORMATION

1. Spanish words

Most Spanish words are derived from Latin. However, it is interesting to note that the evolution of the language from Latin has been subject to two opposing tendencies, one which has sought to preserve words in a latinate form, and one which has allowed free transformation from vulgar Latin, as part of the natural evolutionary process. This has resulted in Spanish often possessing two terms derived from the same Latin root, one a common word, the other a *high* or educated variant which may or may not have a similar meaning:

acre • acrid   agrio • sour
afiliado • member   ahijado • godchild
directo • direct   derecho • right, law
ínsula • island   isla • isle
mácula/mancha • stain, spot

Spanish also possesses words derived from other languages:

* **Iberian**, a language which disappeared before the Roman conquest.
* **Basque**, which has given the language words such as *izquierdo (left), ascua (hot coal), pizarra (slate),* etc.
* **Greek**, which has provided a constant source of enrichment: *baño (bath), idea (idea), fantasma (ghost), bodega (wine cellar), filosofía (philosophy),* etc.
* **Germanic languages:** *guerra (war), guardar (to keep), robar (to steal), espuela (spur),* etc.
* **Arabic**, which was spoken for centuries in the Iberian peninsula along with Spanish: *alférez (second lieutenant), atalaya (watchtower), algodón (cotton), aldea (hamlet), alcalde (mayor), cifra (figure, number),* etc.
* **French**, which was particulary important during the Middle Ages and in the 17th and 18th centuries: *ligero (light), linaje (lineage), peaje (toll), hostal (hostal), salvaje (wild),* etc.
* **Italian**, whose effect was felt especially during the Renaissance: *escolta (escort, guard), fragata (frigate), balcón (balcony), novela (novel), soneto (sonnet),* etc.
* **English**, which has been very influential in the last few decades: *parking (car park), misil (missile), computadora (computer), pub, club,* etc.

Languages always need to adapt and expand to find words to express new discoveries and ideas. Taking words from other languages is only one way in which Spanish does this, another is by using the creative potential provided within itself to form new words. This does not happen in a haphazard way, but follows set procedures existing in the language for deriving words from other words. These are:

— the use of suffixes
— the use of prefixes
— combining two words together

2. Word formation

2.1. The use of suffixes

Suffixes can be used to turn one type of word into another, or one group of words into another which performs a different function. For instance:

María es bella • *María is beautiful.*

can be reformulated as a noun phrase:

*La bell**eza** de María* • *María's beauty.*

In this way abstract nouns can be generated from adjectives which describe a quality attributed to a noun:

Carlos es bueno • *Carlos is good.*   *La **bondad** de Carlos* • *The goodness of Carlos.*
Pepa es feliz • *Pepa is happy.*   *La **felicidad** de Pepa* • *Pepa's happiness.*
Miguel es valiente • *Miguel is brave.*   *La **valentía** de Miguel* • *Miguel's bravery.*

Nouns which refer to an action or a state can be derived from participles:

Pablo ha llegado • *Pablo has arrived.*   *La llegada de Pablo* • *Pablo's arrival.*
Pablo se ha abatido • *Pablo has got depressed.*
El abatimiento de Pablo • *Pablo's depression.*

And adjectives can be formed from nouns and noun phrases:

Luis es de Madrid • *Luis is from Madrid.*
Luis es madrileño • *Luis is a Madrileño.*
La campaña del presidente • *The president's campaign.*
La campaña presidencial • *The presidential campaign.*

Spanish has a very wide range of suffixes which can be used to turn nouns into adjectives:

-able	-ario	-í	-ita
-aco	-eno	-iaco	-ol
-ado	-ense	-ico	-oso
-al	-ento	-iento	-ota
-án	-eño	-il	-udo
-ano	-és	-ino	-uzco
-ar	-estre	-ío	-uzo

(and the feminine variants of all the above).

The suffixes **-or, -ero, -in, -sta** and **-nte** and their feminine forms can turn a verb into a noun describing the person or thing which performs the action. Thus nouns can be derived from relative clauses:

El que canta • *The one who sings*   *El cant**or*** • *The singer*
El que cocina • *The one who cooks*   *El cocin**ero*** • *The cook*
El que anda • *The one who walks*   *El andar**ín*** • *The walker*
El que invierte • *The one who invests*   *El inversion**ista*** • *The investor*
El que oye • *The one who hears*   *El oy**ente*** • *The hearer*

Some suffixes can be used to reduce a verb phrase to a single verb:

Ponerse verde • *To become green.*   **Verdear.**
Ponerse dulce • *To become sweet.*   **Dulc(ifi)car.**
Poner de lado • *To tilt.*   **Ladear.**

The prefix **en-** can also fulfil this function:

Ennegrecer • *To become black.*
Endulzar • *To sweeten*

2.2. Prefixes

Prefixes are especially useful in providing an alternative to certain phrases with prepositions:

El que está a favor de los americanos: **pro**americano.
  • *A person in favour of the Americans* (pro-American).
El que está en contra de la guerra: **anti**belicista.
  • *A person who is against war.*
Quitar la estabilidad de/a algo: **des**estabilizar.
  • *To take away something's stability:* (to destabilise)
Más desarrollado de lo normal: **super**desarrollado.
  • *More developed than the norm.*

As may be seen from the following table, Spanish possesses a wide range of prefixes, which can be used to form different types of words. Not all prefixes can be used to form verbs:

Prefix	Noun	Adjective	Verb
a-	*anormalidad* • *abnormality*	*aséptico* • *aseptic*	*alinear* • *to align*
ab-	*absolución* • *absolution*	*absorto* • *absorbed*	*abjurar* • *to abjure*
ante-	*anterior* • *previous*	*antedicho* • *aforesaid*	*anteceder* • *to precede*
anti-	*antídoto* • *antidote*	*antibiótico* • *antibiotic*	*anticipar* • *to advance*
archi-	*archiduque* • *archduke*	*archifamoso* • *world famous*	
co-(m/n/r)	*competición* • *competition*	*conciso* • *concise*	*corresponder* • *to correspond*
des-	*desunión* • *disunion*	*deshonesto* • *dishonest*	*desatar* • *to untie*
dis-	*distensión* • *distension*	*dispar* • *different*	*dislocar* • *to dislocate*
em-	*empalme* • *joint*	*embutido* • *stuffed*	*empanar* • *to bread*
en-	*enmienda* • *correction*	*endiablado* • *fiendish*	*envejecer* • *to age*
entre-	*entresuelo* • *mezzanine*	*entrecano* • *greyish*	*entrever* • *to glimpse*
ex-	*exalumno* • *ex-pupil*	*externo* • *external*	*expulsar* • *to expel*
hipo-	*hipótesis* • *hypothesis*	*hipoalérgico* • *hypoallergic*	*hipotecar* • *to mortgage*
hiper-	*hipertrofia* • *hypertrophy*	*hiperfocal* • *hyperfocal*	*hipertrofiar* • *to hypertrophy*
i-	*irradiación* • *irradiation*	*irreal* • *unreal*	*identificar* • *to identify*
im-	*impuesto* • *tax*	*imberbe* • *beardless*	*impedir* • *to prevent·*
in-	*inconveniente* • *objection*	*incorrecto* • *incorrect*	*inducir* • *to lead into*
inter-	*interdicción* • *interdiction*	*interino* • *interim*	*intervenir* • *to intervene*
infra-	*infractor* • *infractor*	*infrahumano* • *sub-human*	*infradotar* • *to under provide*
omni-	*ómnibus* • *omnibus*	*omnívoro* • *omnivorous*	—
pan-	*panacea* • *panacea*	*panafricano* • *pan-African*	—
para-	*parapsicología* • *para-psychology*	*paramilitar* • *paramilitary*	
pre-	*preguerra* • *pre-war*	*prehistórico* • *prehistoric*	*presentir* • *to forebode*
pos(t)-	*posdata* • *postscript*	*postimpresionista* • *post-impressionist*	*posponer* • *to postpone*

Prefix	Noun	Adjective	Verb
re-	*revuelta* • *revolt*	*revoltoso* • *rebellious*	*revivir* • *to revive*
so-	*soporte* • *support*	*sometido* • *submitted*	*socavar* • *to undermine*
sobre-	*sobresalto* • *fright*	*sobresaliente* • *outstanding*	*sobreponer* • *to put on top*
sub-	*submarino* • *submarine*	*subnormal* • *subnormal*	*subestimar* • *to underesti-mate*
trans-	*tránsito* • *transit*	*transitorio* • *transitory*	*transportar* • *to transport*

The following prefixes come from Greek words and have a lexical meaning, as in English:

auto- gastro- geo- helio- hemo- hidro- neo- pseudo- tele-, etc.

2.3. Compounding

New words can be formed by combining:

— A noun and an adjective to form a new noun or adjective:

> *Nochebuena* • *Christmas Eve*
> *pelirrojo* • *red-headed*

— An adjective and a noun to form a noun:

> *mediodía* • *midday*
> *salvoconducto* • *safeconduct*

— Two adjectives to form another adjective or a noun:

> *altibajos* • *ups and downs*
> *agridulce* • *sweet and sour*

A very common way of forming words for new objects or concepts in Spanish is by combining a verb form with its complement:

abrelatas • *tin opener*
portaaviones • *aircraft carrier*
sacacorchos • *corkscrew*
tragaperras • *fruit machine*
buscavidas • *hustler, wheeler-dealer*

1. What is a sentence?

A sentence can be defined as a linguistic structure consisting of two parts in a *predicative relationship* to each other, and which has a communicative purpose.
Thus:

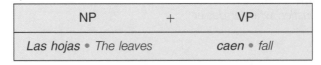

NP	+	VP	
El sol • *The sun* *Los pájaros* • *The birds*		*luce* • *shines* *cantan* • *sing* *dulcemente* *sweetly*	= bipartite structure = communicative purpose

Sentences have the following characteristics:

— They have a linear structure: the forms follow on from one another in time and space.
— They have a hierarchical structure, with lesser elements embedded into more important ones. Thus the morphemes **hoja** and **-s** combine to form the word **hojas**, and the words **las** and **hojas** combine to form a Noun Phrase, a higher category again. Hierarchical rules operate within the noun phrase, with the dominant element (in this case *hojas*) imposing its number and gender on the other elements (*las* = feminine, plural). (However, the NP must combine with other elements to make a sentence.)

When two elements of equal status are combined, for instance NP and VP, their *predicative relationship* is marked by grammatical agreement between them in number and person:

NP	+	VP
Las hojas • *The leaves*		*caen* • *fall*

It is this relationship, and in particular the establishment of agreement as regards *person*, which is fundamental to the communicative function.
The hierarchical structure of a sentence can be represented as follows:

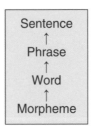

Sentence
↑
Phrase
↑
Word
↑
Morpheme

Morphemes are the smallest unit of grammatical description and cannot be subdivided into smaller units of meaning. The sentence is the highest level of syntactical description, although paragraphs and whole texts can also be analysed grammatically.

A sentence can also function *recursively* as a group or clause within another sentence. This possibility of *recursiveness* means that an infinite number of sentences can be generated from a limited number of elements.

Sentences can also be linked together by means of other elements which either *co-ordinate* or *subordinate* them:

$$\frac{\textit{Sofía canta y Laura baila}}{NP + VP \ y \ NP + VP} \bullet \frac{\textit{Sophie sings and Laura dances}}{NP + VP \ and \ NP + VP}$$

Sentence + Coordination + Sentence

$$\frac{\textit{Sofía canta si Laura baila}}{NP + VP + si + \ NP + VP} \bullet \frac{\textit{Sophie sings if Laura dances}}{NP + VP \ if \ NP + VP}$$

Sentence + Subordinating element + Sentence

2. Syntactic categories

If sentences are analysed according to syntactic categories, the structure produced is non-linear:

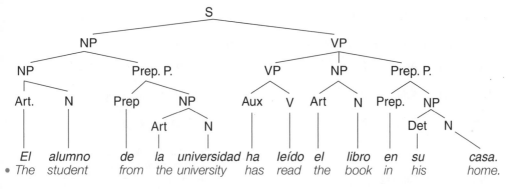

The NP and the VP are the *immediate constituents* of the sentence in that they are the highest category structures after the sentence itself. This is seen more easily in less complex sentences:

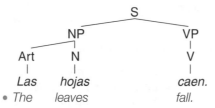

The basic structure of a sentence consists of a (NP) and a VP:

149

Sentence			
Categories	(NP)	+	VP
Functions	(subject)	+	predicate

Note that the NP is placed in brackets to indicate that the subject is often, in practice, omitted in Spanish.

The order of the constituents may vary as follows:

— Spanish allows either NP + VP, or VP + NP:

Los pájaros cantan/Cantan los pájaros • *The birds sing.*

If the NP is omitted, there is only one possible word order:

Hace frío • *Not *Frío hace.*
Es de día • *Not *De día es.*

— If the structure involves a NP, a VP and a complement, there are six different word order permutations:

Julia vive en Madrid.	*En Madrid vive Julia.*	*Julia en Madrid vive.*
Vive Julia en Madrid.	*Vive en Madrid Julia.*	*En Madrid Julia vive.*

(They may not, of course, all be used necessarily in the same context, and in some cases there may be other syntactic restrictions on their use.)

— The NP, is its simplest form, consists of a determiner + a noun:

Mi lápiz escribe bien • *My pencil* writes well.

It may also have more complex structures, such as the following:

Det. + N + Adj. + Prep. = *El libro sagrado de Buda*
 • *The sacred book of Buddah.*

Det. + N + Adv. + Adj. = *Un libro muy antiguo*
 • *A very old book.*

Det. + N + Prep. + N = *Un café con leche*
 • *A coffee with milk.*

Det. + N + N = *La capital, Madrid*
 • *The capital, Madrid.*

Det. + N + Clause = *El año que viene* • *Next year.*
Det. + N + Conj. + Det. + N = *La pluma y el lápiz*
 • *The pen and pencil.*

Det. + N + Prep. + N + Conj. + Prep. + N = *El libro de Juan y de Luis.*
 • *Juan and Luis's book.*

Det. + N + Prep. + Clause = *La duda de si el libro era suyo.*
 • *The doubt whether the book was his.*

The VP is very variable because of the different varieties of verb:

V = *Hiela* • *It is freezing.*
V + PrepP. = *Es de día* • *It is day(time).*
  = *Se acuerda de mí* • *He remembers me.*
V + AdvP. = *Está bien* • *It's OK.*
  = *Vive tranquilamente* • *He lives quietly.*

V + NP + PrepP. + AdvP. = *Dio un beso a Laura amorosamente.*
- *He gave Laura a kiss lovingly.*

V + NP + PrepP. = *Dejó el lápiz sobre la mesa.*
- *He left the pencil on the table.*

All the examples above are *simple sentences* in that they consist of only one predicate. Some sentences involve one predicate being embedded within another. These are known as *complex sentences*:

V + clause = *Dijo que no lo haría* • *He said he wouldn't do it.*
V + AdvP. + Conj. + V + AdvP. = *Vendrá pronto si trabajas bien.*
- *He will come soon if you work hard.*

3. Syntactic functions

Different syntactic categories fulfil different functions within a sentence, as illustrated in the following diagram:

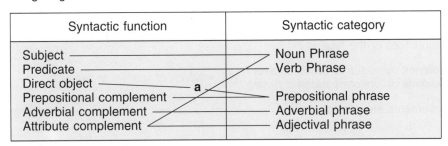

Syntactic function	Syntactic category
Subject	Noun Phrase
Predicate	Verb Phrase
Direct object	
Prepositional complement	Prepositional phrase
Adverbial complement	Adverbial phrase
Attribute complement	Adjectival phrase

The main functions are those of *subject* and *predicate*, the rest are complementary.

3.1. The subject

This is a function restricted to the NP. It may be accomplished *lexically,* by means of a NP (***Las hojas*** *caen*) or a pronoun (**Ella** *ríe*).

Or it may be carried out by the verb ending (*Canto* = I *sing/Escriben mucho* = **They** *write a lot*).

Or it may be carried out by another sentence functioning recursively as a clause within a larger structure:

*Me encanta **que baile*** • *I love her to dance.*
Que lo diga Teresa *es muy significativo.*
- *It is very significant that Teresa should say that.*

The subject agrees in number and person with the verb:

Los niños *se divierten* • *The children are enjoying themselves.*
El niño *se divierte* • *The boy is enjoying himself.*

Sometimes problems of agreement occur when the form and the meaning make more than one interpretation possible. This may occur when the subject consists of:

— Concrete nouns:
*Chocaron **un tren** y **un autobús*** • *A train and a bus collided.*

— Collective abstract nouns:

*Se amotinó **la gente,** pero a la primera descarga huyeron despavoridos.*
- *People started rioting, but at the first shot they fled in terror.*

The verb agrees with the nearest singular subject, even when there are several co-ordinate subjects in the sentence:

*Me gusta **madrugar y hacer ejercicio.***
- *I like getting up early and taking exercise.*
***Lo que ha hecho y lo que ha dicho** concuerda con su manera de ser.*
- *What she has said and what she has done is in accordance with the way she is.*

Sentences such as:

*Yo soy el que lo **hizo*** • *I am the person who did it.*
*Tú eres la que lo **dijo*** • *You are the person who said it.*

are correct in their agreements. This form is preferred over agreement based on sense:

*Yo soy el que lo **hice**/Tú eres la que lo **dijiste.***

In sentences of the type:

¿Quiénes de vosotros estáis a favor? ⎫
¿Quiénes de vosotros están a favor? ⎬ • *Which of you are in favour?*

both agreements are correct.

3.2. The predicate

The predicate function may be performed by:

— A verb phrase (VP):

*El sol **brilla*** • *The sun shines.*

— A VP + AdjP.:

*El sol **es grande*** • *The sun is big.*
*Los niños **están listos*** • *The children are ready.*

In these examples, the verbs *es* and *están* carry the grammatical markers of tense, number and person, while the adjectives *grande* and *listos* carry the semantic information and agree with the subject in gender and number.
This agreement does not take place when the structure is VP + NP:

Las prácticas de química fueron un lío • *The chemistry practical lessons were a mess.*
      NP   VP   NP

but:

Las prácticas de química fueron liosas • *The chemistry practical lessons were confusing.*
      NP   VP   AdjP.

The predicate may also consist of a VP + other secondary functions, as summarized in the following table:

PREDICATIVE FUNCTIONS

	Direct object	Indirect object	Prepositional complement	Adverbial complement
Hiela *(It's freezing)* *Hace* *(It's* *Es* *(It's* *Está* *(It's*	*frío* *cold)*		*de día* *day[light])*	*bien* *OK)*
Bebo *(I drink* *Gusta* *(It pleases* *Se acuerdan* *(They remember* *Vives* *(You live*	*un café* *a cup of coffee)*	*a María* *María)*	*de mí* *me)*	*tranquilamente* *quietly)*
Dieron *(They gave* *Hablas* *(You talk* *Aparcó* *(He parked* *Olvidé* *(I forgot*	*un regalo* *a present* *el coche* *the car* *el libro* *the book*	*a Julia* *to Julia)* *a Blanca* *to Blanca*	*de amor* *about love)* *sobre la mesa* *on the table)*	*mal* *badly)*

4. Types of sentences

Sentences are not just two elements in a predicative relation to each other: they are linguistic structures too designed to communicate or express meaning. In order to do this, they take on different forms and are also complemented by other features such as intonation.

— A **declarative** sentence expresses or announces an idea or thought:

El avión ha aterrizado • *The aeroplane has landed.*

— An **interrogative** sentence is used when the speaker wishes to ask a question:

¿Quieres acompañarme al cine? • *Do you want to come to the cinema with me?*

— An **imperative** sentence gives an order or communicates a request:

Ven a mi casa • *Come to my house.*

153

— An **exclamatory** sentence expresses feelings of indignation, surprise, doubt, admiration, etc.:

¡Qué espectáculo! • *What a scene!*
Quizá lo haga yo • *I may do it.*

Note that *grammatical form* may not always coincide with *communicative function*. An imperative sentence may indeed be expressed using the imperative form of the verb, but this function may also be fulfilled by using different types of construction, for example:

Deja el coche en el garaje • *Leave the car in the garage.*
¿Harías el favor de dejar el coche en el garaje?
• *Would you mind leaving the car in the garage?*
¡Tú dejas el coche en el garaje!
• *You leave the car in the garage!*
¡Te ordeno que dejes el coche en el garaje!
• *I order you to leave the car in the garage!*

Intonation and context, as well as grammatical considerations, have an important role in establishing the communicative function.

The following table gives an idea of the communicative varieties of each type of sentence:

Type of sentence	Communicative function	Examples
Declarative	Announcing	*Mañana iré a Toledo.* • *Tomorrow I'll go to Toledo*
	Ordering	*Irás con ella a casa.* • *You will go home with her.*
	Questioning	*Desearía saber si viene.* • *I would like to know if she is coming.*
	Surprise	*El plato está que quema.* • *The plate is burning hot.*
Interrogative	Questioning	*¿Quién soy yo?* • *Who am I?*
	Requesting	*¿Puedo sentarme contigo?* • *May I sit with you?*
	Exclamation	*¿No es maravilloso?* • *Isn't it wonderful?*
	Ordering	*¿De qué te ríes tú?* • *What are you laughing at?*
Imperative	Ordering	*¡Párate!* • *Stop!*
	Wishing	*Tengamos la fiesta en paz.* • *Let's have the party in peace.*
	Surprise	*¡Piensa en lo que has dicho!* • *Think about what you have said!*
Exclamatory	Request/Wish	*¡Qué pastel tan rico!* • *What a lovely cake!*

5. Simple sentences

A simple sentence is that in which none of the syntactic functions is fulfilled by another sentence, that is, it has no subordinate clauses fulfilling one of the primary functions of subject, predicate or complement.

A simple sentence is always independent, in terms of both structure and function.
For example:

a)   *Juan juega al tenis* • *Juan plays tennis.*
b)   *Que Juan juega al tenis* • *That Juan plays tennis.*
c)   *Cuando Juan juega al tenis* • *When Juan plays tennis.*

Only *a* is independent and a sentence in its own right; *b* and *c* are subordinate clauses which depend on a higher structure and function at a lower level. For example, the higher structure in *b* might be:

Compruebo *que Juan juega al tenis* • *I confirm that Juan plays tennis.*

However, a simple sentence may contain a subordinate clause, either:

— in the NP:

*Ésta es la novela **que** María te regaló*
• *This is the novel that María gave you.*
*Esto no es motivo suficiente **para** enfadarte.*
• *This is not sufficient reason to get angry.*

In these examples, the subordinate clauses function as complements or adjuncts to the NP.

Or:

— in an Adjectival phrase:

*Isabel está muy contenta **de que** haya llegado.*
• *Isabel is very happy that it has arrived.*

Or:

— in an Adverbial phrase:

*Luis no está lejos **de que** la suerte le acompañe.*
• *Luis is not far from having luck on his side.*

5.1. Combination and condensation of sentences

To communicate by using only simple sentences would be uneconomical and involve unnecessary repetition. That is why we tend to combine or condense sentences.

Combination of sentences involves co-ordination of two or more sentences of equal syntactic value:

Pablo estudia y su padre trabaja • *Pablo studies and his father works.*
Ramón es médico, pero no trabaja • *Ramón is a doctor, but he is not working.*

Co-ordination does not break the independence of the simple sentence, despite the fact that two clauses are integrated into a large whole, and that certain elements can be spared (for instance, in the second example, Ramón, the subject, is omitted before *trabaja*).

Condensation is achieved through subordination, that is, by embedding one sentence within another:

Recuerdo. He visto a Luis = Recuerdo haber visto a Luis.
• *I remember. I have seen Luis = I remember seeing Luis.*

In this case, one clause fulfils a syntactic function within a higher level structure:

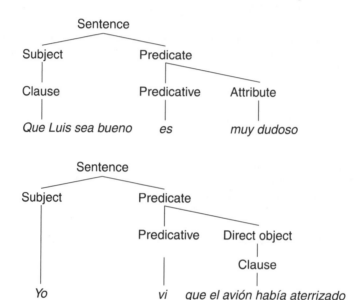

6. Complex sentences

A complex sentence is that where one or more functions are carried out by another sentence (clause), e.g.:

Que estaba enfermo *era obvio.*
• *It was obvious he was ill.*
Recuerdo ***que el niño dijo eso.***
• *I remember the boy saying that.*
Como dice el cartel, *la tienda está cerrada.*
• *As the notice says, the shop is closed.*
Si hace sol*, iremos de paseo.*
• *If it is sunny, we will go out for a walk.*

6.1. Types of complex sentences

Complex sentences may consist of more than one subordinate clause, as follows:

156

Me pregunto si te atreves a decirme por qué piensas que no es verdad.
• *I wonder if you dare tell me why you think it's not true.*

(bracket diagram with labels *a*, *b*, *c*, *d*)

a is the complex sentence, *b, c* and *d* are all in subordinate relationship to *a*, fulfilling the function of direct object to *me pregunto*.

Subordinate clauses can be classified by *structure* or *function*.

Structurally, we can distinguish between the following types of subordinate clauses:

— Those which have a personal form of the verb:

*Temo **que venga antes que tú*** • *I'm afraid he will come before you do.*
***Que haya hecho sol** era esperable.*
• *That it would be sunny was to be expected.*

— Those which have an impersonal form of the verb:

*No recuerdo **haberlo visto*** • *I don't remember seeing him.*
***Hablar en público** es saludable* • *Talking in public is healthy.*

— Those which do not have a verb at all:

***Así las cosas**, desistieron de sus propósitos.*
• *Given the way things were, they abandoned their objectives.*
***Impacientes por la demora**, rompieron el contrato.*
• *Tired of waiting, they broke the contract.*

Alternatively, from a functional point of view, we can distinguish between the following types of subordinate clauses:

— Those where the subordinate clause acts as subject:

***Que hagas ejercicio físico** es saludable.*
• lit. *That you should take exercise is healthy.*

— Where it acts as a direct object:

*Dijo **que lo había perdido todo**.* • *He said that he had lost everything.*

— Where it acts as an indirect object:

*Regalo mi lápiz **a quien lo necesite**.* • *I shall give my pencil to whoever needs it.*

— Where it acts as a complement of circumstance:

*Hablo de política **con quien me pregunta**.*
• *I talk about politics to anyone who asks me.*

— Where it acts as an attribute:

*Eso de **luchar por un ideal noble**.* • *This thing about fighting for a noble ideal.*

157

7. Co-ordinated or Compound Sentences

A compound sentence is one which consists of two or more sentences joined through co-ordination. Each retains its hierarchical status and remains independent, without one being embedded in the other.

Sentence co-ordination

Sentence co-ordination is the joining together, usually by means of a conjuction, of two or more simple or complex sentences:

Simple sentences:

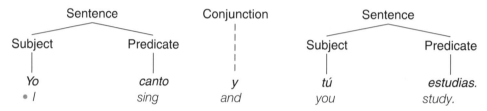

Complex sentences:

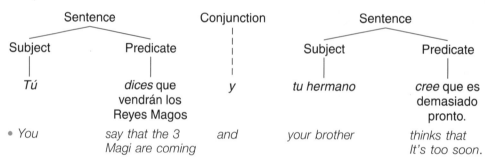

Co-ordination is achieved by means of forms such as **y, o, pero,** etc. Simple sentences may also be combined with complex sentences. (For example, *Tú cantas y yo digo que no me gusta* • *You sing and I say that I don't like it.*)

8. Substitution and ellipsis

Language tends to avoid structures which are uneconomical or unnecessarily repetitive by using *substitution* or *ellipsis*:

Substitution is the use of pronouns or other *pro-forms* instead of part or all of a preceding clause.

Instead of: *María dijo que María estaba acatarrada.*
            • **María said that María had a cold.*

we would say: *María dijo que (**ella**) estaba acatarrada.*
- *María said she had a cold.*

María is substituted by the pronoun **ella**, which in Spanish, as we have seen earlier, may be omitted altogether if the context makes quite clear who is the subject of the sentences.

In the same way: *Paula viajó a Madrid y Marta viajó a Madrid.*
- *Paula travelled to Madrid and Martha travelled to Madrid.*

The verb phrase in the second clause may be substituted by the *pro-form* **también**:

*Paula viajó a Madrid y Marta **también**.*
- *Paula travelled to Madrid and so did Martha.*

In the exchange: *¿Vino Paula? - No.* • *Did Paula come? - No.*

No is a *pro-form* which substitutes a second sentence: *Paula no vino.*

Spanish allows for the following types of substitutions:

— A Noun Phrase may be substituted by a personal pronoun (as in the first example above).
— An Adjectival Phrase may be substituted by **lo**:

Juan parece inteligente y realmente es inteligente.
- *Juan seems intelligent and he really is intelligent.*
*Juan parece inteligente y realmente **lo** es.*
- *Juan seems intelligent and he really is.*

— A complete sentence or clause may be substituted by an adverb such as *sí* or *así*, or by the pronoun *ello*:

*¿Ha venido el cartero? - **Sí.*** • *Has the postman come? - Yes.*
*Hizo una operación óptima en la bolsa y **ello** me alegra.*
- *He made a very good move on the Stock Exchange and I'm pleased about that.*

Ellipsis is the omission of certain structures where the context makes them unnecessary:

Juan compró un ordenador y Luis compró un vídeo.
- *Juan bought a computer and Luis bought a video.*
Juan compró un ordenador y Luis, un vídeo.
- *Juan bought a computer and Luis a video.*

Ellipsis is different from **substitution** in that no *pro-forms* are used, the space left by the structures omitted is simply left empty. It would seem, therefore, that the condition on which **ellipsis** may be used is simply that this empty space should be easily reconstructable by the context. **Ellipsis** may affect:

— the subject:

La juventud ama la libertad, pero (...) no la respeta tanto.
- *Young people love freedom but (...) don't respect it much.*

— the subject and part of the predicate:

Deseábamos ir a Madrid y (...) visitar el Rastro.
- *We wanted to go to Madrid and (...) visit the flea market.*

— the predicate:

Mis amigos fueron a León y sus padres (...) a Valencia.
  • *My friends went to León and their parents (...) to Valencia.*

— the predicate and the complement:

Picasso fue famoso en este siglo y Goya (...) en el anterior.
  • *Picasso was famous in this century and Goya (...) in the last one.*

1. Sentences and Communication

There are three elements implicit in any act of linguistic communication: the **code,** the **speaker** (or transmitter) and the **hearer** (or receiver). The structure of the sentence is always accompanied therefore by what we call *sentence modality,* that is the communicative purpose of the linguistic structure in the act of communication between **speaker** and **hearer.**

There are two types of sentence modalities:

— *obligatory modalities* and
— *non obligatory* or *optional modalities.*

Obligatory sentence modalities are phonemic resources which the **speaker** uses in combination with syntactic structures in order for them to fulfil the communicative purpose. They can be classified as follows:

— Declarative modality - *to report or inform.*
— Interrogative modality - *to ask or seek information about.*
— Imperative modality - *to give an order.*
— Exclamatory modality - *to express the emotions of the speaker.*

Optional sentence modalities are syntactic devices which affect the quality of the message emitted, and which appear in combination with the *obligatory modalities.* There are two types:

— Negation.
— Emphasis.

2. Declarative sentences

These affirm or negate the reality or possibility of something. To affirm a reality, the indicative mood is used:

Luis tiene cuarenta años • *Luis is 40.*

The intonation pattern of this type of sentence is a rising curve with a final fall:

Y todo estaba tranquilo • *And all was quiet.*

If the sentence has two phonic groups, the first ends in a rising curve and the second in a fall:

Se puso el sol, y nos marchamos • *The sun set and we went away.*

Declarative sentences may also contain words or phrases which reinforce the communicative purpose, be it an assertion, a negation or a hypothesis.

The following adverbs and adverbial phrases are used to reinforce an affirmative sentence:

ciertamente • *certainly*   *efectivamente* • *indeed, in fact*
evidentemente • *obviously*   *exactamente* • *exactly*
a decir verdad • *to tell the truth*   *claro (que)* • *of course*
en efecto • *in fact*   *por cierto* • *of course*
etc.

These are used to reinforce a negation:

nunca, jamás • *never*   *en absoluto* • *absolutely not*
en parte alguna • *nowhere*   *en mi vida* • *never in my life*

The following negative pronouns are also used in this way:

nada • *nothing*   *nadie* • *no-one, nobody*
ninguno • *none, no-one*

Similarly, adverbs and adverbial phrases can be used to weaken the assertion:

difícilmente • *hardly*   *posiblemente* • *possibly*
probablemente • *probably*   *seguramente* • *surely*
a lo mejor • *perhaps, maybe*   *casi seguro* • *almost certainly*
quizás, tal vez • *perhaps*

Declarative sentences have the following structural features in common:

— They involve the basic elements of the sentence (subject and predicate):

Juan escribe • *Juan writes.*

— They follow a set logical order of subject-predicate-complement:

Juan escribe una carta • *Juan writes a letter.*

— They use the indicative mood:

• to assert the reality of something:

*El día no **está** lluvioso* • *The day is not rainy.*
*Ricardo no **escribió** una carta* • *Ricardo did not write a letter.*

• to indicate possibility or probability in the present or immediate past:
Serán *las doce* • *It must be about 12.*
Estarán *en casa* • *They will (probably) be at home.*
*Tus amigos **habrán llegado** ya* • *Your friends will (probably) have already arrived.*

• to express possibility or probability in relation to a past or future event:

Serían *las doce* • *It must have been about 12.*
Viviríais *muy contentos en ese país.*
• *You must have been happy living in that country.*
*Nunca me lo **habría imaginado*** • *I would never have thought it.*

- to express courtesy:

Querría ver al Director • *I wanted (= would like) to see the Director.*

— They use the subjunctive mood:

- to refer hypothetically to something:

Hubiera estado *más tiempo de vacaciones, si el tiempo hubiera sido bueno.*
• *I would have stayed longer on holiday if the weather had been good.*
- to indicate a minor doubt:

Tal vez **se hayan enterado** *ya* • *They may have found out already.*
Quizá **no vuelva** • *He may not come back.*

- to emphasize a doubt:
Tal vez **conozcas** *a este hombre* • *You might know this man.*

2.1. Negative declarative sentences

These should not be seen as belonging to a different category from affirmative sentences. Their particular characteristics derive from the use of certain negative particles. In Spanish there are two types of negative words:

— Those which are negative in origin:

No:	*No salí de casa* • *I did not go out.*
Ninguno:	*Ninguno lo vio* • *No one saw him.*
Nunca:	*Nunca lo dijo* • *He never said it.*
Sin:	*Entró sin ruido* • *He came in without a sound.*
Sin que:	*Pasó la noche sin que mejorara.*
	• *He passed the night without any improvement.*

— Those which are not etymologically negative in origin:

nada • *nothing*   *nadie* • *no one*
jamás • *never*   *en mi vida* • *never in my life,* etc.

These words and expressions take on a negative meaning as a result of being used in phrases incorporating the particle *no*:

No tengo nada ⎫
Nada tengo ⎭ • *I have nothing.*

— The particle **no**:

This generally precedes the verb:

Eso **no** *es verdad* • *That is not true.*

However, certain pronouns may come between **no** and the verb:

No se *sabe lo que pasó* • *Nobody knows what happened.*
No lo *quiere decir* • *He/she doesn't want to say so.*

As may a whole phrase or clause affected by the negation:

No a todos *es dado expresarse bien.*
• *Not everyone has the talent to express themselves well.*
No porque aprobase *merecía tal nota.*
• *It wasn't because he passed that he deserved that mark.*

The position of **no** may affect the meaning of the sentence:

*La gramática **no puede** aprenderse bien en la niñez.*
● *Grammar cannot be learnt well in childhood.*
*La gramática **puede no** aprenderse bien en la niñez.*
● *Grammar may not be learnt well in childhood.*

When **no** is preceded by **que** and used in a comparative sense, it loses its negative sense:

*Más quiero exponerme a sus críticas **que no** resignarme a estar callado.*
● *I prefer to expose myself to their criticism than to accept that I should remain silent.*

When followed by the adverb *sólo*, the negation does not affect the verb:

***No sólo** le gusta, sino que la quiere por esposa.*
● *He not only likes her, but he wants her as his wife.*

— The following elements may be used after **no**:

   — *Nunca* and *jamás*, which reinforce the negation adverbially:
     No** lo he visto **nunca }
     No** lo he visto **jamás } ● *I have never seen him.*

   — The indefinite pronouns *ninguno, nadie* and *nada*:

     No** he visto a **ninguno ● *I have not seen anyone.*
     No** ha engañado a **nadie ● *He/she has not deceived anyone.*
     No** ha hecho **nada ● *He/she has not done anything.*

   — Phrases which reinforce the negation in an absolute sense:

     No** lo he visto **en mi vida ● *I have never seen him in my life.*
     No** he dormido **en toda la noche ● *I haven't slept all night.*

— *Nada* and *nadie* are sometimes used in their original positive sense:

*¿Crees que **nadie** lo sabe?* ● *Do you think that nobody knows?*
***No** espero que se logre **nada** por ese camino.*
● *I don't expect anything to be gained by going down that road.*

By extension, words which are etymologically negative are also used in this positive sense:

*Ésta es la obra más notable que hombre **ninguno** haya realizado en su vida.*
● *This is the most remarkable work ever done by any man in his life.*

— Spanish allows several negatives to appear in the same sentence without cancelling each other out:

No** pide **nunca nada** a **nadie ● *He never asks anything from anyone.*

— *Nunca* and *jamás* can appear together to reinforce the negative sense:

***Nunca jamás** lo haría* ● *I would never ever do that.*

— Two negatives are only equivalent to an affirmative in the following cases:

   — where one of the negatives belongs to a subordinate clause:

     ***No** puedo **no** admitirlo* ● *I can't but admit it.*

— where *no* is used with *sin,* or with a word having a prefix with a negative sense:

Lo hizo **no sin** dolor por su parte.
• *He did it not without grief on his part.*
Lo hizo **no des**interesadamente.
• *He did it not disinterestedly.*

— Colloquial Spanish has a number of words or phrases which carry a negative value:

Le importa **un bledo** ⎱
Le importa **un comino** ⎰ • *He/she doesn't give a damn.*

— In interrogative sentences there is a correlation between question words and their negative answers:

qué • *what* = **nada** • *nothing*
quién • *who* = **nadie** • *no one*
dónde • *where* = **ninguna parte** • *nowhere*
cuándo • *when* = **jamás** • *never*
cómo • *how* = **de ningún modo** • *in no way*

2.2. Uses of declarative sentences

Declarative sentences can be used to express:

— a command:

Estarás a las 12 en casa • *Be home by 12.*

— a question, expressing doubt or possibility:

Ignoro lo que habrá ocurrido.
• *I don't know what might have happened.*
Es probable que sean las dos.
• *It is probably about 2 o'clock.*

— an exclamation:

La sopa está muy caliente • *The soup is very hot!*

3. Interrogative sentences

Although interrogative sentences are generally used to ask something which the speaker wishes to know, an interrogative structure may also be used in other contexts, for example giving emphasis to an affirmation or negation:

¿No es verdad que la tierra gira alrededor del sol?
• *Isn't it true that the earth revolves around the sun?*

Interrogative sentences are often pronounced with rising intonation towards the end, especially when the question begins with a verb:

¿Habrá venido mi padre?
• *Will my father have arrived?*

However, the intonation curve may also be that of a rise followed by a fall, especially when the question begins with a pronoun:

¿De quién es esta maleta?
* Whose is this suitcase?

Interrogative sentences have the following syntactic features:

— The subject follows the verb:

¿Has sido tú? • Was that you?

This also occurs when the question begins with an interrogative pronoun:

¿Quién es tu profesor? • Who is your teacher?
¿Qué esperas (tú) del examen? • What do you expect from the exam?

— The verb may be either in the indicative or subjunctive mood:

¿Qué hora es/será/sería?
* What time is it/would it be/would it have been?
¿Quién se hubiera atrevido a hacerlo?
* Who would have dared to do it?

— A declarative structure (i. e., with the subject preceding the verb) can be used interrogatively in order to emphasize the subject:

*¿**Ustedes** están conformes?* ⎫
*¿Están **ustedes** conformes?* ⎭ • Do you agree?

— Certain interrogatives presuppose a negative reply:

De la pasada edad, ¿qué ha quedado? (Nada)
* What remains from the past age? (Nothing).
¿Cómo pudimos imaginarlo? (De ninguna manera).
* How could we have imagined that? (In no way).

3.1. Uses of interrogative sentences

As with declarative sentences, interrogative sentences perform different functions according to the context in which they occur. The can be used:

— As exclamations:

¿No es maravilloso? • Isn't it wonderful?

— As commands:

¿De qué te ríes? • What are you laughing at? = Don't laugh at me.

— As statements:

¿No sería mejor irnos? • Wouldn't it be better to leave? = We'd better go.

— As rhetorical questions:

¿Qué hacer? • What is to be done?

This type of question does not require a reply on the part of the listener. Indeed, rhetorical questions are not necessarily addressed to any listener, but refer back to the subject (*What should I do?*, etc.).

3.2. Interrogative words

Quién • *Who*

Requires a declarative reply identifying human countable nouns, or their equivalent:

¿Quién llama? - Juan • *Who is calling? - Juan.*
Juan es el que llama • *Juan is the person calling.*

The following forms occur in answer to **quién:** *alguien (someone), nadie (nobody), cualquiera (anyone), uno (one), alguno (someone), ninguno (no-one).*

Qué • *What*

Requires a reply involving identification of the object or person being referred to:

¿Qué es Luis? - Es médico • *What is Luis? - He is a doctor.*

Compare this with:

¿Quién es Luis? • *Who is Luis?*
—Es el médico del pueblo • *—He is the village doctor.*

Words which can appear in answer to **qué:** *algo (something), nada (nothing), todo (everything), mucho (much, a lot of)* and *poco (little).*

Qué can be used as a pronoun in place of a noun or noun phrase:

*Ocurrió una desgracia - ¿**Qué** ocurrió?*
• *A terrible thing happened. What happened?*

It can also be used as a determining adjective:

*Ésta es una piedra - ¿**Qué** piedra es ésta?*
• *This is a stone. What stone is it?*

It is sometimes equivalent to a neuter indefinite pronoun:

*No sé nada. —¿**Qué** sé yo?*
• *I don't know anything. What do I know?*

Cuál • *Which*

Requires the listener to identify one object from a group:

*¿**Cuál** es la casa en que vive?* • *Which house does she live in?*
La casa en que vive es este palacio.
• *The house she lives in is this mansion.*

Uses of **cuál** and **qué:**

Cuál is used:

— when followed by a preposition and a plural noun:

*¿**Cuál** de las dos ciudades te gusta más?*
• *Which of the two cities do you like better?*

as opposed to:

¿Qué ciudad te gusta más?
* *Which city do you like best?*

— when followed by a choice between countable nouns:

*¿**Cuál** es mejor, mi coche o el tuyo?*
* *Which is better, my car or yours?*

but with abstract nouns, **qué** is used:

*¿**Qué** es mejor, el sufrimiento o la alegría?*
* *What is better, suffering or joy?*

Qué is used:

— before countable or mass nouns in the singular without a preposition:

*¿**Qué** ciudad prefieres?* * *What city do you prefer?*
*¿**Qué** café te gusta más?* * *Which café/coffee do you like best?*

— before verbs:

*¿**Qué** harás hoy?* * *What will you do today?*
*¿**Qué** estudias a estas horas?*
* *What are you studying at this time of day/night?*

Cuál is almost always used as a pronoun. Its use as an adjective is very rare:

*¿**Cuál** libro prefieres?* * *Which book do you prefer?*

Cuánto * *How much/many*

Cuánto can be used as a pronoun, referring either to persons or things:

*¿**Cuánto** cuesta este libro?* * *How much does this book cost?*
*¿**Cuántos** llegaron a la meta?* * *How many reached the finish?*

It can also be used as a determining adjective with countable or mass nouns:

*¿**Cuántos** coches tienes?* * *How many cars do you have?*
*¿**Cuánta** cerveza eres capaz de beber?* * *How much beer are you capable of drinking?*

Dónde * *Where*

Dónde is a relative pronoun, and can be used as follows:

— Before verbs which describe actions which are capable of being carried out in a particular place:

*¿**Dónde** duerme el niño?* * *Where is the child sleeping?*
*¿**Dónde** trabajamos esta tarde?*
* *Where are we working this afternoon?*

— Before verbs of movement. In cases where the question concerns movement towards, it generally appears in the form **adónde**:

*¿**Adónde** vas?* * *Where are you going (to)?*

In other cases, **dónde** may be combined with *de, por, hacia* or *hasta*:

*¿**Hasta dónde** llega la carretera?* * *How far does the road go?*

Cómo • *How*

The question **¿cómo?** may mean either *with what instrument?* or *in what way*?

*¿**Cómo** lo hicieron? Con una máquina.*
• *How did they do it? With a machine.*
*¿**Cómo** escribe? A máquina.*
• *How is he writing? On a typewriter.*

Cómo is only used with a preposition when asking about the price:

*¿**A cómo** están las naranjas?* • *How much do oranges cost?*

¿Cómo? can be answered with an adverb of manner: *well, badly,* etc.

Cuándo • *When*

Cuándo takes the place of a noun phrase relating to time. It may be preceded by a preposition:

*¿**Desde cuándo** trabajas?* • *How long have you been working?*
*¿**Cuándo** llega el avión?* • *What time does the plane arrive?*

The reply to questions with **cuándo** can be an adverb of time (*hoy, ayer, nunca,* etc.).

4. Imperative sentences

Imperative sentences are used to express a command, prohibition, exhortations, desire, request or granting of permission. The action of the verb is always focused on the listener:

***Ven** pronto* • *Come soon.*
***No** lo **dejes** para mañana* • *Don't leave it till tomorrow.*
***Que tengáis** buen viaje* • *Have a good trip.*

Imperative sentences tend to be pronounced with a rising intonation which then falls:

Ven *a las cinco.*

Imperative sentences have the following syntactic characteristics:

— The subject is usually omitted:

Ven (tú) a las cinco • *(You) Come at five o'clock.*

— The NP always follows the VP:

Ven (tú)
not: **Tú ven.*

— They cannot be combined with **no** and use instead of subjunctive tenses to form the negative:

No vengas • *Don't come.*
not: **No ven.*

— Pronouns may not be placed before the verb:
Contadlo • *Count it.*
not: **Lo contad..*

— Imperative sentences cannot form subordinate clauses as part of another sentence:

Dijo que vinieras • *He/she said that you should come.*
not: **Dijo que ven.*

— They represent a separate *mood* of the verb which is only used in the second person singular and plural.

— When the verb stands alone, it can indicate only present time:

Escribe (ahora) • *Write (now).*

Past or future time is indicated by using adverbs:

Escribe **siempre** • *Write always.*
Escribe **mañana** • *Write tomorrow.*

4.1. Uses of imperative sentences

Imperative sentences are directed at a listener who is of equal or lesser status than the speaker, and with whom the speaker has a certain degree of familiarity or trust:

Dímelo todo • *Tell me it all.*
Cuéntame esa historia • *Tell me that story.*

If the person being addressed is considered to be of a higher status than the speaker, either because of age or through being in a position of authority, or if the speaker is not on familiar terms with him or her, the third person of the present subjunctive is used:

Baje *usted despacio* • *Go down slowly.*
Cuídese *mucho* • *Look after yourself well.*

To express an order which is not tied to any special place or time, the second person of the future indicative tends to be used:

(Tú) **vendrás** *mañana y pasado y todos los días.*
• *You will come tomorrow, the next day and every day.*
(Tú) **amarás** *a tu prójimo* • *Love thy neighbour.*

In colloquial language, the infinitive is frequently used in an imperative sense:

¡ **Callar** *todos!* • *Everyone be quiet!*
Venir *pronto a verme* • *Come and see me soon.*

Sometimes this is preceded by **a**:

¡A callar! • *Shut up!*
¡A cenar! • *Let's eat!*

To soften the harshness of an order, or to express a wish in a polite way, the imperative form can be substituted by the verbs *querer* or *desear* in the conditional or imperfect subjunctive, followed by the infinitive:

Quisiera *decirle algo* • *I would like to say something to you.*
Querría *pedirle un favor* • *I would like to ask you a favour.*

170

The expression **por favor** is also used, followed either by an imperative or by the present subjunctive.

> **Por favor, dígale** que calle • *Please tell him to be quiet.*
> **Por favor**, que **venga** pronto • *Please may he come quickly.*

When imperative sentences express a wish or desire, the imperative is accompanied by one of the following elements:

Que

> **Que** te **vaya** bien • *I hope it goes well for you.*
> **Que venga** • *Let him come.*

Ojalá, Ojalá que

> **Ojalá** te **toque** la lotería • *If only you win in the lottery.*
> **Ojalá que llegue** a tiempo • *If only he arrives in time.*

Así

> **Así** te ayuden a ti • *I hope they help you.*
> **Así** Dios te oiga • *May God hear you.*

In these structures, the preferred sentence order is V + NP:

> **Que vengan** todos • *Let them all come,*

rather than:

> **Que** todos **vengan.**
> **Ojalá que** apruebe mi hermana • *I hope to God my sister passes.*

rather than:

> *Ojalá que mi hermana apruebe.*

In these sentences, the present subjunctive is used to express a desire which is realizable at the moment of speaking:

> **Despiértenme** los pajarillos y los rayos del sol.
> • *May little birds and sunbeams awaken me.*

The imperfect subjunctive is used to express a wish difficult to be fulfilled, not to refer to past time:

> **Diera** yo mi vida por salvarlo • *I would give my life to save him.*
> ¡Ojalá **lloviera** pronto! • *If only it would rain soon!*

Note that these sentences frequently have an exclamatory form.

5. Exclamatory sentences

These express the speaker's state of mind towards the message:

> ¡**Qué** estatua tan bonita! • *What a lovely statue!*
> ¡**Qué** pena! • *What a pity!*

They are pronounced with a rising intonation curve, which begins at a higher point than normal voice tone, and ends by falling fairly abruptly:

¡Qué bello ocaso! • *What a beautiful sunset!*

The tone in which they are pronounced is probably the most notable feature of exclamatory sentences.

They may begin with words such as:

Quién: *¡Quién iba a saberlo!*
                   • *Who could possibly know!*
Qué: *¡Qué bien lo pasamos!*
                   • *What a good time we had!*
Cuál: *¡Cuál le dejaron los ladrones!*
                   • *What did the thieves leave him with!*
Cuánto: *¡Cuánto me alegra oírte!*
                   • *How pleased I am to hear you!*
Cómo: *¡Cómo llorabas!*
                   • *How you cried!*

Or they may use the structure: **lo** + adjective/adverb + **que**:

*¡**Lo** fuerte **que** eres!* • *How strong you are!*
*¡**Lo** bien **que** lo hace!* • *How well he does it!*

Some exclamatory sentences are only differentiated from declarative sentences in the way they are pronounced:

¡Parece mentira que se haya arruinado tan pronto!
• *It's unbelievable he should have bankrupted so quickly!*

They are characterised by the fixed order VP + NP:

*¡**Lo que** sabe Juan!*
• *The things Juan knows!*

Although in some cases one element may be omitted:

*¡**Qué** bello día (es)!*
• *What a beautiful day (it is)!*

5.1.   Uses of exclamatory sentences

Qué as an exclamatory form expresses degree, and is used as a determiner:

*¡**Qué** bello!* = *Es muy bello.*
• *How beautiful!* = *It is very beautiful*

Cuánto (without a preposition) can take the place of a NP:

*¡**Cuánto** sabe Juan!* • *How much Juan knows!*

or a determiner which serves to identify or intensify:

172

*¡**Cuánto** dinero has gastado en vicios!*
- *The money you have spent on your bad habits!*

or and adverb:

*¡**Cuánto** me divertí! = Me divertí mucho.*
- *What a good time I had!*

Cuánto can also be preceded by prepositions:

*¡**A cuánto** obliga el amor!* • *The things we do for love!*
*¡**Con cuánto** dinero contáis!* • *What a lot of money you have!*

Cuán is used as an intensifier of adjectives or adverbs:

*¡**Cuán** silencioso venías!* • *How quiet you came!*
*¡**Cuán** bien lo pasé!* • *What a good time I had!*

In these sentences, **lo** + **que**, with the adjective or adverb between the two elements, can substitute *cuán*:

¡Lo silencioso que venías! • *How quiet you came!*
¡Lo bien que lo pasé! • *What a good time I had!*

Cómo is equivalent to an adverb:

*¡**Cómo** llorabas! = Llorabas mucho.*
- *How you cried! = You cried a lot.*

Since exclamatory sentences express the attitude of the speaker towards the message, they can be said to be equivalent to superlative constructions:

*¡**Qué** valor tiene! = Tiene muchísimo valor.*
- *How brave she is! = She is very brave.*

They cannot be used in the negative:

¡Qué** no bello es!*

To express a negative sense, other adverbs, such as *poco* or *mal* are used:

*¡**Qué poco** alegre es Juana!* • *How cheerless Juana is!*
*¡**Qué mal** canta!* • *How badly she sings!*

In some contexts, exclamatory sentences can be equivalent to negative declarative sentences:

*¡**Qué** me dices! = No me digas eso.*
- *What are you saying! = Don't tell me that!*

or to a sort of gentle request:

*¡**Qué** sabrosa carne! = Sírvame más, por favor.*
- *What lovely meat! = Give me some more please.*

14 | COMPLEX SENTENCES

1. General features

We have already seen in previous chapters how sentences are composed of two essential groups of words —Noun Phrases and Verb Phrases— which perform the functions of subject and predicate respectively. The Noun Phrase, but not the Verb Phrase, may consist of a separate clause:

Quien calla, otorga.
* He who is silent gives something away.

In this example the verb *otorga* can never be substituted by a clause fulfilling an equivalent function.

However, *elements within* the Verb Phrase (complements of the verb) may be substituted by clauses:

Dio pan **a los que lo necesitaban** • He gave bread to those who needed it.
Dijo **que vendría** • She said she would come.

The following tree diagram illustrates this:

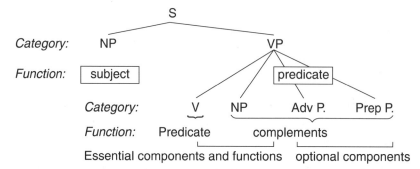

If the NP of the predicate, or the subject, or one of the complements is a clause, the sentence is classified as a *complex* one:

No me gusta **lo que dices** • I don't like what you are saying.
Dio un premio a **los que destacaron** más.
* She gave a prize to the ones who were the most outstanding.

1.1. Functions

Complex sentences perform one of the following functions:

— Relating a subject which is a subordinate clause to a Verb Phrase:

174

El que diga tal cosa, está mintiendo • *Whoever says so is lying.*

      Subject   +   VP

— Within a Verb Phrase, relating a verb to obligatory complements or a noun phrase to an attribute:

*Nos reveló **que había sido el ladrón**.*
• *He told us that he had been the thief.*
*Habló **a quien nunca debería haber hablado**.*
• *She talked to someone she should never have spoken to.*
*La solución es **que no aparezcas por aquí**.*
• *The solution is for you not to show up around here.*

— Relating subordinate clauses of the NP to subordinate clauses of the VP:

***Me trae sin cuidado que hayas decidido** no hacer ese trabajo.*
• *I couldn't care less that you've decided not to do that job.*

1.2. Structure

In these type of complex sentences relations are established between obligatory or constant elements. However, when an optional element —an Adverbial Phrase— is introduced, an obligatory element is then related to an optional element, producing different semantic and syntactic characteristics. These sentences are known as *complex adverbial sentences* (see chapter 15).

In these types of sentences, the elements related are not of the same hierarchical status. The subordinate clause in the adverbial phrase is dependent on the predicate of the main clause and forms a *subpredicate*:

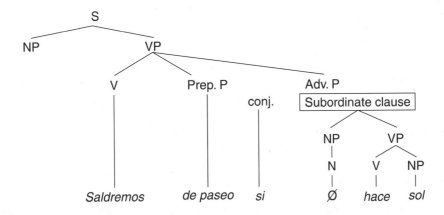

Here the sentence is a complex one because the adverbial function is being performed by a subordinate clause. The subordinate clause expresses the manner by which the predicate is performed (*si hace sol*).

1.3. Typology

Simple and complex sentences have similar forms and structures, although moods and sometimes tenses may vary due to restrictions imposed on these in complex sentences where one element is being related to another.

Complex sentences can be:

— Declarative.
— Interrogative.
— Volitional.
— Exclamatory.

Unlike simple sentences, complex sentences do not have distinctive intonation patterns, but tend rather to use verbs and adverbs to perform these functions.

2. Declarative complex sentences

These simply enunciate a situation or an idea. They usually include **que** after the verb:

*No entiendo **que** llegue tan tarde* • *I can't understand how he is so late.*

2.1. Functions

Declarative complex sentences are transpositions or amplifications of simple declarative sentences which come to perform a NP function (subject, direct object, etc.) in a more complex structure.

2.2. Structure

Simple declarative sentences which become transposed in this way retain the same verbal patterns:

Simple sentence	Complex sentence	
Yo sé la lección. • *I know the lesson.*	*Dice que sabe la lección.* • *He says that he knows the lesson.*	*Dijo que sabía la lección.* • *He said that he knew the lesson.*
Quizá yo lo sepa hacer. • *Perhaps I know to do it.*	*Dice que quizá lo sepa hacer.* • *He says that perhaps he knows...*	*Dijo que quizá lo supiera hacer.* • *He said that perhaps he knew...*
Con anticiclón no llovería. • *If there were an anticy-clone, it wouldn't rain.*	*Dice que con anticiclón no llovería.* • *He says that if... it wouldn't rain.*	*Dijo que con anticiclón no habría llovido.* • *He said that if... it wouldn't have rained.*

Complex declarative sentences tend to include lexical elements (adverbs in **-mente** or adverbial phrases) to reinforce what they are trying to express.
For example:

indudablemente • *undoubtedly*
naturalmente • *naturally*
lógicamente • *logically*
seguramente • *certainly, surely*
por supuesto • *of course*
sin duda • *doubtless*

Naturalmente que él sabía lo que hacía • *He of course knew what he was doing.*

They may also be headed by verbal constructions such as:

Es claro. • *It's clear.*
Está claro. • *It's clear.*
Es lógico. • *It's logical.*   } *... que (that)*
Es evidente. • *It's obvious.*
Es seguro. • *It's certain.*
etc.

Other adverbial words and phrases can give different weights to the opinion being expressed:

Realmente • *Really.*
Verdaderamente • *Really.*
Ciertamente • *Certainly.*
Efectivamente • *Indeed.*
En realidad • *Actually.*
Francamente • *Frankly.*
De verdad • *Really.*
De veras • *Really.*
En efecto • *Indeed.*
Por cierto • *Certainly, by the way.*

These can be positioned at the beginning or end of the sentence:

Realmente *no sé lo que pasa*   }
No sé lo que pasa **realmente**   } • *I don't really know what's happening.*

Similarly, the following can be used to assure the listener of the objectivity of the assertion being made:

Exactamente • *Exactly.*
Precisamente • *Precisely.*
Efectivamente, en efecto • *In fact.*
Realmente • *Really.*
Es verdad que • *It's true that.*
La verdad es que • *The truth is that.*
La realidad es que • *The reality is that,* etc.

Other adverbs and adverbial phrases may be used to create the opposite effect: doubt or uncertainty:

Difícilmente • *Hardly.*
Posiblemente • *Possibly.*
Probablemente • *Probably.*
Seguramente • *Probably.*

In the negative, complex declarative sentences show little regularity. Some verbs require the subjunctive in the subordinate clause, and this tendency is more marked when the main verb is in the negative:

anhelar • *to long for*	*dudar* • *to doubt*
desear • *to wish*	*implorar* • *to implore*
lamentar • *to regret*	*intentar* • *to try*
esperar • *to hope, expect*	*merecer* • *to deserve*

pedir • to ask	*necesitar* • to need
procurar • to ensure	*provocar* • to provoke
proponer • to propose	*querer* • to want
rogar • to beg	*resistir* • to resist
solicitar • to ask	*tolerar* • to tolerate

No tolero que hables en voz alta.
• I can't/won't put up with you raising your voice.
Intento que duerma solo.
• I try to make him sleep alone.

Another group of verbs normally take the indicative, but when in the negative, they can take either the indicative or the subjunctive:

Notifica que **llegará** el viernes.
• She says she will arrive on Friday.

but:

*No notifica que **llegará** el viernes.
• She doesn't say that she will arrive on Friday.
No notifica que **llegue** el viernes.
• She doesn't say whether she will arrive on Friday.

It these two negative examples, the first, using the indicative, merely states a fact; the second, with the subjunctive, leaves the question open.

Other verbs only take the indicative, whether they are in the negative or not:

aclarar • to clarify	*aparentar* • to appear, pretend
apuntar • to point out	*aseverar* • to assert
captar • to understand, catch	*divulgar* • to disclose
mentir • to lie	*ocultar* • to hide
olvidar • to forget	*presuponer* • to presuppose
resaltar • to stress	*transmitir* • to pass on a message

No oculta que **tendrá** que ayudarle.
• He doesn't hide (the fact that) he will have to help her.

Some verbs indicating speech or expression may be followed by either the indicative or the subjunctive, plus the infinitive:

acordar • to agree	*admitir* • to admit
celebrar • to celebrate	*comprobar* • to check
decir • to tell/say	*escuchar* • to listen
decidir • to decide	*estimar* • to consider
garantizar • to guarantee	*indicar* • to indicate
negar • to deny	*sentir* • to feel
sugerir • to suggest	*ver* • to see

Veo que **dice** la verdad • I see she is telling the truth.
No veo que **diga** la verdad • I don't see she is telling the truth.
Veo que **admite haber comido** demasiado.
• I see she admits having eaten too much.
No veo que **decida comprar** el piso.
• I don't see him deciding to buy the flat.

Some cannot be followed by the infinitive:

advertir • *to warn, notice*   *avisar* • *to notify, warn*
balbucear • *to stammer*   *comprender* • *to understand*
contestar • *to answer*   *criticar* • *to criticize*
entender • *to understand*   *asentir* • *to agree, consent to*
gritar • *to shout*   *hablar* • *to speak*
informar • *to inform*   *oponer* • *to oppose*
repetir • *to repeat*   *responder* • *to respond, reply*
verificar • *to check*

*Advirtió que **conducía** muy deprisa.*
• *He noticed that she was driving very fast.*
*No entiende que le **critiquen.***
• *He doesn't understand that they should criticize him.*

3. Interrogative complex sentences

3.1. Formal description

These are what are generally known as *indirect questions*. They are formed with:

Verbs of perception: *saber, ver, pensar, imaginar, juzgar,* etc.
Verbs of communication: *decir, avisar, preguntar, entender, informar,* etc.

Complex interrogative sentences are transpositions of simple questions and always keep the indicative form:

Simple sentences	Complex interrogative sentences	
¿Qué pretendes? • *What are you playing at?*	*Pregunta...* • *She asks...* *qué pretende él.* • *what he is playing at.*	*Preguntó...* • *She asked.* *qué pretendía él.* • *what he was playing at.*
¿Irías tú ahora? • *Would you go now?*	*si iría él ahora.* • *if he would go now.*	*si habría ido entonces.* • *If he would have gone then.*

3.2. Structure

Complex interrogative sentences are formed with:

— the interrogative particles *qué, quién, quiénes, cuál, cuáles, cuánto, cuánta, cuántos, cuántas, dónde, cómo,* etc.

— **si** + a personal form of the verb (not the infinitive) if the question falls upon the predicate:

*No sé **si llegará** Juan* • *I don't know whether Juan will come.*

— **que** followed by an interrogative:

*Preguntó **que** qué le iba en ello* • *She asked what he was getting out of it.*

(This construction is only possible with *decir* and *preguntar*.)

Indirect questions only take the infinitive when the subject is the same in both clauses:

*No saben qué **decir*** • *They don't know what to say.*
*No ven con quién **aconsejarse*** • *They don't see who can advise them.*

4. Volitional complex sentences

These express a command, wish, prohibition, exhortation, request, etc. and are always formed by using *que* and the subjunctive:

Simple sentences	Complex volitional sentences	
Ojalá vaya • *If only he would go*	*Dice...* • *He says...*	*Dijo* • *He said...*
	que ojalá vaya • *If only he would go*	*que ojalá fuese* • *If only he would go*
Estudiarás • *You will study*	*que estudie* • *that he should study*	*que estudiara/-iase* • *that he should study*
Ojalá hubiera ido • *If only he had gone*	*que ojalá hubiera ido* • *If only he had gone*	*que ojalá hubiera ido* • *if only he had gone*
Vete fuera • *Get out*	*que vaya fuera* • *to/that he should get out*	*que fuese fuera* • *to get out/that he should get out*
Pasen • *Come in*	*que pasen* • *come in/that they should come in*	*que pasasen* • *come in/that they should come in*

4.1. Uses of volitional complex sentences

There are two types of complex volitional sentences:

Those expressing inclination:

Verbs such as *desear, imaginar, pretender, decidir, decretar, procurar, conseguir,* can take the infinitive if the subject is the same in both clauses:

*Pretenden **escalar** la cumbre de la montaña.*
• *They intend to scale the mountain peak.*

If the subject is different, they require the subjunctive:

*Desean que su hijo **pague** menos.*
• *They wish their son to pay less.*

Verbs of inducement, such as *mandar, rogar, persuadir, exigir,* etc., can take either the infinitive or the subjunctive:

*Les permito **ir***
*Les permito **que vayan**.*   • *I let them go.*

*Les mandó **salir**.*
*Les mandó **que salieran**.*   • *He ordered them out.*

Verbs expressing agreement such as *pactar* and *convenir* can take either the infinitive or the future indicative if the subject is the same:

Pactan **ir**
Pactan **que irán.**   • *They agree to go.*

Convienen **que irán** a la votación • *They agree to go to the vote.*
Convienen **que vayan** a la votación
Convinieron **que fuesen** a la votación
• *They agreed to go/that they would go to the vote.*

Those expressing aversion:

Verbs such as *rehusar* and *evitar* can take the infinitive if the subject is the same:

Rehusaron **marcharse** • *They refused to go.*
Evitaron que el incendio **se propagase**.
• *They prevented the fire from spreading.*

Verbs indicating *fear* may also take the infinitive if the subject does not change:

Temo **venir** • *I'm afraid of coming.*
Teme que **vengas** • *He's afraid of you coming.*

Verbs of prohibition (*prohibir, impedir*) take either the infinitive or the subjunctive:

Te prohíbo **viajar** en avión
Te prohíbo **que viajes** en avión.   • *I forbid you to travel by plane.*

5. Exclamatory complex sentences

These are used to express the speaker's attitude or emotional reaction to a particular situation. They are often complemented by adverbs and adverbial phrases such as *desgraciadamente, lamentablemente, por desgracia (unfortunately)* or *por suerte (luckily)*.
These sentences are commonly produced with the following verbs:

Me alegra • *I'm happy*
Me extraña • *I'm surprised*
Siento • *I'm sorry*
Me satisface • *I'm satisfied*
Me pesa • *I regret/lit. It burdens me*
Es interesante • *It's interesting*
Me agrada • *I'm pleased*

Me gusta • *I like*
Es una lástima • *It's a pity*
Me asombra • *I'm astonished*
Lamento • *I'm sorry*
Me encanta • *I'm delighted*
Me fascina • *I'm fascinated*
Me hace feliz • *It makes me happy*
Me importa mucho • *It's very important to me.*
Lo peor es • *The worst thing is*

que • *that*
cómo • *how*
cuánto • *how much*

Complex exclamatory sentences use the same tenses and moods as simple ones:

Simple sentences	Complex exclamatory sentences	
	Exclama... • *She exclaims...*	*Exclamó...* • *She exclaimed...*
¡Tú me insultas! • *You're insulting me!*	*que cómo le insulta* • *that he is really insulting her*	*que cómo le insultaba* • *that he was insulting her*
¡Qué yo vaya! • *Me go?!*	*que cómo va a ir él* • *that it's very difficult for him to go*	*que cómo iba a ir él* • *that how was he to go*
¡Qué bonito es! • *How pretty it is!*	*que cuán bonito es* • *how pretty it is*	*que cuán bonito era* • *how pretty it was*
¡Quién lo hubiera hecho! • *Who would have done that.*	*que quién lo hubiera hecho* • *that who would have done that*	*que quién lo hubiera hecho* • *that who would have done that*

6. Relative clauses

These are clauses introduced by a relative which function as an adjective describing the antecedent:

*El hombre **que corría velozmente** no era de aquí.*
• *The man who ran fast wasn't from here.*

In this example for instance, *que corría* is equivalent to an adjective (*corredor*) and refers to the antecedent (*el hombre*).

However, in other sentences the relative performs a function different from that of its antecedent:

*Recogió al niño, **que** lloraba desconsolado.*
• *He picked up the child, who was crying disconsolately.*

Here **que** is the subject of *lloraba*, whilst the antecedent (*niño*) is the direct object of *recoger*.

6.1. Types of relative clauses

There are two types:

— *Restrictive* or defining relative clauses limit the meaning of the antecedent by specifying it in a more exact way, so that without them the meaning of the sentence would be incomplete:

*Los alumnos **que aprueben** irán de excursión.*
• *Pupils who pass will go on a trip.*

Here *only* these pupils will go on the trip.

— *Non-restrictive* or non-defining relative clauses simply give additional information about the antecedent, without limiting its meaning:

*Los alumnos, **que aprobaron el examen**, irán de excursión.*
  • *The pupils, who passed the exam, are going on a trip.*

In this example it is implied that *all* the pupils passed the exam, and the relative clause is placed between commas because even if it were removed it would not affect the meaning of the main clause, whereas commas are never used in writing to separate restrictive relative clauses from the antecedent, as this would change the meaning of the sentence.

See also section on relative pronouns.

1. General description

Most complex sentences are the result of NP + VP structures being embedded within another Noun Phrase or Verb Phrase, as we have seen above. Complex sentences are not, therefore, linguistically superior to simple sentences, they are merely structures in which one or more constituent parts is a separate clause.

Complex sentences can be broken down by using different levels of analysis, as shown by a tree diagram:

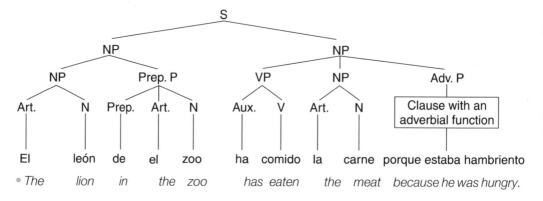

• *The lion in the zoo has eaten the meat because he was hungry.*

Complex sentences can be classified into three types:

Substantive: where the NP is a subordinate clause.
Relative: where the Adjectival Phrase is a subordinate clause.
Adverbial: where the Adverbial Phrase is a subordinate clause.

In this final category, the subordinate clause is marked by the fact that:

— It is optional.
— Its position is not fixed.

2. Adverbial clauses of place

These indicate the place where something happened or is happening:

*Aquí es **donde yo vivo*** • *This is where I live.*

They are introduced by an adverbial relative, which may be accompanied by a preposition expressing different place relationships:

a donde • to where, whither
de donde • from where, whence
por donde • where, through
hacia donde • towards where
hasta donde • until where, up to where

e.g.:

*Suele ir **a donde** va la gente.*
• She usually goes where people go.
*Fueron a la ciudad, **de donde** volvieron tarde.*
• They went to the town from where they returned late.
*Pasaron **por donde** habían empezado las obras.*
• They passed by/through where building work had started.
*Aquél es el límite **hasta donde** debes llegar.*
• That is as far as you should go.

In sentences such as these, the antecedent may be:

— an adverb:

Aquí es **donde** pasé mi juventud • Here/This is where I spent my youth.

— a noun:

Éste es el **salón donde** celebramos las reuniones.
• This is the room where we hold the meetings.

— a neutral pronoun:

Comprendo **esto, de donde** deduzco las consecuencias.
• I understand this, from which I can infer the consequences.

— a whole clause:

Al atardecer llegaron muchas personas, de donde deduzco que se celebró la reunión.
• As it was getting dark many people arrived, from which I imagine that the meeting took place.

The antecedents are often omitted when they are easily reconstructible from the context:

*Cené **donde** siempre* • I ate in the same place as usual.

Clauses of place may be constructed by using the indicative, the subjunctive and, when the subject is the same in both clauses, the infinitive:

*Pasará **por donde** quiere pasar.*
• He will pass through where he wants to pass through.
*Señale una habitación **donde** duerman más de dos personas.*
• Show me a room where more than two people (can) sleep.
*Los pobres no tienen **donde** dormir.*
• The poor have nowhere to sleep.

3. Adverbial clauses of time

Adverbial clauses of time indicate the time at which the action of the clauses in which they are embedded takes place.

The most common words used to form them are:

cuando • *when*   *antes de que* • *before*
mientras que • *whilst, while*   *después de que* • *after*
tan pronto como • *as soon as*   *siempre que* • *whenever*
en cuanto • *when, as soon as*   *desde que* • *since*
hasta que • *till, until*   *una vez que* • *once*

Cuando

This may be preceded by the preposition *para*:

*Estaremos preparados **para cuando** lleguéis.*
• *We will be ready by the time you arrive.*
*Estaremos preparados **cuando** lleguéis.*
• *We will be ready when you arrive.*

If there is an explicit antecedent, a relative construction is usually preferred (instead of *cuando*):

*Fue el día **en que** llegué a este país.*
• *It was the day that I arrived in this country.*

not:

Fue el día **cuando llegué a este país.*

Apenas, no bien (*hardly*)

These have an adverbial function if followed by *cuando*:

***Apenas** se había sosegado la gente **cuando** llegó la policía.*
• *People had only just quietened down when the police arrived.*

Without *cuando*, they function as conjunctions:

***Apenas** aparece la primavera, los campos se cubren de flores.*
• *As soon as spring arrives, the fields are covered with flowers.*

Como

Como may be used alone, or with *tan pronto* as an antecedent:

***Tan pronto como** vino la noche, nos metimos en casa.*
• *As (soon as) night fell, we went indoors.*

The same sense is achieved by using *así, luego* or *tan luego* combined with **que**:

***Luego que** llegamos, tomamos un respiro.*
• *As soon as we arrived, we had a break.*
***Así que** llegó, se acostó en la cama.*
• *As soon as she got in she went to bed.*

Cuanto

This indicates the duration of an action, and may be used with or without a preposition:

*Has de trabajar **cuanto** dura el día.*
• *You have to work all day long (lit. as long as the day lasts).*

When used with *en, cuanto* can have different senses:

En cuanto *vivió, fue amante de la pobreza.*
 * *Whilst he lived he loved poverty.*
En cuanto *llega a casa, se sienta en el sillón.*
 * *As soon as he gets home, he sits down in the armchair.*

Considerable subtlety of meaning can be achieved with adverbial clauses of time. They can be used to indicate:

— Something which happens at the same time as something else, over a period of time: *mientras* (que), *en tanto* (que), *entretanto* (que) * *whilst, as long as.*

Mientras *yo viva, siempre se hará lo mismo.*
 * *As long as I live we'll always do the same thing.*

— Something which happens with momentary simultaneousness with something else: *al tiempo, al punto y hora que* * *at the same time/moment as.*

Llegué **al punto y hora** *que quedamos.*
 * *I arrived at the exact moment we had arranged.*

— Something which happens before something else:

Se levantó **antes de que** *se lo ordenasen.*
 * *He got up before they told him to.*

(Note that the subjunctive is required in this case.)

— Something which takes place after something else. If the event refers to the future, the subjunctive must be used:

Después de que *coma te dará la noticia.*
 * *He/she will tell you the news after he/she has eaten.*

but if the event refers to the past, the indicative is correct:

Después de que *comió, le dio la noticia/***Una vez que** *comió...*
 * *After he had eaten he told her the news/Once he had eaten...*

— Something which takes place immediately after something else: *así que, luego que* *
as soon as.

Así que *se supo la notica, cundió el desorden.*
 * *As soon as the news got out, disorder spread.*

— The beginning or end an action:

desde que * *since*   *hasta que* * *until*
hace... que * *It's... since*

Desde que *lo vio, no se separó de su lado.*
 * *Since she saw him, she hasn't been parted from him.*
No paró **hasta que** *lo consiguió.*
 * *She didn't stop until she got it.*
Hace *diez días* **que** *lo vi* * *It's ten days since I saw him.*

— Repetition of an action:

siempre que * *whenever*
todas las veces que * *every time that*
cada vez que * *each time that*

*Lo saluda **siempre que** lo encuentra por la calle.*
* She says hello whenever she meets him in the street.

3.1. Tense and mood in adverbial time clauses

If the action takes place in present or past time, the present or past tense must be used in both verbs:

Canto mientras **como** * I sing whilst I eat.
Escucho música cuando **estudio** * I listen to music when I study.
*Apenas **llegó**, le **saludó*** * As soon as he arrived he said hello.
*Después que **comía**, se **lavaba** las manos.*
* After he had eaten, he would wash his hands.

If the action takes place in the future, the subjunctive is needed:

*Le invitaré **siempre que venga.***
* I'll invite him whenever he comes.
*Promete abrazarlo **en cuanto llegue.***
* He promises to give him a hug as soons as he arrives.
*El juez mandó que le encarcelasen **cuando aterrizase el avión.***
* The judge ordered him to be taken prisoner as soon as the aeroplane landed.

The imperative also requires the subjunctive:

Ven cuando puedas * Come when you can.

The idea of one action taking place at the same time as another can also be conveyed by using **al** + infinitive:

Al entrar, se cayó por la escalera.
* As she came in she fell on the stairs.

The idea of an action taking place before or after another one can be expressed by using **antes de** + infinitive or **después de** + infinitive:

Después de abrir la puerta, saluda.
* Say hello after you have opened the door.
Antes de entrar, deje salir.
* Before you go in, let people out.

Note: A construction with the participle can also express a sequence of actions:

Vistos los expedientes, se dictó sentencia.
* After the files had been seen, the verdict was given.

4. Adverbial clauses of manner

These express the way in which the action of the verb is carried out. They often use the following conjunctions **como, que, cual, cuanto, según, conforme**.

Como

This may have an adverb of manner as an antecedent:

*Se portó noblemente, **como** convenía a su caballerosidad.*
* He behaved nobly, as befitted his gentlemanly status.

Or a noun such as *manera* or *modo (way)*:

*Te contaré luego la manera **como** ocurrió el accidente.*
* I will tell you later how the accident happened.

In some cases, the antecedent may be omitted:

*En lo que toca a **como** has de gobernar, no esperes mi consejo.*
* As regards how you have to govern, don't expect my advice.

Como may also be used in combination with *para*, especially in colloquial Spanish, signifying real or imagined purpose:

*Le habló al oído **como para** consolarle.*
* He said something in his ear as if to console him.

Según

This should not be confused with the preposition **según** (as in: *Según el hombre del tiempo* [*according to the weather man*]). In clauses of manner it may be used with or without **que**:

*Lo hace **según** lo piensa* • She does it how she thinks.
*Se deteriora su salud **según** (que) pasan los días.*
* His health is getting worse as the days go by.

Según may also be combined with *como* and *conforme*:

*Tiende a hacer las cosas **según y como** le indican.*
* She generally does things exactly as instructed.

Clauses of manner can also be formed by using:

— Relative particles:

*Quiero explicarte el modo **con que** has de proceder.*
* I want to explain to you how you have to proceed.

— The gerund:

Caminando así, *no llegará muy lejos.*
* He won't get far walking like that.

— The past participle in an «absolute» construction:
Arrodillado, *suplicó clemencia.*
* On his knees, he pleaded for mercy.

5. Comparative sentences

Two clauses may be linked together to express a comparison of *manner, quality,* or *quantity*. The comparison may be one expressing *equality, superiority* or *inferiority*.

The following elements are used to form comparative clauses:

— To express equality:

así... como/cual	• *as (much)... as*
tal... cual	
tanto... cuanto	
tanto... como	
tal... como	

— To express superiority:

más... que	• *more... than*
(comparative adj.) + **que**	• *-er... than*

— To express inferiority:

menos... que	• *less... than*
(comparative adj.) + **que**	• *-er... than*

Comparison of manner is expressed by using:

así... como
así... cual
tal... cual

Como *el pobre que no recibe dinero no come,* **así** *la paloma que no recibe su grano de trigo sufre ayuno involuntario.*
  • *Just as the pauper who receives no money doesn't eat, so the dove which does not receive its grain of wheat is forced to starve.*
Cual *manada de ovejas,* **así** *caminaban los prisioneros por la estepa.*
  • *Just like a flock of sheep, so the prisoners made their way over the steppe.*

Comparison of *quality* is expressed by using *tal...cual:*

Cual *es María,* **tal** *hija cría.*
  • lit. *Just as María is, so is the daughter she brings up.*

Comparison of *quantity* can be expressed by using *tanto... cuanto:*

Tiene **tanto cuanto** *necesita* • *He has as much as he needs.*

5.1. Equal comparisons

Cual and **cuanto** are used in combination with *tal, tanto* and *cual,* which act as their antecedents:

La reunión fue **tal cual** *se esperaba.*
  • *The meeting was just as it had been expected.*
Consiguieron **tanto cuanto** *pidieron.*
  • *They got as much as they asked for.*

Sometimes the antecedent is omitted:

*Dame **cuanto** tengas* • *Give me as much as you have.*

Según expresses a comparison of equality when followed by *así*:

Según *sea el día, **así** será la noche.*
• *Just as the day is, so the night will be.*

Como is used with *así, así también, así bien, tan, tal* or *tantos*, in order to express equality:

Como *el grano cae en la tierra y germina, **así también** el alma...*
• *As the seed falls on to the earth and germinates, so too the soul...*
*Tus hijos serán **tantos como** estrellas hay en el firmamento.*
• *Your children will be as numerous as the stars in the sky.*
*Fue **tal** su valentía **como** nunca se había visto.*
• *Lit. Her bravery was such that had never been seen.*

When the comparison is conditional, the comparative clause following on from **como** is omitted:

*Le respeta **como** (le respetaría) si fuera su padre.*
• *He respects him as (he would respect him) if he were his father.*

A conditional comparison can also be formed by using the gerund preceded by *como*:

*Marcharon **como** mirándose.*
• *They went as if looking at each other.*

Other forms used to express a comparison are *igual... que, lo mismo... que*:

Igual *talento requiere la tragedia **que** la comedia.*
• *The same talent is necessary for tragedy as for comedy.*
Lo mismo *dice hoy **que** dirá mañana.*
• *She says the same today as she will say tomorrow.*

5.2. Unequal comparisons

There are three types:

— Those using adjectives such as *diverso, distinto, diferente* and adverbs derived from these:

    *Esto es **distinto** de lo que te había contado.*
    • *This is different from what I had told you.*

— Those using *más, menos, mayor, menor, mejor, peor, primero, antes*:

    Primero *es la obligación **que** la devoción.*
    • *Obligation comes before devotion.*
    Más *vale pasar frío **que** pedir prestado.*
    • *It is better to be cold than to borrow.*

191

— Those using *el más, el menos, el mayor, el menor, el mejor, el peor, el primero, el último, el postrero*, etc.:

*Hizo **el más** grande de los esfuerzos (que podía hacer).*
* He made the greatest effort (that he could).

The most commonly used term of comparison is *que*:

*Diversamente obra la naturaleza **que** la gracia.*
* Nature works differently to grace.
*No me fío de otro **que** de ti.*
* I don't trust anyone other than you.

De is less frequently used in comparisons:

*Más costumbres tiene **de las que** confiesa.*
* He has more habits than he admits (to).

No added to **que** has the effect of reinforcing the comparison:

*Más quiero mojarme **que no** quedarme encerrado en casa.*
* I would rather get wet than stay shut up at home.
***Mejor** es decirlo **que no** amargarse uno la vida.*
* It is better to say it than to make your life a misery.

Que and **de** as terms of comparison.
When a relative clause is involved, only **de** is used as a term of comparison, in order to avoid confusion in the double use of **que**:

*No hay en el mundo hombres **más hábiles de** lo que tú eres.*
* There are no men in the world more skillful than you (are).
*Al fin llegaron **más recursos de** los que se habían pedido.*
* In the end more resources arrived than had been requested.

When **más** is followed by a cardinal number, a partitive or a multiple (i. e. when it refers to an *amount*), **de** is always used:

*Se perdieron **más de** trescientos hombres.*
* More than three hundred men were lost.
*Me prestó **más de** una docena de libros.*
* She lent me more than a dozen books.

However, if the sentence is in the negative, then either **que** or **de** may be used, although the sense is different:

*No se gastó **más que** mil pesetas.*
* She only spent 1.000 pesetas.
*No se gastó **más de** mil pesetas.*
* She didn't spend more than 1.000 pesetas.

With verbs such as *ser* and *parecer*, only *que* followed by a predicate can be used:

*Fue para el niño **más que** un amigo.*
* He was more than a friend to the child.

De, entre

When these are used in making comparisons, they must be followed by a noun, usually in the plural:

*El primero **de los reyes** es Gustavo V.*
• *The first of the kings is Gustavo V.*
*Cicerón fue el más elocuente **de los oradores.***
• *Cicero was the most eloquent of orators.*

Comparative sentences can be described according to four types:

— Conditional:

*Me respeta **como si** fuera mi hijo.*
• *He respects me as if he were my child.*

— Causal:

*Bondadoso **como** era, perdonó la vida a sus enemigos.*
• *Generous as he was, he showed mercy on his enemies' lives.*

— Consecutive:

*Son demasiados **para que** nos atrevamos a ofenderles.*

or:

*Son demasiados **para** atrevernos a ofenderles.*
• *There are too many of them for us to dare offend them.*

— Restrictive:

*Ayúdame **cuanto** puedas.*
• *Help me as much as you can.*

6. Consecutive sentences

In these, the action described in the subordinate clause happens as a result or consequence of that referred to in the main clause:

*Dio **tal** puntapié **que** derribó la puerta.*
• *He gave such a kick that he knocked the door down.*

Consecutive clauses are usually headed by:

tanto/tan... que
tal... que   } • *so much/such... that*
así... que
de modo... que } • *in such a way... that*
de manera... que

*Sentí **tanto** frío **que** me acosté.*
• *I felt so cold that I went to bed.*
***Tan** oscura era la noche **que** no pudimos continuar caminando.*
• *The night was so dark that we could not continue walking.*
*Toca la guitarra **de modo/manera que** casi la hace hablar.*
• *He plays the guitar in such a way that he almost makes it speak.*

Así estaba enfadada *que no quiso ni hablar.*
* *She was so angry that she didn't even want to talk.*

Sometimes the antecedent may be omitted, and **que** alone establishes the consecutive relation:

*Toca la guitarra **(de modo) que** la hace hablar.*

6.1. Tense and mood in consecutive constructions

If the consequence is real, the indicative is used. If it is being presented as unreal, or as yet unfulfilled, then the subjunctive must be used:

*Es **tanto** el calor **que invita** al baño.*
* *The heat is such that it makes you want to go for a swim.*
*Hace **tanto** calor **que** uno se **hubiera bañado** con gusto.*
* *It is so hot that one would gladly have gone for a swim.*

If the first verb is in the negative, the second must be in the subjunctive:

*No hizo **tanto** frío **que** se **helase** el estanque.*
* *It wasn't so cold as to make the pond freeze.*

7. Conditional sentences

With these, one clause is presented as a condition for the other to be fulfilled. The conditional clause is linked to the main clause by means of the conjunction **si**.

7.1. Types of conditional relationship

The relationship between the two clauses may be *necessary, impossible* or *contingent.*

Necessary relation

In this case the conditional clause uses the indicative mood, and the consequent clause may take any tense:

Si (yo)	*vengo* • If I come *he venido* • have come *venía* • came *vine* • came	*él se va* • he goes *él se ha ido* • he has gone *él se iba* • he would go *él se irá* • he will go *él se fue* • he went

Impossible relation

If this refers to present or future time, the imperfect subjunctive is used in the conditional clause and the conditional in the consequent clause:

Imperfect subjunctive	Conditional
*Si **tuviera** dinero* • *If I had money*	***podría** comprarme un coche.* • *I could buy myself a car.*

If it refers to past time, the past perfect subjunctive is used in the conditional clause, and either the past perfect subjunctive or a conditional tense in the consequent clause:

Past perfect subjunctive	Past perfect subjunctive/conditional
*Si **hubiera tenido** dinero,* • *If I'd had money,*	*me **hubiera comprado** un coche.* *me **habría comprado** un coche.* • *I would have bought myself a car.*

Contingent relation

Here the conditional clause is expressed as something doubtful, over which the speaker has no control. The tense and mood used in the consequent clause are subject to greater variation:

Imperfect subjunctive	Present/conditional/imperative
*Si te **pidiese** dinero,* *Si te **pidiere** (fut. subj.) dinero,* • *If he should ask you for money,*	*se lo **das.*** ***dáselo.*** • *give him some.*
*Si te **pidiera** dinero,* • *If he should ask you for money you would give him some.*	*se lo **darías.***

The following linking devices are used in forming conditional sentences:

a)   **si** (if) - the most common.
b)   Conjunctive expressions:

Dado que	***Dado que** tienes dinero, hazme un regalo.* • *As you've got money, buy me a present.*
Supuesto que	***Supuesto que** es verdad, confiesa tu culpa.* • *Given that it's true, confess your guilt.*
Ya que	***Ya que** no hay remedio, esperaremos.* • *Since there is no choice, we will wait.*
Con tal que	*Lo sabrás, **con tal que** me prometas no decirlo.* • *I will tell you, provided you promise not to tell anyone.*
En caso de que	***En caso de que** cobre, pagaré la casa.* • *If I get paid, I will pay for the house.*

Caso de que	**Caso de que** viniese solo, le invitaría a cenar.
	• If he should come alone, I shall invite him to dinner.
A menos que	Su conducta es inconcebible **a menos que** esté drogado.
	• It is inconceivable that he should behave like that, unless he was/were drugged.
Con que	**Con que** me lo digas, basta.
	• If you tell me, that's enough.

c) Relative sentences such as:

El bien **que** viniere, para todos sea y el mal, para **quienes** lo fueren a buscar.
• If good should come, let it be for all and if bad, for those who look for it.

d) Conditional sentences may also be formed using the infinitive, preceded by **a, de** and sometimes, **con**:

A juzgar por sus observaciones, ha leído el libro.
• Judging by his comments, he has read the book.
De venir, ven cuanto antes.
• If you come, come as soon as possible.
Con presentarte tú, es suficiente.
• If you show up, that's enough.

e) Gerunds may also be used to form conditional sentences:

Siendo favorables los vientos, llegaremos pronto a puerto.
• If the winds are favourable, we will reach port soon.

8. Concessive sentences

A concessive clause describes an objection or obstacle which prevents the action of the main verb from being carried out. They are formed by using:

> aunque, si bien • although
> a pesar de que • in spite of
> por más que • much as...
> aun cuando • even when
> por + adj. + que... • though...

A wide range of possibilities exists as regards use of mood and tense, depending on the meaning the speaker wishes to convey. Use of the indicative means that the obstacle which prevents the action of the main verb from being carried out is real:

Aunque **tiene** dinero, no lo gasta.
• Although she has money, she doesn't spend it.
Aunque **tenga** dinero, no lo gastaba.
• Although she had money, she didn't spend it.

If the subjunctive is used, the obstacle may or may not be a reality:

*Aunque **tenga** dinero, no lo gastará* • *Even if she has money, she won't spend it.*
*Aunque **tuviera** dinero, no lo gastaría.*
• *Even if she had money, she wouldn't spend it.*

As may be noted from the examples given above, the tense used in the concessive clause determines which tenses may be used in the main clause. These may be summarised as follows:

Concessive clause	Main clause
INDICATIVE	INDICATIVE
Present *Aunque trabaja mucho,* • *Although she works hard,*	**Present, future** *no gana mucho dinero.* • *she does not earn much money.* *no ganará mucho dinero.* • *she will not earn much money.*
Imperfect *Aunque trabajaba mucho,* • *Although she worked hard,*	**Imperfect, simple past** *no ganaba mucho dinero.* *no ganó mucho dinero.* • *she didn't earn much money.*
Future *Aunque trabajará mucho,* • *Although she will work hard,*	**Future** *no ganará mucho dinero.* • *she won't earn much money.*
Conditional *Aunque estudiaría más allí,* • *Although I would work more there,* *Aunque ganaría más en esa empresa,* • *Although I would earn more with that firm,* *Aunque trabajaría mucho,* • *Although I would work hard,*	**Present, future, conditional** *no quiero gastar tanto dinero.* • *I don't want to spend so much money.* *no cambiaré de trabajo.* • *I won't change my job.* *no ganaría mucho dinero.* • *I wouldn't earn much money.*
SUBJUNCTIVE	INDICATIVE
Present *Aunque trabaje mucho,* • *Even if he/she works hard,*	**Future** *no ganará mucho dinero.* • *He/she won't earn much money.*
Imperfect *Aunque trabajase mucho,* • *Even if she were to work hard,*	**Conditional** *no ganaría mucho dinero.* • *she wouldn't earn much money.*
SUBJUNCTIVE	IMPERATIVE, SUBJUNCTIVE
Present *Aunque trabaje mucho,* • *Even if she works hard,*	**Present** *págale poco* • *pay her little.* *no le pagues mucho* • *don't pay her much.*

Not all words used to introduce concessive clauses allow all the possibilities referred to above:

— **Aunque** is the commonest used form.

— **Por... que** requires the subjunctive:

Por sabios que sean, este problema no lo resolverán.
- *Wise though they might be, they won't solve this problem.*

— **Si bien** requires the indicative:

Si bien sus modales son suaves, su carácter es enérgico.
- *Although his manners are gentle, his character is forceful.*

— **Aun cuando** can take either the indicative or the subjunctive:

Aun cuando todos le odien, él no cejará en su empeño.
- *Even if everyone hates him, he won't be daunted.*
Aun cuando todos conspiran contra él, el ministro no dimite.
- *Even if everyone is conspiring against him, the minister will not resign.*

— **Con lo** + adverb or adjective + **que** takes the indicative:

Con lo poco que come, todavía engorda.
- *Even eating so little, she is still getting fat*
Con lo simpático que es, no tiene novia.
- *Even though he's so nice, he doesn't have a girlfriend.*

— **Todo** is used in the following way, without the presence of a gerund, to form a concessive clause:

Enfermo y todo, sigue/siguió/seguirá trabajando.
- *Even though he was ill, he continues/continued/will continue to work.*

— **que** + subjunctive + **que** can also be used to express a concessive sense:

que quiera que no, lo haré.
- *I will do it, whether he likes it or not.*

— **con** + infinitive:

Con ser mayor, todavía tiene mucha energía.
- *Even though she is getting old, she still has a lot of energy.*

— **aun** + gerund:

Aun pidiéndotelo yo, no lo haces.
- *Even though I am asking you, you won't do it.*

— **siquiera** requires the subjunctive:

Hazme este favor, siquiera sea el último.
- *Do me this favour, even though it may be the last.*

— A repetition of the verb in the subjunctive also produces a concessive sense:

Escribas lo que escribas, nadie lo leerá.
- *Write what you may, no one will read it.*

9. Causal sentences

These express what caused the action of the main verb to take place. It may be a *logical* cause, or a *real* cause.

A logical cause is that which is deduced from what has been stated:

*Ha enfermado, **porque** no ha venido.*
- *He's been taken ill, because he's not come.*

A real cause is that explicitly expressed to be the cause of the action:

*Ha enfermado **porque** ha comido demasiado.*
- *He's been taken ill because he's eaten too much.*

9.1. Words expressing cause

The following words are used to express cause:

porque
ya que
pues/pues que
puesto que
supuesto que
como/como que
comoquiera que   } • *because, since, as, seeing that,* etc.
por cuanto
es que
en vista de que
a causa de que
cuando
etc.

Cause may also be expressed by using:

— the infinitive preceded by **por** or **de**:

*Estoy castigado **por** no **haber** cumplido con mi deber.*
- *I am being punished because I haven't done my duty.*
*Se ha vuelto loco **de** tanto **estudiar.***
- *He has gone mad through too much studying.*

— the gerund:

***Atendiendo** al bien de todos, se ha de castigar al delincuente.*
- *In order to ensure the welfare of all, hooligans must be punished.*

— a relative:

*Feliz de mí, **que** he hallado el perdón.*
- *Happy I am to have found pardon.*

— **que**:

*Duerme, **que** si no, mañana estarás cansado.*
- *Go to sleep, because otherwise you will be tired tomorrow.*

*Ten paciencia, **que** ya llegará el día.*
* *Be patient, that day will come.*

— **Es que** is usually used after a conditional clause:

*Si no ha venido, **es que** se le ha estropeado el coche.*
* *If she hasn't come, it's because her car has broken down.*

Or after a question:
*—¿Por qué no escribes? —**Es que** no tengo lápiz.*
* *Why aren't you writing?— Because I haven't got a pencil.*

Porque, pues, puesto que, ya que. Their use is fairly straightforward:

*No viene **porque** está enfermo.*
* *He's not coming because he's ill.*
*Ponte una manta más, **pues** hará frío esta noche.*
* *Put another blanket on, it'll be cold tonight.*
*Vayamos todos juntos, **puesto que** la unión hace la fuerza.*
* *Let's go all together, since unity is strength.*
*No se hará nada, **ya que** todo depende de él.*
* *Nothing will be done, since it all depends on him.*

Como, apart from its other uses, can also be used in a causal sense:

***Como** oyó ruido, salió a ver lo que pasaba.*
* *Since he heard a noise, he went out to see what was happening.*

De + adverb + infinitive:

***De tanto leer**, se le ha deteriorado la vista.*
* *His eyesight has got bad through so much reading.*

Causal sentences can be formed by using either the subjunctive or the indicative, according to the communicative intention of the speaker:

*No ha llegado porque **está** enfermo.*
* *He has not come because he is ill.*
*No vino, porque le **habrían castigado**.*
* *He did not come because they would have punished him.*
*No vino, porque le **hubieran castigado**.*
* *He did not come because they might have punished him.*

10. Clauses of purpose

These express the objective or intention with which the main action is carried out. They may be formed by using:

— **Conjunctions:**

a que	
para que	• in order that, so that
porque	
a fin de que	

*Vengo **a que** me ayudéis.*
* I'm coming so that you can help me.
*No dice nada, **porque** no le oigan.*
* He isn't saying anything so they don't hear him.
*Se esconde de la policía **a fin de que** no le metan en la cárcel.*
* He is hiding from the police so that they don't put him in prison.
*Escribe **para que** le lean.*
* He writes in order to be read.

— Prepositions: **a, para, por** + infinitive:

*Vengo **a hablar** de negocios.*
* I have come to talk business.
*La ataron **para forzarla** a hablar.*
* They tied her up to force her to speak.
*No te lo pido **por** no **molestarte.***
* I'm not asking you so as not to bother you.

— Phrases such as *a fin de que, en razón de, en orden a* + infinitive:

*Lo hicieron público **en orden a** no tener que ir ante los tribunales.*
* They made it public so as not to have to go to court.

— Relatives:

Le asignaron un despacho en el que estudiara.
* He was given an office in which to work.

10.1. Verbal tenses and moods

If the main verb and the subordinate verb have different subjects, then the subordinate verb takes the subjunctive:

*La llamo para que me **responda.***
* I'm calling in order for her to answer.
*Han contratado a más obreros con el fin de que **adelanten** las obras.*
* More workers have been taken on to get ahead with the building.

If the subject is the same in both clauses, the infinitive may be used:

*Iremos a clase **para** aprobar.*
* We will go to class in order to pass.
*Come poco **para** no engordar.*
* He eats little in order not to get fat.

11. Absolute constructions

These can be formed by means of the past participle, the gerund, or the infinitive.

11.1. Absolute constructions with the past participle

When the participle is equivalent to a separate clause, it forms what is known as an absolute construction:

Dicho *esto, se levantó la sesión.*
* *This having been said, the meeting came to an end.*

When used in this way, it is syntactically disconnected from the rest of the sentence and does not agree with the other elements (except those belonging to its clause):

Los jugadores, ***perdido el partido,*** *se desanimaron.*
* *Since the game had been lost, the players got discouraged.*

It may be equivalent to a clause expressing:

— time:

Dicho *esto, se levantó la sesión* * *This having been said, the meeting came to an end.*

— condition:

Disuelto *el Parlamento, no habrá más problemas.*
* *Once the Parliament has been dissolved, there will be no more problems.*

— manner:

Calada *la boina, marchó silencioso.*
* *With his beret firmly on his head, he went away in silence.*

— concession:

Conocida *la desgracia, reaccionó con serenidad.*
* *Although he was aware of the unhappy event, he reacted calmly.*

11.2. Absolute constructions with the gerund

The gerund, which need not agree with the subject of the sentence, can be used to indicate:

— manner:

Siendo *ella así, su marido la adoraba* * *Being as she was, her husband adored her.*

— condition:

Haciéndolo *tú, estamos tranquilos* * *If you do it, we are happy.*

— cause:

Hablando *tan alto, le abuchearon* * *They hissed him because he was talking so loudly.*

— time:

Viajando *a la luna, tuve experiencias únicas.*
* *Whilst travelling to the moon, I had some unique experiences.*

11.3. Absolute constructions with the infinitive

These may indicate:

— time:

Al salir *el sol, nos levantamos.*
* *When the sun rose, we got up.*

— intention:

Para tener *éxito, hay que esforzarse.*
- *In order to be successful you must try hard.*

— cause:

Por haber *llegado tarde, le han castigado.*
- *He has been punished for being late.*

— condition:

De ser *así, lo aceptaría.*
- *If it were so, I would accept it.*

— concession:

Con *tanto* ***trabajar****, no consiguió lo que quería.*
- *Even though he worked so hard, he did not get what he wanted.*

16 CLAUSE COORDINATION

The basic fact that linguistic communication takes place in time and space gives rise to the need to order the various elements used and to link them together in logical succession. Clause co-ordination is the linkage of two or more clauses of equal status without one being subordinate to the other. According to the type of conjunction used, this linkage may express the similarity or divergence of the two clauses.

1. Copulative coordination

This structure implies a similarity or unity in the ideas contained in each of the two clauses:

*Juan **come** y **duerme** bien.*
* *Juan eats and sleeps well.*

In this example the similarity exists at a structural level as well as at the level of ideas. Similarly:

*Juan **compró** un lápiz y Luis lo **gastó** escribiendo.*
* *Juan bought a pencil and Luis used it up writing.*

However, this similarity need not necessarily exist except in the mind of the speaker:

*La esperaremos media hora: yo **leeré** el libro, tú **tomarás** una cerveza y Paula **verá** la televisión.*
* *We will wait half an hour for her: I shall read the book, you will have a beer and Paula will watch TV.*

Conjunctions used to form this type of coordination are:

— **y** • **and:**

*Vinieron Juan **y** su madre* • *Juan and his mother came.*

— **e** • **and:**

*Llegaron padre **e** hijo* • *Father and son came.*

— **ni** • **neither/nor:**

*No llegó **ni** el padre ni el hijo* • *Neither the father nor his son came.*

— **que** • no literal translation:

*Dale **que** dale* • *Over and over again.*

These conjunctions frequently occur with adverbs such as *también (also), igualmente (in the same way), tampoco (neither), asimismo (likewise),* etc.

Note: **Y** becomes **e** if the following word begins with the sound **(i) (hi** or **i)**.

— Copulative coordination may be negative or affirmative.

1.1. Affirmative coordination

In affirmative coordinations, if each clause contains similar elements or ones which have a similar function, these are frequently omitted, in order to avoid unnecessary repetition:

Tu amigo *llegó alegre/***Tu amigo** *llegó cansado* = **Tu amigo** *llegó alegre* **y** *cansado.*
* *Your friend arrived happy/Your friend arrived tired =Your friend arrived happy and tired.*

Los niños *juegan en el patio/***Las niñas** *juegan en el patio* = **Los niños y las niñas** *juegan en el patio.*
* *The boys are playing in the yard/The girls are playing in the yard = The boys and girls are playing in the yard.*

Los niños *juegan/***Los niños** *se divierten* = **Los niños** *juegan* **y** *se divierten.*
* *The children are playing/The children are having fun = The children are playing and having fun.*

Juan *entró en la sala/***Andrés** *entró en la sala furtivamente* = **Juan y Andrés**, *furtivamente, entraron en la sala.*
* *Juan came into the room/Andrés came into the room stealthily = Juan and Andrés, the latter stealthily, came into the room.*

When there are more than two components to be linked, only the last is linked with **y**, the rest are linked by juxtaposition only:

Los libros, los cuadernos, los bolígrafos **y los lápices** *son útiles para el alumno.*
* *Texts, exercise books, biros and pencils are useful for pupils.*

However, **y** may be repeated between each element for stylistic reasons in order to emphasize each element:

En la calle **y** *en la casa* **y** *en la escuela no hacen más que hablar.*
* *In the street and at home and at school all they do is talk.*

Similarly, **y** may be left out altogether:

Llama, grita, llora, se desespera...
* *He calls, shouts, cries, despairs...*

This occurs especially when a list of elements is later taken up in one word by way of recapitulation:

Riqueza, honra, bienestar, todo lo sacrificó.
* *Wealth, honour, well-being, she gave up everything.*

When the speaker wishes to emphasize the unity of the two elements, **y** is sometimes replaced by **con** or **como**:

El reo, **con** *todos sus cómplices, fueron ejecutados.*
* *The culprit, (along) with all his accomplices, was executed.*

*Los libros, **como** las películas, aportan algo de cultura.*
- *Books, like films, are carriers of culture.*

When coordination is achieved by means of commas and there is a preposition, this only appears in the first example:

Era de talla alta, color moreno, pelo negro,...
- *She was of tall build, dark, with black hair...*
Viajaba por España, Italia, Francia...
- *She travelled in Spain, Italy, France...*

Where there are verbs which differ in tense or mood from one part of the sentence to the other, these should strictly be repeated and not left out.

*Estamos seguros de que tienes esta intención/Nos alegramos de que tengas esta intención = Estamos seguros de que tienes esta intención **y** nos alegramos de que la tengas.*
- *We are sure you have that intention. We are happy that you have that intention = We are sure that you have that intention and are happy that you do.*

However, in practice this rule is often ignored and the more usual way of coordinating the above two sentences would be:

*Estamos seguros **y** nos alegramos de que tengas esta intención.*

1.2. General rules affecting affirmative coordination

— If the subject includes more than one grammatical person, the verb takes the first person or preference, of the second person if there is no first:

*Tú, ella y yo **podemos** viajar juntos.*
- *You, she and I can travel together.*
*Tú y ella **podéis** salir juntos.*
- *You and she can go out together.*

— If the nouns being coordinated are of different genders, the adjective takes the masculine plural:

*La casa tenía puertas y balcones **blancos.***
- *The house had white doors and balconies.*

— Verbs may be coordinated in two ways:

*Pedro y Juan **cantan*** ⎱
***Cantan** Pedro y Juan* ⎰ • *Pedro and Juan are singing.*

In the first example the subjects are coordinated and the verb appears in the plural. In the second, the verb in the second clause simply disappears, and the verb in the first clause remains in the singular.

— With adverbs ending in **-mente**, all but the last drop this ending:

*Isabel vive **modesta** y pobre**mente.***
- *Isabel lives modestly and in poverty.*

206

— If the elements coordinated are preceded by more than one preposition or adverb, then it is not necessary to repeat them:

*En el grupo venía gente **con y sin** sombrero.*
- *There were people in the group with and without hats.*
*Lo hace **donde, como y cuando** quiere.*
- *He does it where, how and when he likes.*

— Verbs and other elements may be left out in the second clause rather than being repeated:

*Al enfermo la noche le parece **eterna** y el día **breve.***
- *To an invalid the night seems never-ending and the day short.*

Repetition may also be avoided by using pronouns:

*Lo que depende de otra cosa y está asido **a ella.***
- *What depends on something else and goes hand in hand with it.*

— If the verbs used require different prepositions, these must be included:

*Providencias exigidas **por** y acomodadas **al** estado actual de la nación.*
- *Provisions demanded by and adapted to the present state of the nation.*

1.3. Negative coordinations

— Negative coordinations are different from affirmative ones because they use the particle **ni** rather than **y**. If the verb appears before the coordinated elements, it must also be in the negative:

Ni** Pedro **ni** Juan **pintan.
- *Neither Pedro nor Juan paint.*
***No** pintan **ni** María **ni** Laura.*
- *Neither María nor Laura paint.*

— Verbs and adjectives may be in the singular or plural:

***Ni** Juan canta, **ni** Marta.* }
***Ni** cantan Juan **ni** Marta.* } • *Neither Juan nor Marta sing.*

— The first **ni** may be substituted by **no** if the coordinated elements are verbs:

***Ni** era riço, **ni** tampoco sabio* • *He was neither rich nor wise.*
***No** era rico, **ni** tampoco sabio* • *He wasn't rich, or wise either.*

— If the verb is already in the negative, the first **ni** may be omitted:

***No** te lo daré **(ni)** hoy ni mañana.*
- *I shan't give it to you either today or tomorrow.*

— **Ni** is also omitted if the first phrase is implicitly in the negative:

***En mi vida** le ofenderé **ni** le daré motivo para ofenderse.*
- *I shall never offend him (n)or give him reason to take offense.*

— Sometimes there is an implied progression in the list of elements:

*Leones, tigres, monos **y hasta** elefantes huían del fuego.*
- *Lions, tigers, monkeys and even elephants fled from the fire.*
***Ni** mis amigos, **ni** mis hermanos **y ni siquiera** mis hijos le vinieron a ver.*
- *Neither my friends, nor my brothers and not even my children came to see him.*

2. Explanatory coordination

When the second phrase expresses the same as the first but in a different way, this in known as *explanatory coordination:*

*Detuvieron al juez, **es decir**, prendieron a la justicia.*
• *They detained the judge, that is to say, they captured justice.*
*La cooperación, **o** acción conjunta, contra el terrorismo.*
• *Cooperation, or joint action, against terrorism.*

In some cases the second phrase may explain the first by giving more detail:

*Pocos son los españoles a quienes les preocupa no cumplir las leyes, **mejor dicho**, son pocos los que no se jactan de haberlas infringido.*
• *There are few Spaniards who worry about not abiding by the law, or rather, there are few who don't boast about having broken it.*

The following phrases and expressions are used:

es decir • *that is to say*   *mejor dicho* • *rather*
como si dijera • *in other words*   *por ejemplo* • *for example*
a saber • *that is*   *esto es* • *that is*
en otros términos/dicho con otras palabras • *in other words*
etc.

3. Disjunctive coordination

This type of sentence expresses the notion of alternatives:

***O** vienes hoy **o** no vienes nunca.*
• *Either you come today or you don't come at all.*
*Comes conmigo **o** comes solo.*
• *Either you eat with me or you eat alone.*

Words used are: **o, u**, or **o bien.**

U takes the place of **o** when the following word begins with the sound **(o) (o-** or **ho-):**

*Tengo siete **u** ocho libros* • *I have seven or eight books.*
***O** son mujeres **u** hombres* • *They are either men or women.*

The alternatives expressed can be mutually exclusive:

***O** lo tomas **o** lo dejas* • *Either you take it or you leave it.*

or inclusive:

*Creyentes **o** no creyentes, todos coincidimos en los deseos de paz.*
• *Believers or unbelievers, we all agree on the desire for peace.*

4. Distributive coordination

This presents non-exclusive alternatives, and uses expressions such as:

unos... otros • *some... others*
bien... bien • *either... or*
este... aquel • *the former... the latter*
ora... ora/ahora... ahora • *now... now*
tal... tal/cual... cual • *like... like*
que... que • *whether... or*
ya... ya • *now... now/whether... or*

Unos *venían cantando,* **otros** *llorando.*
• *Some came singing, others crying.*
Bien *leen,* **bien** *escriben.*
• *Either they read or they write.*
Ahora *dicen esto,* **ahora** *dicen lo otro.*
• *Now they say this, now they say that.*
Nadie debe jactarse de ello, **que** *sea el dueño,* **que** *sea el gerente.*
• *No one should boast about that, whether they're the owner or the manager.*

5. Contrastive coordination

In this type of sentence two ideas are presented as contrary. A range of words can be used, depending on the meaning the speaker wishes to convey:

— To correct an idea:

sino, sino que, antes, antes bien, más bien • *rather, not... but.*
No es tonto, **sino** *caprichoso* • *He's not stupid, just whimsical.*

— To limit an idea:

mas, empero, pero, aunque, sin embargo, con todo, a pesar de, si bien, bien que, no obstante... • *but, although, however, nevertheless, despite...*

Es joven, **pero** *maduro* • *He is young, but mature.*
La fruta ya está buena, **si bien** *todavía conviene que madure un poco más.*
• *The fruit is good to eat now, although it would still be a good idea to let it ripen a little more.*

— To express a gradation of ideas:

No sólo... sino *también...* }
no *solamente...* **sino** *que...* } • *not only... but (also)...*
No *sólo compra coches,* **sino** *también helicópteros.*
• *He not only buys cars, but helicopters too.*

The elements being contrasted can be affirmative, negative, or a combination of both:

No sólo *había hombres y niños,* **sino también** *mujeres.*
• *There were not only men and boys, but women too.*
No sólo *no conseguimos bajar,* **sino tampoco** *subir.*
• *Not only did we not manage to get down, but we didn't manage to get up either.*

No sólo no me alabó, *sino que* me criticó.
- *Not only did he not praise me, but he also criticized me.*

No sólo me hirió, *sino que* ni siquiera me dejó hueso sano.
- *Not only did he injure me, but he left me with not even a bone unbroken.*

The contrast can be reinforced by the use of adverbs such as *al contrario (on the contrary)*, *en cambio (instead)*.

No caminan, *pero en cambio*, se cansan
- *They don't walk, and yet they get tired.*

The most commonly used conjunction expressing contrast or opposition is **pero** *(but)*. **Mas** (without accent) is less frequent. **Pero** must always precede the second clause and may not start a sentence*:

*Lo vi, **pero** no lo toqué* • *I saw it but I did not touch it.*
*Pero no lo toqué, lo vi.

* In exclamations, where the context supplies the contrast of ideas, it is sometimes heads a sentence:

¡Pero si ha llegado! • *But he has arrived!*

Pero and aunque

Their meanings are slightly different:

*Tu hermano es fuerte, **aunque** pálido.*
- *Your brother is strong, although/despite being pale.*
*Tu hermano es fuerte, **pero** pálido.*
- *Your brother is strong, but pale.*

Sino

Sino is always used when the first clause is negative, to express a positive meaning in contrast to it:

*No come carne, **sino** fruta* • *He doesn't eat meat, but fruit.*

Its meaning expresses a progression of ideas if the first phrase begins with **no sólo**:

*No sólo come dos veces al día, **sino** tres* • *He not only eats twice, but thrice a day.*

Sino que

It is used to coordinate verbs:

*No llueve, **sino que** nieva* • *It's not raining, but snowing.*

However, **sino** may also be used alone with verbs:

*No corre, **sino** vuela* • *He's not running, he's flying.*

INDEX